Speaking of God in an Inhumane World, Volume I

Speaking of God in an Inhumane World,
Volume 1

*Essays on Liberation Theology
and Radical Christianity*

Christopher Rowland

EDITED BY
David B. Gowler

CASCADE Books • Eugene, Oregon

SPEAKING OF GOD IN AN INHUMANE WORLD, VOLUME I
Essays on Liberation Theology and Radical Christianity

Copyright © 2024 Christopher Rowland. All rights reserved. Except for brief quotations in critical publications or reviews, no part of this book may be reproduced in any manner without prior written permission from the publisher. Write: Permissions, Wipf and Stock Publishers, 199 W. 8th Ave., Suite 3, Eugene, OR 97401.

Cascade Books
An Imprint of Wipf and Stock Publishers
199 W. 8th Ave., Suite 3
Eugene, OR 97401

www.wipfandstock.com

PAPERBACK ISBN: 978-1-6667-5385-1
HARDCOVER ISBN: 978-1-6667-5386-8
EBOOK ISBN: 978-1-6667-5387-5

Cataloguing-in-Publication data:

Names: Rowland, Christopher, author. | Gowler, David B., editor.

Title: Speaking of God in an inhumane world, volume 1 : essays on liberation theology and radical Christianity / by Christopher Rowland ; edited by David B. Gowler.

Description: Eugene, OR: Cascade Books, 2024. | Includes bibliographical references.

Identifiers: ISBN 978-1-6667-5385-1 (paperback). | ISBN 978-1-6667-5386-8 (hardcover). | ISBN 978-1-6667-5387-5 (ebook).

Subjects: LCSH: Liberation theology. | Bible—Hermeneutics. | Theology—Doctrinal.

Classification: BT28 R85 2024 (print). | BT28 (epub).

Scripture quotations marked (KJV) are taken from the King James Version of the Bible, which is in the public domain.

Scripture quotations marked (NRSV) are taken from the New Revised Standard Version of the Bible © 1989 National Council of the Churches of Christ in the United States of America. Used by permission. All rights reserved worldwide.

Scripture quotations marked (RSV) are taken from Revised Standard Version of the Bible, copyright © 1946, 1952, and 1971 National Council of the Churches of Christ in the United States of America. Used by permission. All rights reserved worldwide.

The following essays are reprinted
in this volume with permission

"Theology of Liberation and its Gift to Exegesis." *New Blackfriars* 66.778 (Apr. 1985) 157–72.

"In Dialogue with Itumeleng Mosala: A Contribution to Liberation Exegesis." *Journal for the Study of the New Testament* 15.50 (Apr. 1993) 43–57.

"Liberation Theology." In *The Oxford Handbook of Systematic Theology*, edited by John Webster, Kathryn Tanner, and Iain Torrance, 634–52. Oxford: Oxford University Press, 2007.

"Liberation Theology and Politics." In *Religion in Public Life*, edited by Daniel Cohn-Sherbok and David McLellan, 74–90. New York: St. Martin's, 1992.

"The Bible and Politics." In *Scripture and Its Interpretation: A Global, Ecumenical Introduction to the Bible*, edited by Michael J. Gorman, 365–76. Grand Rapids: Baker Academic, 2017.

"How the Poor Can Liberate the Bible." *Priests & People* 6.10 (Oct. 1992) 367–71.

"That We Should Remember the Poor." *Scripture Bulletin* 24.1 (Jan. 1994) 2–14.

"'The Gospel, the Poor, and the Churches': Attitudes to Poverty in the British Churches and Biblical Exegesis." In *The Bible in Ethics: The Second Sheffield Colloquium*, edited by John W. Rogerson, Margaret Davies, and M. Daniel Carroll R., 213–31. Sheffield: Sheffield Academic Press, 1995.

"Reflections on the Politics of the Gospels." In *The Kingdom of God and Human Society: Essays by Members of the Scripture, Theology and Society Group*, edited by Robin Barbour, 224–41. Edinburgh: T. & T. Clark, 1993.

"The 'Interested' Interpreter." In *The Bible in Human Society: Essays in Honour of John Rogerson*, edited by Mark Daniel Carroll R. et al., 429–44. Journal for the Study of the Old Testament Supplements 200. Sheffield: Sheffield Academic Press, 1995.

"The Second Temple: Focus of Ideological Struggle?" In *Templum Amicitiae: Essays on the Second Temple presented to Ernst Bammel*, edited by William Horbury, 175–98. Journal for the Study of the Old Testament Supplements 48. Sheffield: JSOT Press, 1991.

"Friends of Albion?: The Danger of Cathedrals." In *Flagships of the Spirit: Cathedrals in Society*, edited by Stephen Platten and Christopher Lewis, 18–34, 181–82. London: Darton, Longman & Todd, 1998.

"Render to God What Belongs to God." *New Blackfriars* 70.830 (Sept. 1989) 365–71.

"Reading the Bible in the Struggle for Justice and Peace." *The Way* Supplement 63 (Fall 1988) 25–37.

"The Revaluation of All Values." *The Way* Supplement 79 (Spr 1994) 84–91.

"Reading the Apocalypse." *The Way* 39/4 (Oct. 1999) 349–60.

For Neville Black, John Vincent, Ched Myers, and
all my friends in Brazil (Christopher)

and

Jerry Stookey, OP (David)

All of whom speak of justice, of peace, and
of God in an inhumane world

Contents

Foreword by David B. Gowler | xi
Acknowledgments | xvii
Introduction | xix

1. Theology of Liberation and its Gift to Exegesis | 1
2. In Dialogue with Itumeleng Mosala: A Contribution to Liberation Exegesis | 19
3. Liberation Theology | 33
4. Liberation Theology and Politics | 55
5. The Bible and Politics | 72
6. How the Poor can Liberate the Bible | 83
7. That We Should Remember the Poor | 92
8. "The Gospel, the Poor, and the Churches": Attitudes to Poverty in the British Churches and Biblical Exegesis | 108
9. Reflections on the Politics of the Gospels | 127
10. The "Interested" Interpreter | 142
11. The Second Temple: Focus of Ideological Struggle? | 158
12. Friends of Albion?: The Danger of Cathedrals | 180
13. Render to God What Belongs to God | 194
14. Three Essays from *The Way*
14.1. Reading the Bible in the Struggle for Justice and Peace | 207
14.2. Reading the Apocalypse | 220
14.3. "The Revaluation of All Values" | 232

Foreword

David B. Gowler

THE QUESTION RAISED BY Gustavo Gutiérrez about how to speak of God in a world that is inhumane (Chapter I.4) is one of the many reasons that I came to study with Chris Rowland over thirty-five years ago and why I believe the publication of these two volumes of his essays on social justice, liberation theology, and Radical Christianity is so essential. How, indeed, can we speak of God as a loving parent in a world that continues to be so inhumane?

To be honest, a decade before I met Chris, I was asking a slightly different question: *whether* we can speak of any God in this inhumane world. Issues involved with that question and its connection to the historical Jesus eventually led me to change my major at the University of Illinois in Urbana-Champaign from chemical engineering to religion, where my academic training in biblical studies was initially ensconced within the historical-critical method. In due course—despite the seeming irrelevance of many of Jesus' sayings for contemporary people that stemmed from my historical and sociocultural research of the first-century contexts—I came to understand the "immediate" relevance of Jesus' teachings especially to those who, in the words of Howard Thurman in his *Jesus and the Disinherited*, live continually with their "backs against the wall."[1]

---

1. See what Chris writes in I.6, "How the Poor Can Liberate the Bible," about how historical-critical study can result in seeing the texts "as part of a strange and perhaps alien culture irrelevant to our modern age." Chris concludes that paragraph by saying,

Thurman helped lay the theological foundation for much of the civil rights movement in the United States and helped paved the way for other contextual theologies, including liberation theology, as he spoke about God in an inhumane world and believing, against all appearances, that the "contradictions of life were not final," in that the justice and peace of God would ultimately prevail.

So for me the question no longer is whether Jesus' ethics can be applicable to modern society, but how they can take their place as one voice among others in contemporary discussions. The essays by Christopher Rowland in these two volumes address these concerns—and more—as he speaks of God in an inhumane world, and they make a significant contribution to contextual theology. These essays take their place in the incredible body of work that Chris produced during his academic career. The importance of Chris's scholarship has been documented in many ways,[2] not the least of which is that not one, not two, but *three* Festschriften have been published in his honor, the first of which, *Radical Christian Voices and Practice*, published by Oxford University Press, I was honored to co-edit with Zoë Bennett.

Chris Rowland's scholarship is as impressive for its breadth as it is for its depth, and his brilliant work deservedly led to his appointment as the Dean Ireland's Professor (now Emeritus) of the Exegesis of Holy Scripture at Oxford University—the most prestigious chair in biblical studies in the UK. At Oxford University, The Dean Ireland's Professorship carries with it certain expectations about "scholarly exegesis" (cf. Chris's discussion of the collection of his essays in the Wissenschaftliche Untersuchungen zum Neuen Testament volume in his Introduction below), something in which Chris excels. In addition to—or, more correctly, as a necessary complement of—his more "traditional" scholarship, however, Chris has a radical passion for contextual theology, for liberation, justice, and equality, that stems from his ethical response to and critique of biblical texts. In Chris's brilliant yet humble, self-effacing way, his exegesis of biblical texts; his concern for those on the margins and with the responses of those like us who are not; and his interest in liberation, radical Christianity, and grassroots movements foster a dialogue in which all voices are heard and valued.

"The Bible is not just an ancient text; it is a Christian Scripture which has informed the lives of men and women down the centuries."

2. The collection of his essays on apocalypticism, for example, *By an Immediate Revelation*, contains forty-four essays and approaches nine hundred pages.

His 1992 Inaugural Lecture as Dean Ireland's Professor clearly stated his belief that exegesis was not "an arcane enterprise properly carried out only in academic institutions."[3] Instead, he declared:

> The interpreter of Holy Scripture will find him or herself engaged in an activity which will need to take cognisance of a wide range of interpretative questions precisely because the object of enquiry is Holy Scripture, the foundation texts of contemporary communities of faith as well as important evidence for ancient religion.[4]

In an example that would have surprised many in his audience—if not stunned or disturbed them—Chris focused on how New Testament exegetes should work alongside the "academically untrained," especially the poor and marginalized:

> I will suggest that the patterns of biblical exegesis which have emerged in parts of Latin America over the last twenty years offer an example of the way in which the academic endeavour and the practical faith of the non-professional reader can be found fruitfully alongside one another, rather than in a relation of mutual hostility.[5]

As Chris notes toward the end of Chapter I.10 below, he believes that interpreters must focus on both the "academic endeavour" of exegeting New Testament texts in their first-century contexts (as best they can) and locating their interpretations "within the quests for meaning and significance that exist within contemporary society." As Chris wrote:

> My location in an academic environment demands certain canons of critical application partly in order to gain a hearing and partly to gain credibility for the enterprise. . . . There is also an assumption that this kind of theoretical activity is worthwhile and that mere practice is insufficient. For me, therefore, there is oscillation between different sorts of worlds, trying to make sense of them, trying to inhabit both and be heard by the inhabitants of both and trying to interpret one to the other.[6]

---

3. Rowland, "'Open Thy Mouth,'" 228.
4. Rowland, "'Open Thy Mouth,'" 228.
5. Rowland, "'Open Thy Mouth,'" 229. Chris's Inaugural Lecture was in 1992, and this essay was published in 1993; at the time of writing this Foreword, the liberation theology perspective has now been informing biblical studies for over five decades, not just twenty years.
6. In this volume see Chapter 10, "An 'Interested' Observer," below (page 155).

The essays in both volumes of *Speaking of God in an Inhumane World* are paradigms of such fruitful complementary dialogues, ones that, if heard and heeded, can make a difference not just in academia but in people's lives.

This Foreword would not be complete, however, without mentioning not only how Chris's first visit to Brazil in 1983 contributed to these developments in his academic and personal life but also how they revolutionized his pedagogy. At its heart is the centrality of learning from the poor, marginalized, and oppressed—those at the base—and modifying—in fact, transforming—his pedagogical practices accordingly. I first experienced how Chris embodied this spirit and process in his teaching in 1987 at Cambridge during our tutorials and in weekly meetings with his doctoral students. Later as a colleague, I observed these practices while attending some of Chris's New Testament doctoral seminars at Oxford University and, especially, when team-teaching a course with him at my own institution, Oxford College of Emory University, in spring 2007. Chris indeed learned from what he calls "the academy of the poor, vulnerable, and outcast"—people in ordinary, everyday settings engaging with the Bible—and it transformed his teaching and pedagogy in ways that never could have happened without those grassroots experiences.[7] It is a tribute to him that he implemented those insights, practices, and that spirit at Cambridge University, the University of Oxford, other echelons of academia, and in his scholarship and teaching with the general public.

I am grateful for the people and resources that facilitated the publication of this volume, some of whom are noted on the Acknowledgements page—Jon-Philippe (JP) Ruhumuliza's editorial work was instrumental, as were the Pierce Program in Religion funds that supported his work. A faculty development grant and my Pierce Chair research funds enabled me to return to Cambridge again to finalize the selection and arrangement of essays and to craft a formal proposal to submit to a publisher. We decided that Wipf and Stock Publishers, who had published two authored books by Chris (*Radical Christianity* and *The Open Heaven*) and two that he coedited, would be the best home for the volume. We were delighted by the positive response of the editorial board and for the productive conversations that ensued (e.g., the recognition that the number, breadth, and depth of these essays necessitated two volumes, not just one).

The people to whom Chris and I dedicate these two volumes all demonstrate in word and deed not only *whether* we can speak of God in an inhumane world but illustrate *how* we should do so. Along with the people

---

7. See, for example, his discussions of the CEBs (*comunidades eclesiais de base*) in numerous chapters throughout these essays.

to whom Chris dedicated these volumes, I add one person, Jerry Stookey (OP), because of how he himself has dedicated his life and career to working for justice and peace, for speaking of God, and in his life demonstrating the love, justice, and peace of God in an inhumane world.

Jerry, one of my wife, Rita's, brothers, studied in Mexico City with the liberation theologian Miguel Concha Malo (OP) and then directed the Denver Justice and Peace Committee in Denver, Colorado, a grassroots organization dedicated to human rights and lasting peace in Latin America. From 1985 to 1991, Jerry lived and worked in a tiny village near Somotillo, Nicaragua, just a few short miles from the Honduran border. Jerry and the people with whom he lived were under constant danger of attack from the Contras, right-wing groups that during that time were supported and illegally funded by members of the Reagan administration in the United States.

Jerry helped open my eyes more fully to the "immediacy of the relationship between biblical narratives and the situation and experiences of the poor" (as Chris writes in Chapter I.14.2 below).[8] In the late 1980s, when Jerry visited the United States during his time in Nicaragua, I shared with Jerry my insights into the past that modern scholarship of first-century social, cultural, political, and economic contexts was continuing to uncover, and Jerry shared with me how many of those aspects—ones that he learned from the Nicaraguan people and that eluded New Testament scholars trained and operating in the "historical" method—were in numerous ways similar to or even the same as the daily life Jerry experienced in a small village in Nicaragua.

I know that I also speak for Chris when I say that it is our wish that these essays similarly can help provide for their readers that "moment of insight which enables us to see the way[s] in which [biblical texts] can illuminate our present circumstances" (Chapter I.6).[9]

Bibliography

Rowland, Christopher. "'Open Thy Mouth for the Dumb': A Task for the Exegete of Holy Scripture." *Biblical Interpretation* 1.2 (1993) 228–45.

---

8. In this volume see Chapter 14.2, "Reading the Apocalypse," below (page 211).
9. In this volume see Chapter 6, "How the Poor," below (page 84).

Acknowledgments

We are grateful for the editorial work of Jon-Philippe Ruhumuliza, who took the original essays—in rough form due to their transition from PDFs—and diligently worked to help transform them in their various manifestations into the single, coherent format required for this volume.

Funds from the Pierce Program in Religion at Oxford College of Emory University were made available to subsidize Jon-Philippe's work.

A faculty development grant from Oxford College of Emory University and research funds from David Gowler's Emory University Distinguished Chair—the Pierce Chair of Religion—permitted David to travel to Cambridge in June 2022 to begin work with Christopher Rowland on this two-volume project.

Introduction

Speaking of God in an Inhumane World

CHRISTOPHER ROWLAND

ONE OF THE TASKS of the years since my retirement has been to respond to the request from one of the editors of the series Wissenschaftliche Untersuchungen zum Neuen Testament to consider and then prepare a collection of published and unpublished articles for the series of which he is editor. This I did, but the reaction to my initial collection was not what I expected. The reason was not too far to seek. In addition to essays on the New Testament and its exegesis there were others which reflected the intellectual interests of a lifetime which had taken me into perhaps unusual areas for a New Testament scholar but which had been integral to my intellectual journey.

It was the result of a visit to Brazil in 1983 that led an increasing part not least in my extracurricular work with UK charities and church-related pedagogy. That meant much intellectual commuting between the political and the theological and between the historical and the contemporary, as I explored the historical antecedents of liberation theology and explored the pedagogy which I had witnessed in the grassroots communities in Brazil and how I might contribute to similar methods at work in the UK. The gap between text and context became a central part of my task as a professor of the exegesis of Holy Scripture, which I became in 1991. That sabbatical visit to Brazil in 1983 introduced me to a significant intellectual stimulus which has been at the heart of what has been central to my intellectual life over the last thirty years, not least a self-involving kind of biblical interpretation which complemented my theological and historical interests. I came back from Brazil wondering how I would integrate that experience into my professional life, first in Cambridge, then in Oxford. That struggle has been ongoing ever since. What I learned in Brazil led to a journey into neglected byways of the Christian tradition in, for example, the writings of Gerrard Winstanley (1609–1676).

The problem is that this dimension of intellectual life was hardly reflected in the collection of essays *By an Immediate Revelation*, published by Mohr Siebeck. In the second Festschrift volume, *Revealed Wisdom*,[10] edited by my dear friend John Ashton, now sadly departed, he wrote as follows in the Introduction:

> Chris Rowland is a man of many parts. This fact alone is sufficient to justify what might otherwise seem the strange decision to dedicate a second *Festschrift* to him only a couple of years after two close friends had put together an admirable collection of essays [*Radical Christian Voices and Practice* Oxford: Oxford University Press 2012] to celebrate his Christian radicalism and his eager promotion of the relatively new discipline of Reception History. It is tempting to say that in that book it was the man who was honoured, in the present volume the scholar; but Chris would be the first to reject, and reject vehemently, such a facile disjunction.[11]

John's comment is accurate to the extent that, for good or ill, the link between my immersion in biblical apocalypticism and its reception and the history and practice of Christian radicalism has been a dynamic which has been crucial to my research, writing, and teaching for the last forty years. I would be first to admit that it is work in progress. Indeed, as the years speed by, the chances of fully comprehending what is required to do justice to the subject become more attenuated. But as with the first two volumes presented to me on my retirement so with essay collections which are put together after retirement—the two areas together reflect the legacy I seek to leave.

It is true that there was one major exception, consideration of the texts and images of William Blake. When articles which reflected my interests in liberation theology and Christian radicalism were excluded from the 2022 Mohr Siebeck volume against my wishes, I found a way to include

---

10. Ashton, ed., *Revealed Wisdom*; see also Sullivan and Knight, eds., *Open Mind*.
11. Ashton, Introduction, 1.

one aspect of that interest in the already published volume (in Section IV: "William Blake: Apocalyptic Poet and Painter"). William Blake is a crucial part of the history of apocalypticism in the history of Christian intellectual thought, and it was accepted that articles on Blake should be included. His work may not have featured in the history of Christian thought, but that absence needs to be rectified as few understood the nature of apocalypticism better than he did, and, what is more, allowed an apocalyptic perspective, inspired by the Bible, to inspire his intellectual life.

The same Introduction prefaces both volumes since the inspiration for the essays in them both stems from my visits to Brazil. The first essay in Volume 2 of *Speaking of God in an Inhumane World* starts with the recollection of a crucial meeting four years before my first visit to Brazil in 1983 and my firsthand experience of liberation theology and the *comunidades eclesiais de base*. The subject-matter of that article is a crucial part of my immersion in the neglected evidence of Christian radicalism, specifically the writings and life of Gerrard Winstanley (1609–1676). Related texts also formed part of a study of the radical interpretation of the Apocalypse in the Mohr Siebeck volume. My attempt to reflect on the Latin American experience of 1983 in my 1988 book *Radical Christianity* indicated the interplay of the contemporary manifestations and the history of Christian radicalism. The first volume of *Speaking of God in an Inhumane World* (e.g., I.1, I.2, and I.13) includes my initial engagement with the biblically orientated writings from the liberation theology movement, my reading of the Bible from the perspective of the poor (I.6, I.7, and I.8), essays characterized by my growing awareness of the political dimensions of biblical texts (I.9), and the exploration of this dimension that the engagement with liberation theology had opened up for me (I.10, I.11, I.12, and I.14). Volume 2 has a more explicit emphasis on Christian radicalism with studies on the writing and life of Gerrard Winstanley and his contemporaries, and essays on Thomas Müntzer (c. 1489–1525); William Blake (1757–1827); the twentieth-century lawyer and exponent of Christian radicals, William Stringfellow (1928–1985; see II.5, II.7, II.8, II.9, II.10, II.12, and II.13); and more general reflections on Christian radicalism (II.1, II.2, II.3, II.4, II.6, and II.11).

So, both volumes are an attempt to complement what has already been published not only to explain my intellectual journey but also to help others understand better how the apocalyptic and radical complement each other and offer a perspective on the basis of Christian theology. The various essays in both volumes explore this theme and seek to demonstrate both its importance and its intellectual originality as a neglected dimension of Christian life and thought down the centuries. The work which I have done in this area makes no claim to be comprehensive, but it does make a claim to be a contribution to a much-neglected subject.

Last but not least: words cannot express the gratitude I owe to David Gowler for his offer to undertake the preparation of the manuscript for publication. I know all too well what a chore it is to check the transformation of pdfs into Word documents ready for publication. Over time I have learned the hard way that whatever contributions I now have to make to learning have been impeded recently by an emergency operation for an undetected spinal abscess followed by four months in the hospital. If it had been left to me to prepare the book, it would have been impossible. David's generous offer allowed the other dimension of my intellectual life to complement the contemporary Mohr Siebeck project, the preparation of which was also seriously affected by my illness. There is an appropriateness about David having taken this on when he, along with Zoë Bennett, had edited a volume of essays presented to me in 2012 in which "radical Christian voices and practice" had been the subject matter (mentioned earlier). David has demonstrated what a good friend he is by making possible what I know I could not have done myself.

Along with David's dedication, I dedicate this book to Neville Black and John Vincent, who welcomed me, and allowed me to share in their work, when I returned from Brazil in 1983, and I saw that what had inspired me in Brazil was already happening in Britain; to Ched Myers, from whom I have learned so much; and to all my friends in Brazil who taught me so much about their work, enabling people at the grassroots to engage with the Bible in the midst of life: "action is the life of all, and if thou dost not act, thou dost nothing."[12]

Bibliography

Ashton, John F. "Introduction." In *Revealed Wisdom: Studies in Apocalyptic in Honour of Christopher Rowland*, edited by John F. Ashton. Ancient Judaism and Early Christianity 88. Leiden: Brill, 2014.

———, ed. *Revealed Wisdom: Studies in Apocalyptic in Honour of Christopher Rowland*. Ancient Judaism and Early Christianity 88. Leiden: Brill, 2014.

Bennett. Zoë, and David B. Gowler, eds. *Radical Christian Voices and Practice: Essays in Honour of Christopher Rowland*. Oxford: Oxford University Press, 2012.

Rowland, Christopher. *By an Immediate Revelation: Studies in Apocalypticism, Its Origins and Effects*. Wissenschaftliche Untersuchungen zum Neuen Testament 473. Tübingen: Mohr Siebeck, 2022.

———. *The Open Heaven: A Study of Apocalyptic in Judaism and Early Christianity*. 1982. Reprint, Eugene, OR: Wipf & Stock, 2002.

12. Winstanley, *Works*, 315–16.

———. "'Open Thy Mouth for the Dumb': A Task for the Exegete of Holy Scripture." *Biblical Interpretation* 1.2 (1993) 228–45.

———. *Radical Christianity: A Reading of Recovery*. 1988. Reprint, Eugene, OR: Wipf & Stock, 2004.

Sullivan, Kevin, and Jonathan Knight, eds. *The Open Mind: Essays in Honour of Christopher Rowland*. London: Bloomsbury, 2015.

Thurman, Howard. *Jesus and the Disinherited*. 1949. Reprint, Boston: Beacon, 1996.

Winstanley, Gerrard. *The Works of Gerrard Winstanley*. Edited by George H. Sabine. Ithaca: Cornell University Press, 1941.

1

Theology of Liberation and its Gift to Exegesis

Finding the Biblical World

THE FUTURE OF THE theology of liberation is hidden in a cloud of controversy.[1] Nevertheless, I have a shrewd suspicion that, whatever the aspirations of the religious authorities might be, we are dealing with an approach to the Bible and a way of Christian discipleship which is so deep-rooted that it will be difficult to dislodge, at least in some areas of Latin America. This is not to suggest that the way ahead for the liberation theologians is going to be an easy one. But the fact is that in a country like Brazil there is an intimate link between this theological approach and the life of the church. The importance of the Basic Christian Communities in the lives of ordinary Christians and in the work of the theologians of liberation themselves cannot be overestimated. They have provided the framework and the foundation on which its edifice has been built. There may be moves against practitioners of the theology of liberation, but there will still be the setting for that theological reflection. What is more, there are signs that the theological method has been appropriated in certain quarters of North American and European theology. But what most concerns us here is the fact that the theology of

---

1. See notably the Vatican document "Instruction on certain aspects of the 'Theology of Liberation'" issued by the Sacred Congregation for the Doctrine of the Faith, Rome, September 1984.

liberation is producing distinctive approaches to biblical interpretation which in my view demand a hearing from us.

It is probably fair to say that in the first instance the theology of liberation inherited many of the approaches of North American and European biblical scholarship.[2] It is true that from the start there was a concern to emphasize the importance of the site of reading and interpreting of the exegete and theologian.[3] Those of us in Europe were asked to examine the impact of our setting and traditions on our exegetical concerns. But initially the treatment of the early Christian sources flowed in fairly traditional channels, albeit with an increased concern for the political dimension of the gospel. There was little that was new in the interpretative methods adopted. Few of the liberation theologians well known in this country would regard themselves as biblical specialists (Jose Porfirio Miranda is an exception).[4] Consequently, in their New Testament exegesis they have tended to take over the methods and many of the conclusions of those biblical scholars who adopt the historical-critical method, a method of interpretation which dominates the exegesis of our era, and which is infrequently subjected to critical scrutiny.

Alongside the emergence of liberation theology there has been a resurgence of interest in the social world of the biblical writers. Such interest, of course, is nothing new. Pioneers like Deissmann[5] earlier in this century provided a wealth of material on the basis of which the world of early Christianity could be constructed. What is different about much of the recent inquiry into the social world of the biblical writings is that it has been done with sociological tools. In other words, we have, in addition to the study of social history, sociologies of early Christianity in which a variety of paradigms familiar to the sociologist and social anthropologist have been deliberately and explicitly used to examine Christian origins. Thus, we find the theory of cognitive dissonance (i.e., analysis of responses to the failure of beliefs to be fulfilled in experience) being used in the study of the Hebrew Bible prophetic literature by Robert Carroll[6] and in the study of early Christian literature by John Gager.[7]

I do not know enough about the various interpreters involved in this enterprise to be sure that the emergence of interest in the sociology of the

2. See, for example, Sobrino, *Christology*; Boff, *Jesus Christ, Liberator*.
3. See Segundo, *Liberation of Theology*.
4. Miranda, *Marx and the Bible*.
5. Deissmann, *Light from the Ancient Near East*.
6. Carroll, *When Prophecy Failed*.
7. Gager, *Kingdom and Community*.

biblical communities initially had any links with the theology of liberation. Nevertheless, as both have developed there has clearly emerged a confluence of interest. We find in a recent collection edited by Norman Gottwald[8] that contributions from several of the major figures in the discussion of the social world of the biblical communities stand alongside those of feminist biblical exegetes like Elisabeth Schüssler Fiorenza and Third World interpreters.

Much of this exegesis still follows fairly conventional patterns, albeit with an explicit concern to spell out the site of reading of the different interpreters. The difference of perspective provokes different concerns, though the interpretation itself still treads ground that would be fairly familiar to us all. Thus, in the feminist/liberationist exegesis (manifest particularly in Schüssler Fiorenza's *In Memory of Her*) there is a concern to shed light on the place of women in the earliest Christian communities. But as well as elucidating neglected features of biblical literature, this approach has revealed how much mainstream biblical exegesis has led to an excessive concentration on various types of theological discourse at the expense of the elucidation of the social world and the character of the ethical response. So an outcome of the new approach is a change of interest: away from the theology of the writers to a concern for their social world and practices.

There is in my mind little doubt that these developments have been to the benefit of biblical study. Others better equipped than I am will be able to assess the contribution of Norman Gottwald's massive *Tribes of Yahweh* to the study of Israelite origins, but, as far as the New Testament is concerned, I have found the discussions of various aspects of early Christianity by Gerd Theissen enlightening.[9] The contrast between the social setting of the Pauline churches and that of Jesus' followers in rural Palestine has opened up a new basis for understanding the religious and social development of primitive Christianity. Similarly, Wayne Meeks's *The First Urban Christians,* while not exactly revolutionizing Pauline studies, has sought to ask pertinent questions about the organization and belief-systems of Paul and his communities.

One of the features of the resurgence of interest in the social world of the early Christians, however, has been the conspicuous lack of an explicitly Marxist interpretation of early Christian literature. There is little doubt that the influence of Marx lurks in the background of some recent writing on the social world of early Christianity, whether it be acknowledged or not, but it is probably fair to say that, apart from the work of Heinz Kreissig[10]

---

8. Gottwald, *Bible and Liberation.*
9. Theissen, *First Followers of Jesus*; Theissen, *Social Setting of Pauline Christianity.*
10. Kreissig, *Geschichte des Hellenismus.*

and Milan Machovec,[11] Kautsky's *Foundations of Christianity* is still a rather lonely, and dated, monument to such an enterprise. In the light of the stimulating work of Geoffrey de Sainte Croix *(The Class Struggle in the Ancient Greek World)*[12] it may well be time to explore such an avenue again. But there is one significant exception to which I would now like to turn, Fernando Belo's *A Materialist Reading of the Gospel of Mark*.

Introducing Belo

Compared with the reading of most of the books and articles mentioned so far, the reading of Belo's book comes as something of a shock to one who has been schooled in the historical-critical method. Its significance is that it offers an entry into a rather different interpretative world, which has connections with mainstream exegesis and with some of the distinctive exegetical approaches now emerging in Latin America. As such it offers a convenient introduction to types of biblical exegesis influenced by liberation theology. Clearly Belo feels himself to be an outsider, and his hermeneutical approach betrays an idiosyncratic amalgam of interpretative tools which is as daunting as it is thought-provoking.[13] He writes from a clear Marxist perspective, in which concern to elucidate the relationship between the ideological superstructure in the religious language and the economic base is an important datum. As far as he is concerned, the Gospel of Mark is a product of the social formation of its day, and the text needs to be examined in this light. Belo is not interested in getting behind the text of Mark to ask what really happened either in the life of Jesus or in the life of the Markan community. His approach is to examine the Gospel as a story which takes place in a particular historical setting and for the proper understanding of which knowledge of the wider setting is important. Belo's analysis proceeds along lines similar to those used in the interpretation of, say, a Dickens novel. Questions of the historicity or otherwise of the events described are ignored, though the wider historical setting of the narrative is explored and explained. Belo's concern with the social setting is linked to a form of structural analysis of the text which tends to play down the role of the author and his concerns. Nevertheless, Belo's use of interpretative tools is eclectic, and he does not entirely ignore the author and his community (what Belo terms the "narrator/readers level"). But before I explain

11. Machovec, *A Marxist Looks at Jesus*.

12. De Ste. Croix, *Class Struggle in the Ancient Greek World*. Cf. Jameson, *Political Unconscious*.

13. Cf. a similar thesis in Pixley, *God's Kingdom*.

the character of Belo's structuralist method, let me say a little more about his treatment of the social setting of the Markan narrative.

Belo's book is in three major parts. The first includes a theoretical discussion of his interpretative method; an examination of the economic, political, and ideological setting in first-century Palestine; and a discussion of the function of the Torah within Jewish society. The second, and most substantial, part of the book consists of a commentary on the Gospel of Mark, in which the complicated method of reading is put into practice. The book concludes with an essay in materialist ecclesiology, in which the main strands of the commentary are brought together and amplified.

In his discussion of the mode of production in biblical Palestine, Belo starts off with an examination of the Torah. He makes a distinction between two systems which he can find in the Torah, one based on Leviticus (what he calls the pollution system) and one based on Deuteronomy (the debt system). It is the system found in Deuteronomy which Belo argues is concerned with social equality. The fact that the two systems are found juxtaposed in the Torah is in Belo's view indicative of a class conflict in postexilic Judaism. The Levitical system, centered as it is on the cult and the privileges of the priests, contrasts with the Deuteronomic system, in which is found the old ethic of brotherhood of the nomadic tribes, which promoted social equality.[14] In the canon of the Hebrew Bible it is the Levitical system which occupies a more prominent position. That is indicative of the fact that it was the priestly caste which was responsible for the final form of the text of the Torah and thus gave their class power a solid foundation in the sacred text.[15] The distinction between the two systems has a prominent role to play in Belo's interpretation of Mark. It is with a radicalized version of the system based on Deuteronomy that Belo considers that Jesus sides, in the narrative of Mark, over against the system which promoted the cult.

In a chapter on Palestine in the first century CE, Belo considers the economics, politics, and ideology of the area. He suggests that the sub-Asiatic mode of production was dominant in Judea and contrasts this with Galilee, which he considers was more intimately linked with the dominant slave-based mode of production of the Roman empire. There is a short discussion of the various political and regional tensions (e.g., Galilee versus Judea and the village versus the city) as well as the importance of the cult-dominated life of Jerusalem and its environs. Belo then turns to what he calls the production in writing, circulation, and consumption of texts of the social formation. His major concern in this section is an outline of the biblical

---

14. Belo, *Materialist Reading*, 44, 56.
15. Belo, *Materialist Reading*, 55–56.

books, and in particular the growth of Jewish eschatology, though he does not explore in any depth the reasons for the production of this literature and its relationship to the socioeconomic situation he describes. In the ideological field the Temple is singled out as an object of considerable importance. In making this statement Belo signals that in his view the words of Jesus against the Temple have to take full account of the challenge to the economic as well as the religious life of the Jewish people.

As far as the class struggle in Palestine is concerned, Belo repeats the opinion of many scholars that the economic situation in the first century CE provoked the emergence of Zealot-type groups, whose enemies were both the Romans and the priestly aristocracy. The goal of the Zealots, he claims, was not a revolution which would completely abolish the existing economic order but a rebellion which would restore it in its pure form.

As we might have expected, consideration of the economic and social setting of the narrative is an important component of Belo's reading, but it is not sufficient for him to embark immediately on an interpretation of the text without further reflection on the question: how is Mark to be read? Belo refuses to follow the path of mainstream New Testament exegesis, whether it be redaction criticism and its concern with the relationship of the various parts of the narrative to the needs of the community for which it was written, or the historical Jesus approach which ascribes the words and events to the situation in Jesus' ministry. As we have seen, a concern for the general historical setting of the story is of central importance for Belo's approach. Indeed, he would not want to exclude the possibility that some parts of the text are best understood as evidence of what he calls the "narrator/readers level," by which he means the traditional concerns of the redaction critics. But it is clear that, unlike most exegetes, the intention of the author is rejected as a single overriding interpretative key. Belo prefers to follow the pattern of reading suggested by Barthes, particularly in the latter's textual analysis of the Balzac story *Sarrasine*. Belo sets out an elaborate system of reading based on the different types of textual material. In his view, the text is a complex in which different types of textual material are juxtaposed and play differing functions within the narrative as a whole. The interpretative method is rather elaborate. A number of textual functions, which Belo calls codes, act as signals to the reader to read the narrative in particular ways.

When summarized, Belo's reading of the Gospel of Mark seems very strange, because it plays down what has been dominant in most study of Mark, the cross. The conclusion of Belo's reading is that the strategy of Jesus as set out in the narrative was to proclaim the kingdom and by his mighty deeds to convince disciples that he was the Messiah. After the recognition of his messiahship by Peter, Jesus' strategy alters, firstly to an articulation of his messiahship over against the view of the Zealots, and secondly to a journey to Jerusalem as a prelude to the extension of his message to the pagan world and his consequent absence from the circle of his disciples. In the process of the narrative Jesus' subversion of the symbolic order, particularly of the system based on Leviticus, is stressed. Thus, for example, Jesus touches a leper, and far from becoming unclean himself, he cures the leper (Mark 1:40–45). In the early part of the narrative there is gradually articulated a division between Jesus and the disciples on the one hand and the crowds on the other. Jesus' strategy is to avoid the towns, centers of both the crowds and the authorities, and, when he cannot escape them, to create a space for himself and his disciples. The problem with the crowds is that their understanding of messianism is dominated totally by the Zealot strategy, which seeks to find a military leader to fight the Romans, and into which mold they seek to fit Jesus. The orders given to the people who have been cured to remain silent have as their function prevention of the precipitation of a messianic movement of a Zealot type, and the same is also true of the silencing of the demons.

Contrary to what one might expect, Belo argues that a part of the Gospel is dedicated to the articulation of an alternative strategy of Jesus over against the Zealots. Jesus' strategy is more radical, in that it challenges the centrality of the Temple in the economic and religious life of Israel. He also repudiates the means whereby the Zealots sought to implement their strategy, namely armed revolt against Rome. Belo notes the way in which Jesus seeks to escape from the crowds, and, in the last days in Jerusalem, seeks refuge away from the city (e.g., Mark 11:11).[16] According to Belo he does this to escape death and so pursue his mission to the pagans. In his absence the practice of the disciples will no longer be focused on the body of Jesus but on the practice of sharing bread.

Belo argues that Jesus did not go up to Jerusalem to die, though he was aware of the possibility of death. He came to Jerusalem to preach in the Temple, to proclaim that the vineyard would be given to others, and to begin his exodus to the pagans. It is only the transfer of Judas back from the circle of Jesus to the circle of the dominant class which enables the authorities to put an end to the strategies of Jesus. Jesus is engaged in a radical subversion of the codes of society. He challenges the current conception of the family, the centrality of the temple and the hegemony of the priests, current conceptions of messiahship and wealth, and he rejects the master/servant relationship. In Belo's view Jesus' message as found in this narrative is non-violent communism. He suggests that there was only

---

16. Belo, *Materialist Reading*, 247.

one way in which Jesus' non-revolutionary communism could have been extended in a situation where the Roman economic and political system was so powerful, other than by marginalization like the Essenes, and that was by means of opening up the gospel to other nations; hence the exodus to the pagans. The resurrection narrative indicates that the narrative of Jesus did not end with his death but started up again: the mission to the pagans was renewed by way of Galilee.

As the narrative unfolds, the ability to understand the strategy of Jesus not only as a messianic practice but also as one which had to be distinguished from the Zealots is a matter of importance. In this, parables play an important role. The parable of the Sower, for example, offers a way of understanding the narrative of Jesus. Belo contrasts the first soil, where the hearers—by being linked with Satan—are Jesus' adversaries, and the last soil, which refers to those who break completely with the prevailing system and transfer into the kingdom.[17] It is of central importance, if the transference is to be made, that a conversion takes place. The problem with the authorities is that their presuppositions prevent them from understanding the true character of Jesus' mission. Indeed, eventually they understand Jesus' deeds not as a messianic practice but as one diametrically opposed to the ways of God, a way of violence which threatens the entire economic, political, and ideological system upon which their power is based.

A major feature of Belo's interpretation is his view that in the Gospel of Mark we have the juxtaposition of what he calls the messianic narrative, based on the miracles and the radical teaching, and a theological discourse, which permeates the second half of the narrative and explains the necessity for Jesus' death. He contrasts the two by giving them the labels pre- and post-paschal discourse. As is evident from these labels, the pre-paschal narrative is not dominated by the cross and the divine necessity of Jesus' suffering, whereas the post-paschal discourse is shot through with an understanding of Jesus' death as predestined. In a rather complicated discussion, Belo argues that in the text of Mark's Gospel the post-paschal elements have erased features of the messianic narrative, though he thinks that its full character can be restored. He stresses that the restoration of the pre-paschal text is not restoration of something originally in a source available to the evangelist. He considers that the narrator erased elements of the pre-paschal narrative in the very process of writing. In so doing the narrator changed the execution of Jesus by the authorities, which originally was devoid of any doctrinal significance, into a death with profound theological meaning.[18]

17. Belo, *Materialist Reading*, 259.
18. Belo, *Materialist Reading*, 280.

Thus, the narrator gave the messianic/post-paschal narrative a significant push in the direction of the dominance of the theological discourse. This is a first step on the road to Christianity, in which, according to Belo, the ideological instance is dominant. The reason for this development he traces to the political powerlessness of the emerging Christian communities in the face of the all-powerful Roman economic system. Charity as a practice, argues Belo, will soon simply become a consequence of ideology. This stands in direct contrast to what Belo believes is the major thrust of the Markan messianic narrative: the practice of power in relation to the bodies of those afflicted with uncleanness; the practice of teaching, that is, of reading the practice of power; the practice of subversion of the Israelite symbolic field and a strategy for dealing with the crowds and the authorities.[19] The messianic practice, in Belo's words, is a process of transforming a given raw material (economic, political, and ideological relations) into a product (a new ecclesial relation in the circle of the disciples), a transformation which is effected by human labor.[20] This is a splendidly provocative sentence which raises a host of interpretative and critical questions. According to Belo the messianic practice of Jesus represents a radicalization of the system based on Deuteronomy and the prophets and a rejection of the system based on Leviticus. In this emphasis on the practice of Jesus and the detection of the shift towards the primacy of the ideological in the account of Jesus' life one can detect a distinctive emphasis of the theology of liberation applied to a particular problem in the Markan narrative.

A summary can hardly do justice to the complexity and wide-ranging character of the reading of Mark offered by Belo. For one thing, such an attempt to summarize makes the various interpretations seem wildly improbable. Indeed, I would not want to pretend that I found the whole edifice convincing, and in detail the analysis can be faulted at several places. The preoccupation with the sub-Asiatic mode of production has been criticized,[21] and many biblical scholars will take exception to Belo's polarization of the Levitical and Deuteronomic systems. The conflict between the messianic narrative and the theological discourse may at first seem far-fetched, though it has to be said that Belo is merely putting a new gloss on a disjunction in the Markan narrative which has for a long time fascinated interpreters. In speaking about the messianic narrative and the theological discourse which he believes partly displaced it he is only using alternative terminology to discuss a long-familiar feature: the change of tone after Peter's confession.

19. Belo, *Materialist Reading*, 127.
20. Belo, *Materialist Reading*, 253.
21. E.g., see de Ste. Croix, *Class Struggle in the Ancient Greek World*, 157–59.

While there has been a tendency in recent scholarship to concentrate on what Belo calls the theological discourse as the heart of the evangelist's message, Belo wants to rehabilitate the central place of the first part of the narrative and so attempt to do justice to the proclamation and practice of the kingdom within the story as a whole. But to relegate the material about suffering merely to a theological discourse which is at odds with the first part of the narrative seems to me to be unnecessary.

Firstly, while it can be said that there are elements in the theological discourse in which the seeds of a developing interest in the significance of Jesus' death as a primary element of what constitutes the messianic circle are to be found, it is not apparent that this discourse necessarily undermines entirely the messianic narrative. Secondly, as Belo points out, there are two economic fields which impinge on the Markan narrative: the Jewish and the Roman. The main thrust of the words and deeds of Jesus concerned the Jewish economic system, centered in Judea on the Temple (though there may also have been a rejection of the Roman slave-based system in Mark 12:13–17, if aspects of Belo's reading are correct). But overarching the Jewish system was the big Roman system. While there may have been a slight possibility of changing the balance in favor of the "Deuteronomic" and against the prominence of the Temple, the extension of such a change outside Palestine would have to contend with the dominant Roman system. While it would be wrong to suggest that the emphasis on suffering in the second half of the Gospel indicates acceptance of that system, it could be argued that in terms of the strategy of the kingdom as set out in the Markan narrative there had to be acceptance that any challenge of it, even if it be non-violent, would involve suffering and death. This is in fact to take up a point made towards the end of Belo's study, where he suggests that the resort to the theological discourse took place precisely because of the powerlessness of the Christian within the Roman empire. Even if this theory be discounted, it is surely part of the messianic practice as set out in Mark to accept the division and hostility which emerge from the proclamation and practice of the kingdom. According to Belo's own reading Jesus reflects throughout the Gospel on the consequences of his practice. As the story unfolds, that reflection inexorably points towards the acceptance of death and martyrdom. Thus, within the narrative of the messianic practice there exists the soil in which the later "theological discourse" could develop, where the focus of attention switches from a narrative of practice to discussion about ideas. So whatever impetus there may have been to elaborate the theological discourse, it must be questioned whether its presence in the Gospel is quite as much at odds with the messianic narrative as Belo supposes.

What, however, is surely the most common criticism of the book is that both Marx and structuralism are being allowed to contaminate the interpretation of biblical texts. I suspect that even those of us who do not react negatively to Belo's use of Marxist tools will want to question how far unadulterated Marx can really be helpful in interpreting the biblical narrative without ending up with a gross distortion of the text. I suspect that Belo himself may recognize this, as it is interesting that his discussion of the resurrection would be totally unacceptable to orthodox Marxists and in fact is more akin to an outlook influenced by Ernst Bloch.

Yet, with all its blemishes, I would echo the comment of Robin Scroggs, who stated unequivocally that Belo needs a hearing.[22] It seems to me that what is most important about this book is not the specific results of the interpretation so much as the suggestive character of the method adopted. Thus, the interplay of different textual functions within the narrative and the contrast between the strategies of the various actors suggest new possibilities in discussions of the Gospel. Belo's interpretative method, eclectic as it is, shows the way in which a wide range of tools can be used, without there being any feeling that by opting for a form of structural interpretation all concern with the historical context is abandoned.

Ideological Superstructure and Economic Base

Why should we use the theory of a nineteenth-century atheist to interpret a first-century theological text? I am not sure that I can offer an easy answer to that question. But I would like to make two comments in connection with it. First of all, it seems to me that the emerging interest in the social world of the New Testament, particularly the relationship between the development of ideas and their social formation, owes a debt to the Marxist tradition which is not always acknowledged. In my view, the fact that Belo makes a clean breast of his Marxist presuppositions should not make us suppose that the influence of Marx is absent in at least an indirect form in other sociological approaches to biblical literature. Second, it is incumbent upon all of us engaged in biblical interpretation to engage more readily than we are prepared to in an analysis of the theoretical basis of our interpretations, however widely practiced a particular interpretative method may be. That is one thing that Belo's book has compelled me to examine.

Of course, one of the great difficulties confronting not only the Marxian approach to early Christian literature but also the renewed interest in the social world of the New Testament is that we do not possess sufficient

22. Scroggs, Review of *A Materialist Reading*.

information about the specific social formations in which particular texts were written. Indeed, we are really in no position to write a reliable social and economic history of first-century Palestine. Those who have tried to do so have had to rely upon isolated pieces of evidence in order to draw far-reaching conclusions about particular areas and periods. For example, the contrast between the situation in Galilee as compared with Judea is clearly important, and yet the information we have at our disposal upon which we can base our assessment of first-century Galilee is extremely limited. When we add to this the fact that we know so little about the specific circumstances in which the extant literary works originated, it will be seen that the material for relating literature and its content to its social formation is meager. Some would probably have us accept the severe limitations placed upon us by the evidence and resist the temptation to speculate about the relationship between the ideological superstructure and the economic base. While accepting the force of the arguments of those who are reluctant to move beyond the limits placed upon them by the evidence, I would hope that, assuming such approaches to the biblical literature are taken further, we may move towards a position in which we can examine the relationship between the ideological plane and the underlying social formation. Some New Testament exegetes have been willing to accept a link between the ideas and the social formation, though they have tended to ignore wider economic and political considerations, not to mention the possible contribution of a class struggle to the formation of the text. The work of Belo has reminded us that a complete indebtedness to the insight of Marx will involve testing the hypothesis that the textual product may itself manifest the contradictions of the class struggle.

There is in my view room for a contribution from a Marxist influenced literary criticism, which takes seriously the social setting and specifically the economic struggles as a potent force in the origin and development of religious ideas, though I would want to add that I myself could not accept the Marxist interpretative edifice without important qualifications. In stressing the contribution that such an approach may make we must not be guilty of supposing a simple and direct connection between the economic base and the ideological superstructure, what Geoffrey de Sainte Croix has aptly called "making leaves grow on roots." The form and content of all literature have a degree of autonomy which cannot be completely explained by reference to the social formation. In considering the literary products of first-century Judaism, the dominance and the influence of the Scriptures, whatever the conflicts which led to their production and canonization, make it difficult to suppose that naive Marxist interpretations can adequately explain ideas. The peculiarities of the Jewish religion and the specific character of its religious tradition must not be ignored. We must not underestimate the influence of the ideas themselves on the emergence of the social formation itself.[23]

We saw reason to question whether there is such a fundamental contradiction between the whole of what Belo calls the theological discourse and the messianic narrative. It seems to me, however, that in posing the question of the relationship between the messianic narrative and the theological discourse Belo has laid before us an issue of some importance for the discussion of christology. I think that it is probably fair to say that the christology of the New Testament has concentrated almost exclusively on the questions: who was Jesus, and how did the first Christians express and develop their convictions about him? The relationship between christology and the community's self-understanding becomes so attenuated that christology becomes a series of statements whose relationship to the human existence of the writers and readers is not always apparent. For a writer like Paul the experience of the Spirit in the believer and the convictions about the person of Christ are closely related, and it would be unwise to suppose that christological convictions can and should be separated from the understanding of the impact of the social world on the disciple and the character of his response.

Few would want to assert that to be a Christian consisted either solely or principally in maintaining the validity of a particular collection of beliefs, but in writing about early Christianity we frequently give the impression that what is most important in discussing the early church is the relationship between ideas and the development of ideas without necessarily examining the relationship between those ideas and the social matrix in which they were formulated.

An important step in the direction of redressing the balance was taken by Wayne Meeks in what I consider to be a significant contribution to our understanding of christology and its relationship to its social world, his article "The Man from Heaven in Johannine Sectarianism."[24] In this article Meeks concentrates on the pattern of descent/ascent of the heavenly Christ. It is not his concern to establish the relationship of this pattern either to Jewish or gnostic material (though he does conclude that it is at least plausible that Johannine christology helped to create some of the gnostic myths). Rather, his concern is to explain the function of the mythical pattern within the Fourth Gospel. In particular, he wants to investigate the dialectic between the symbolic world of the Johannine community and the group's historical experience. This dialectic, he argues, served both to

23. Cf. Lash, *Matter of Hope*, 120.
24. Meeks, "Man from Heaven."

explain that experience and to motivate and form the reaction of group members to that experience. The pattern of descent/ascent, Meek argues, depicts Jesus as the Stranger from Heaven. He states:

> So long as we approach the Johannine literature as a chapter in the history of ideas, it will defy our understanding . . . the reader cannot understand any part of the Fourth Gospel until he understands the whole book functions for its readers in precisely the same way that the epiphany of its hero functions, within its narratives and dialogues.[25]

The book is seen by Meeks as an etiology of the Johannine group. In telling the story of the Son of Man who came down from heaven and then ascended after choosing a few of his own out of the world, the book defines and vindicates the existence of the community that saw itself as unique, alien from its world, under attack, misunderstood, but living in unity with Christ and through him with God. The symbolic universe was not only the reflection or projection of the group's social situation. The christological claims of the Johannine Christians resulted in their becoming alienated and finally expelled from the synagogue, but that alienation was in turn explained by the further developments of christological motifs, which in turn drove the group into further isolation.[26] It was a case of continual, harmonic reinforcement of real experience and ideology.

Even if you cannot go the whole way with Meeks in his analysis of this particular theme, it has to be admitted that he has put his finger on the relationship between ideas and their social formation which could bear fruit in the study of christology.

As has been noted, there is a great danger in rushing to simplistic conclusions on the basis of such treatment of the emerging doctrine of early Christianity. Nevertheless, it seems to me that the study of christology, soteriology, and ecclesiology needs to explore how far its function on what de Ste. Croix terms "the ideological plane" can help us illuminate particular aspects of the social setting of early Christian groups.[27] I would have thought that the emergence of developed christology ought to be considered in this light. It is a well-known fact that during the first century CE early Christian use of the title Messiah underwent quite a profound change, so that within a very short time the term was being used virtually as a proper name with little or no relic of its messianic significance. While it may be true that in the Fourth Gospel the title Messiah still retains some of its original Jewish

---

25. Meeks, "Man from Heaven," 68.
26. This issue is explored in Radcliffe, "'My Lord and my God.'"
27. de Ste. Croix, *Class Struggle*, 409–52.

eschatological significance, its importance has receded, compared with titles like the Son of Man, the Son of God, the descent/ascent formula, and the sending formula. The reason for the eclipse of the messianic title used of the eschatological role of Jesus is a phenomenon which certainly deserves to be considered in the light of the socio-economic situation and practice of emerging Christianity. In the past it has been easy to explain the retreat from messianism and eschatology in purely religious terms (e.g., compensation for the delay of the Parousia). In the future I suspect that we shall want to take more seriously the relationship between such ideological shifts and the developing pattern of the life of the Christian church. While it would be naive to suppose that the shift from rural Palestine to the urban Hellenistic world was entirely responsible, the character of the Christian response appropriate, indeed possible, within the latter may well have affected the form of the developing Christian confession.

Some studies of emerging Jewish eschatology have not ignored the link between the development of ideas and the social setting. Thus, for example, Otto Plöger[28] has argued that in post-exilic Judaism there was a conflict between a priestly group and a group whose views can be found in some prophetic texts; the former being content to see the fulfilment of the prophetic hope in the restored Temple, where the latter still looked forward to the fulfilment of the prophetic promises. More recently P. D. Hanson has argued that a particular form of the eschatological hope has its origins in the struggles that were going on in the post-exilic community.[29] What is clearly stressed here is the importance of the social matrix for understanding the development and conflict of ideas. Hanson believes that it is possible to trace a development in the use of mythological language from Deutero-Isaiah, where it is used to speak of actual historical events, to Trito-Isaiah, where it is used literally of God's actual irruption into the present state of affairs to establish a new heaven and a new earth. He believes that this change took place because of the marginalization of visionary groups in the Isaianic tradition, and the emerging hegemony of the priestly group supported as they were by Ezekiel's vision. With this marginalization there was a progressive despair that the hopes for Israel could be fulfilled while society was ordered as it was, and consequently there was a need to retreat into another world as the only appropriate arena for the fulfilment of divine promises.

This is an extremely suggestive thesis. While I am not convinced that Hanson has solved the problem of apocalyptic origins, I do think that he has offered an intriguing reconstruction of the post-exilic period, but it may

28. Plöger, *Theocracy and Eschatology*.
29. Hanson, *Dawn of Apocalyptic*.

well be possible to go further. As we have seen, Belo has reminded us that this was the period when the Torah was receiving its final formation and was emerging as the definitive authority within Israelite life, probably at the expense of the prophetic vision. The cultic dominance of the Torah and the economic consequences of that for the priestly groups are clearly of some importance both for the population at large and for those whose vision of society neither focused on the Temple nor accepted the economic consequences of that particular settlement.

Beyond the Historical-Critical Method

One issue which Belo's materialist reading has thrown into the sharpest possible relief is the way in which the historical-critical method has dominated the reading of biblical texts in the last century. There are many reasons for this, all of which should be a matter for reflection and acknowledgement by all practitioners of this method. I suspect that the factor which impels this type of reading is the belief that it can get at the original meaning of the text, which will then exercise control on the readings of the text and thus limit the role of the text in wider interpretative questions. Whatever may have been the conscious intention of the author (assuming that we are in a position to ascertain this, at least in general terms), what a Marxist-inspired reading of the Bible compels us to do (and not only this reading, of course) is to reckon with the possibility that in addition to the conscious intention of the author we may be in a position to explore other levels of meaning, specifically those dealing with the socio-economic setting of the text. Thus, while in a particular instance the conscious or manifest concern of the author may have been a religious issue, the socio-economic concerns which may have been largely unacknowledged by the author may show through and be of as much importance to us. In saying this I would accept that we are imposing a particular worldview on our text, which may well have serious shortcomings, and which may be subject to considerable refinement and expansion before it can function adequately as an interpretative key within Christian discourse. It does remind us that we need not always be preoccupied with the author's conscious intention as the sole determinative concern in our reading. In addition, we should be more concerned to lay bare those complex constructions which we as readers bring to the text, whether as part of an academic or ecclesiastical environment or, as Belo and the theologians of liberation would have us remember, as part of a First World culture.

Approaches such as Belo's have opened up for me the obligation to look critically at the mainstream practice of biblical interpretation. There is no doubt that liberation theologians sometimes suggest that the conventional ways of reading the Bible in academic circles are deficient and do not take sufficient account of the site of the reading. While liberation theologians are quick to acknowledge their own presuppositions, one sometimes feels that their method, which does justice to the social world of text and reader, is to be preferred to any other. However, is there enough evidence to suggest that the liberationist reading of biblical texts can demonstrate that the Bible is the literary memory of the poor? This, in my view, is an inadequate assessment of the diversity of the biblical material. The liberationist reading cannot be elevated without further ado to the place of a normative reading, though that is not to exclude the possibility that a hermeneutic could be developed which might in fact do that; that, I hope, can be done, but it is still to come. What is clear is that liberationist exegesis has placed a question-mark against a hermeneutic based on a naive acceptance of the historical-critical method both with regard to its narrow concern with a normative overriding meaning of the text and its neglect of the cultural base of the early Christian theological discourse.

Bibliography

Belo, Fernando. *A Materialist Reading of the Gospel of Mark*. Translated by Matthew J. O'Connell. Maryknoll, NY: Orbis, 1981.

Boff, Leonardo. *Jesus Christ, Liberator.* Translated by Patrick Hughes. Maryknoll, NY: Orbis, 1978.

Carroll, Robert P. *When Prophecy Failed: Reactions and Responses to Failure in the Old Testament Prophetic Traditions*. New York: Seabury, 1979.

Deissmann, Adolf. *Light from the Ancient Near East*. Translated by Lionel R. M. Strachan Rev. ed. New York: Doran, 1927. Reprint, Eugene, OR: Wipf & Stock, 2004.

De Ste. Croix, G. E. M. *The Class Struggle in the Ancient Greek World from the Archaic Age to the Arab Conquests*. London: Duckworth, 1981.

Gager, John G. *Kingdom and Community*. Prentice-Hall Studies in Religion Series Englewood Cliffs, NJ: Prentice-Hall, 1975.

Gottwald, Norman K., ed. *The Bible and Liberation: Political and Social Hermeneutics*. Maryknoll, NY: Orbis, 1983.

———. *The Tribes of Yahweh: A Sociology of the Religion of Liberated Israel, 1250–1050 B.C.E.* Maryknoll, NY: Orbis, 1979.

Hanson, Paul D. *The Dawn of Apocalyptic: The Historical and Sociological Roots of Jewish Apocalyptic Eschatology*. Philadelphia: Fortress, 1975.

Jameson, Fredric. *The Political Unconscious: Narrative as a Socially Symbolic Act*. London: Methuen, 1981.

Kautsky, Karl. *Foundations of Christianity: A Study in Christian Origins*. New York: Monthly Review, 1972.

Kreissig, Heinz. *Geschichte des Hellenismus*. Berlin: Akademie, 1984.
Lash, Nicholas. *A Matter of Hope: A Theologian's Reflections on the Thought of Karl Marx*. London: Darton, Longman, & Todd, 1981.
Machovec, Milan. *A Marxist Looks at Jesus*. Philadelphia: Fortress, 1976.
Meeks, Wayne. *The First Urban Christians: The Social World of the Apostle Paul*. New Haven: Yale University Press, 1983.
———. "The Man from Heaven in Johannine Sectarianism." *Journal of Biblical Literature* 91 (1972) 44–72.
Miranda, José P. *Marx and the Bible: A Critique of the Philosophy of Oppression*. Translated by John Eagleson. Maryknoll, NY: Orbis, 1974. Reprint, Eugene, OR: Wipf & Stock, 2004.
Myers, Ched. *Binding the Strong Man: A Political Reading of Mark's Story of Jesus*. Maryknoll, NY: Orbis, 1988.
Pixley, Jorge V. *God's Kingdom*. Translated by Donald D. Walsh. Maryknoll, NY: Orbis, 1981.
Plöger, Otto. *Theocracy and Eschatology*. Translated by S. Rudman. Oxford: Blackwell, 1968.
Radcliffe, Timothy. "'My Lord and my God': The Locus of Confession." *New Blackfriars* 65.764 (1984) 52–62.
Sacred Congregation for the Doctrine of the Faith. *Instruction on Certain Aspects of the Theology of Liberation*. Boston: St. Paul, 1984.
Schüssler Fiorenza, Elisabeth. *In Memory of Her: A Feminist Theological Reconstruction of Christian Origins*. New York: Crossroad, 1983.
Scroggs, Robin. Review of *A Materialist Reading*, by Fernando Belo. *Catholic Biblical Quarterly* 45 (1983) 473–74.
Segundo, Juan Luis. *Liberation of Theology*. Translated by John Drury. Maryknoll, NY: Orbis, 1976.
Sobrino, Jon. *Christology at the Crossroads: A Latin American Approach*. Translated by John Drury. Maryknoll, NY: Orbis, 1978.
Theissen, Gerd. *The First Followers of Jesus: A Sociological Analysis of the Earliest Christianity*. Translated by John Bowden. London: SCM, 1978.
———. *The Social Setting of Pauline Christianity*. Edited and translated and with an introduction by John H. Schütz. Philadelphia: Fortress, 1978. Reprint, Eugene, OR: Wipf & Stock, 2004.

2

In Dialogue with Itumeleng Mosala

A Contribution to Liberation Exegesis

THERE IS A WIDESPREAD conviction that something needs to be done about poverty, yet even those who are best equipped to offer reasons for their concern find themselves resorting to the odd proof-text or common humanitarian concern to justify their reaction. Merely to quote Matthew 25:31–46[1] ignores acute problems of exegesis and the wider context in which this judgment scene is to be found. Consequently, not only are contrary indications ignored but the possibility of a more nuanced assessment is lost. How Christians should respond is a matter of debate. For many the limits of concern center on charitable action as the appropriate Christian response, and suspicion attaches to anything more overtly politically committed. In particular, to what extent does the Bible support a critique of sinful structures and constructive engagement to bring about their change? Must we rest content with charitable action[2] to ameliorate the worst effects of these structures and accept them, in Augustinian fashion, as a necessary evil in a fallen world? Some would ask why it is that we should concern ourselves with biblical justification.[3]

---

1. For a survey of interpretations of this passage, see Gray, *Least of My Brothers*.

2. There is a critical assessment of contemporary Christian understanding of development in Graham, *The Idea of Charity*.

3. For a Christian development agency which has part of its mandate the task of persuading its supporters that involvement (including political involvement) in the service of the poor is a central part of its evangelical task, engagement with Scripture and tradition is essential. For this reason, Christian Aid has established a commission

As we seek to find ways of responding to human need which are congruent with the evangelical imperative, various interpretative approaches will need to be explored. One of the most fruitful has been the attempt to find resonances between contemporary struggles and those which led to the formation of the biblical text. Resonances with the ancient communities' quest for obedience to God may offer a ring of authenticity to modern activities. That has been an important feature of liberation theology. Yet there has always been controversy about the way in which the Bible has been used in the service of the poor and marginalized. Critics have not been slow to exploit the variety of Scripture and to indicate the difficulties in exploiting the Bible as a political document which resonates with contemporary concerns. It is all too easy to find oneself quickly running into difficulty when the Bible is read as a literary memory of the poor. The limitations and possibilities of such exegesis are well exemplified by Itumeleng Mosala's book on biblical hermeneutics in a South African context.[4]

Mosala's work has its origin in the difficulty black theology has had in developing links with the popular struggle. He argues that an authentic black theology needs to break ideologically with the hermeneutical assumptions inherited from Western theology which have been unquestioningly assumed by much black and liberation theology. Existential commitments to liberty and justice are themselves inadequate because often those who are committed to the struggle are enslaved to dominant forms of discourse. It is necessary to expose the way in which the biblical texts themselves have been produced under the aegis of those who wielded power in the ancient world.

For Mosala the important interpretative moment comes when one recognizes the agenda which determines one's approach to the text. Commitment to the struggle is the key hermeneutical factor:

> The category of struggle at all levels and through various phases of black history should be taken as the key hermeneutical factor. Thus this study seeks to probe the nature of the struggle behind and beneath the text; the struggles in the pages, lines, and the vocabulary of the text; the struggles that take place when readers engage the text by way of reading it, and the struggles that the completed text represents.[5]

Mosala is as entirely aware as any of the difficulty of writing an account of power struggles in the ancient world on the basis of the scanty evidence available to us. What is daring about his interpretative approach is that his

---

to explore the attitudes and responses to the poor in the British churches.

4. Mosala, *Biblical Hermeneutics*.
5. Mosala, *Biblical Hermeneutics*, 6.

primary basis for an examination of that issue is the modern world and the insight that the perspective of the "underside" of the struggle may offer. The task is an important part of a developing criticism which, he believes, will mark a decisive break with mainstream critical practice. Echoing the concerns of some liberation theologians, he stresses the need for an ideological break with contemporary biblical criticism and theology. He argues that it is essential to understand something of the culture (in the widest sense of that term) out of which the struggle for power comes and in which the biblical interpreter is located. In this the interpreter is not just a passive observer but part of that conflict of interests and concerns which engulf the individual in an increasingly global capitalism. To that end, in the second part of his book, Mosala examines the historical and cultural struggles of black people as a hermeneutical starting point for black theology. The nuanced account that follows throws light on the tensions within the black struggle as the dominant ideology is to varying degrees assimilated or rejected.

In his view a critical examination of the Bible will suggest that accommodation with a dominant ideology has already to a greater or lesser extent pervaded the texts themselves. The search for a biblical hermeneutic must take the form of a critical interrogation of the history, culture, and ideologies of the readers/appropriators of biblical texts. In exploring this Mosala takes issue with some of the ways of reading which have in turn played their part in influencing black theology. He argues that the reason that Christianity has so often been such a conservative force in society is that dominant groups in society have often been able to claim to be grounded in the best traditions of Christianity, simply because the powerful groups have found resources to maintain their hegemony in the outlook of those who constructed texts and canon in their own interests. This has determined the way in which the more "nonconformist" texts of Scripture should be read. So, he argues, if liberation theology presents the text as a divine discourse which unequivocally opts for the poor, it can easily find itself colluding with the submission to a dominant ideology which is not always in the interests of the poor and oppressed. Mosala offers two examples of this in the writing of Allan Boesak and Desmond Tutu. Tutu's appropriation of texts from Second Isaiah, for example, is to collude with passages which reinforce the ideas of the ruling elite which was transported into exile and which then sought to establish their God-given right to lead on their return. Mosala is critical of Boesak's narrative reading of the Cain and Abel story which, in Mosala's view, too easily follows the rhetorical constructs of the interested redactor of the Jerusalem elite.[6]

6. There is an interesting discussion of the contrasting approaches to Genesis 4 in

Mosala's interpretation of the biblical traditions, in light of his account of the history and culture from which he comes, involves a study of Micah and the infancy narratives of Luke. In order to understand the text of Micah he seeks to inquire into the nature of the mode of production, the constellation of groups, and their different ideas and interests. In this he is clearly influenced by the tradition of interpretation pioneered by Norman Gottwald and in particular the work done on Amos by Robert Coote.[7] He situates Micah in the political economy of the Judean monarchy established by David and Solomon in which political power is held by an elite and reinforced by an ideology rooted in Temple, Zion, and royal dynasty. The book of Micah, according to Mosala, is made up of contradictory themes which reflect something of the competing ideas and interests in the society when the text reached its final form rather than the time when the oracles were originally uttered. Only with difficulty is it possible to retrieve from the biblical text an alternative perspective to the dominant ideology which has so permeated the text. Mosala identifies three themes as indicative of the kinds of interests which underlie the text. First, he identifies a group of texts which provide a limited connection with the struggles of the poor and oppressed, reflected in their grief and alternative vision. Second, there are other texts which merely reject the ruling class in the vaguest terms. Third, however, there is a picture of a God who restores power structures that were previously in existence; it is this which provides the overlaid and dominant ideology of the book. Here the former oppressors of the poor see themselves oppressed by foreign captors. Now the nations become the targets of Yahweh's judgment, not the rich and powerful in Judea. Mosala argues that the original message of Micah which was directed at the ruling classes of Judah during the eighth century BCE has been stolen from its concrete situation where it concerned the condition of the poor and exploited and is applied to the Judean ruling class in their relationship with foreign oppressors. Apart from the occasional echo,

> The book of Micah . . . is eloquent in its silence on the ideological struggle waged by the oppressed and exploited classes of monarchical Israel. . . . Micah itself offers no certain starting point for a theology of liberation. There is simply too much ideologization to be unraveled before it can be hermeneutically usable in the struggle for liberation. . . . However, enough contradictions within Micah enable eyes hermeneutically trained in struggle for liberation today to observe the kindred struggles of

---

West, *Biblical Hermeneutics of Liberation*.

    7. Gottwald, *Tribes of Yahweh*; and Coote, *Amos among the Prophets*.

the oppressed and exploited of the biblical communities in the very absence of those struggles in the text.[8]

In the final section there is an interpretation of the first two chapters of Luke's Gospel. Despite its reputation as the Gospel of the poor and marginalized, Mosala presents a picture of a book which has lost direct touch with the poor and their longing for justice. The traditions now serve somewhat different needs and have to embrace the interests of the rich and powerful too. In Mosala's view there is too much in Luke which brings the story of Jesus in line with the status quo. Thus the Temple and the priestly class are introduced to give legitimation to the birth and subsequent mission of Jesus. That now begins to cover up the embarrassment of Jesus' lowly social class. Also, the invocation of Davidic messianism helps suppress Jesus' unacceptable origins by reference to the dominant elite who established their power in Jerusalem and its Temple. Mosala argues that Luke turns the experience of poverty and the story of the marginal Jesus into an ethical challenge for the rich and powerful men who make up his church.[9] Luke offers an option for the rich and powerful to accept what is a necessity for the poor and powerless majority: poverty and homelessness. So Luke writes an orderly account for the consumption of the ruling class and subordinates the narratives of a minority group to the concerns and genres of the dominant elite.

Like the exponents of the quest for the historical Jesus, Mosala sees that there is a need to imagine another narrative which must be told alongside, and indeed in some sense as a corrective to, the Gospel narrative. In his writing Luke is dealing with a movement in first-century Palestine which was a threat to the leading groups in society. In retelling the uncomfortable story of Jesus, Luke's purpose in writing this form of narrative is to prove the acceptability of Christianity. The issue for Mosala is whether, in the course of writing an account which seeks to offer a strategy for accommodation, Luke destroys the critical power of the movement he recommends.

Mosala's work typifies one form of exegesis influenced by liberation theology: a form of the hermeneutics of suspicion.[10] Of course, there are echoes of more conventional historical criticism in Mosala's work also. Rather than engage in a detailed discussion of the minutiae of Mosala's interpretation of the various biblical passages, in my discussion I want to

---

8. Mosala, *Biblical Hermeneutics*, 120–21.

9. Similar views are expressed in Esler, *Community and Gospel*.

10. The recovery of another, liberating narrative behind the received biblical text has been a typical feature of some forms of liberation hermeneutics, see, e.g., Schüssler Fiorenza, *In Memory of Her*.

concentrate on more general matters of interpretative interest. I shall consider his work under three headings followed by a conclusion.

Struggling with the Text as We Have It

Liberation hermeneutics seems at times to mark a resurgence of "biblical theology," particularly in the use of terms like the poor, liberation, and oppression. Mosala's work is clearly a warning to some of his Barthian colleagues who prefer to concentrate on the "surface" of the text and avoid engaging with the origins and influences which contributed to its present form.[11] In many respects his concerns echo those which have long been part of historical scholarship. His work is a reminder not to turn our backs on those tools which have enabled us to ascertain something, however partial, of the way texts are infiltrated with a dominant theology. Mosala offers a way of reading which recognizes the diversity, both religiously and politically, within one text. But the use of this particular interpretative perspective must not ignore or play down the insignificance of those parts of the text which do not espouse the preferred perspective. Certain forms of traditio-historical analysis can ride roughshod over the text as we have it in the search for the favored insight, the pearl of great price compared with which all else may be cast on one side. Mosala's interpretation does not *necessarily* mean ignoring those parts of the tradition which do not conform to his prejudices. But memories of the ways in which the application of the hermeneutics of suspicion have led to the jettisoning of difficult or inauthentic material should make us pause before we embark along that road again.

The doyen of contemporary literary criticism influenced by Marxism, Frederic Jameson,[12] has suggested that we do not have to jettison material in order to practice a criticism which is sensitive to the social and political dimension. Texts do include the dominant ideology, either by way of reaction or by specific espousal alongside their witness to other less conformist traditions. A biblical interpretation which is sensitive to the ideological variety of the Bible will seek to understand its complexity and not move to outright rejection of those sections which fail to meet the criteria of acceptability. Understanding the variety is the basis of the criticism which Mosala beckons us to espouse. Even what appear to be more difficult passages may help us understand something of our own prejudices as we glimpse something of the compromises in the texts of the past. What is more, as Jameson reminds us, even what may appear to be the most reactionary texts may surprise us

---

11. On Barth's biblical interpretation, see Ford, *Barth and God's Story*.
12. Jameson, *Political Unconscious*.

by offering what he calls a "utopian impulse."[13] Criticism has a role in helping lay bare that impulse, but the task of retrieval is not its only, or even its main, function. All facets of texts are revealing about human striving and the compromises which attend it. We are forever destined to use old wine skins for the new wine and to risk losing both. There is no way out of that impasse, however much we may long to grasp hold of the definitive story, whether of the historical Jesus or the authentic memory of the poor. The need is for constant critical vigilance about ourselves and our reading in the same proportion to that which we devote to the texts of which we are seeking to make sense. Perhaps in this way some of the tensions which are so much part of the interpretative task can at least be recognized and be theologically productive, even if they cannot be entirely overcome.

Towards an Understanding of the Ambiguity of Early Christian Textual Production

Mosala's discussion of Luke is more superficial than the treatment of Micah. He is right to remind us that one of the ways whereby Christianity sought to ensure its survival was through seeking to persuade and placate those in power. Part of the task of Christian intellectual production in its earliest phase was to position itself over against the dominant ideology, whether it be a dominant form of Judaism or the ideologies of the wider Greco-Roman world. Thus, legitimation of a controversial movement and practice is going on in many of the texts from Matthew to Hebrews. Perhaps only in the Fourth Gospel do we come close to a theology, which, in the last resort, does not rest on proof on the basis of prevailing traditions, but grounds it in the self-authenticating pronouncement of the one sent from God.

Among other reasons, Luke wrote in order to present an acceptable religion which conformed to the canons of Judaism, and which would not completely exclude the penitent rich and mighty. The writing of the story of Jesus in this form is a product of a particular moment in Christianity when issues of identity became particularly pressing. Despite the concern to give it a conventional setting, the story Luke tells is remarkable in its subordination of the rulers of the contemporary world to the background of rural Galilee, whose populace is confronted with good news which differed markedly from the propaganda of the imperial world.[14] For all its conventional opening and setting in the context of contemporary history,

---

13. Jameson, *Political Unconscious*, 296.
14. There are useful comments on this in Myers, *Binding the Strong Man*.

Luke's Gospel hardly exhibits an unambiguous attitude towards established institutions and beliefs. It is, after all, Luke's Gospel which portrays Jesus as predicting the destruction of city and Temple in the light of its inability to understand what led to its peace. The attitude to Davidic messianism is hardly the unquestioning assumption of the expectation of the Davidic king. The manifesto of Jesus in Luke 4 questions that assumption (looking forward to the detaching of messiahship from David in Luke 20:41–44). In Luke the message to the rich is hardly a very palatable one. The reader of the Gospel is left in little doubt about the appropriate response to those such as Lazarus. The chapters after the infancy narratives have plausibly been seen as a contrast to more militant sentiments earlier in the Gospel. Of course, this may have suited the apologetic aim of a writer who wished to portray a pacific religion. But elsewhere there is little evidence of any obsequious attitude towards Rome; certainly, it is less obvious than in Josephus. Yet even the more obviously sycophantic Josephus enables us to catch a glimpse of another dimension to the story of Second Temple Judaism than what appears to have been the one preferred by him.

However, it seems important that we face up to the contradictory signals which have been picked up by interpreters of Luke–Acts. On the one hand, there is the clarion call to liberation in Luke 4:16, in the uncompromising attitude towards wealth and poverty and the prominence of women in the narrative. On the other hand, there are the apparent nods in the direction of accommodation, particularly in Acts. The account of Cornelius's conversion leaves open the question of the character of life of the newly converted Gentile soldier; Ananias's and Sapphira's sin is deceiving the Holy Spirit rather than refusal to share their property, perhaps a tacit acceptance of the need to move away from the practice of the earliest church in Jerusalem according to Luke's account. The ambiguity is no more evident than in Luke 16 where the utter repudiation of mammon and the disparagement of Dives sits uneasily with assertions that one has to use the mammon of unrighteousness in order to gain access to heaven.

That which is considered important in the eyes of humans (wealth, privilege, etc.) is an abomination. The word βδέλυγμα occurs in Matthew and Mark in the context of the eschatological discourse (e.g., Mark 13:14) and refers to the future desecration of the Temple. In Luke it refers to the idolatrous practice of the worship of mammon which detracts from the worship of God. Even the strange story of the "unjust" steward can be read as an attack on the values of mammon. The wisdom of the steward is in his recognition that human dignity (even if it is his own) transcends the strict rules of accounting and property which go with the service of mammon. The story may suggest that there is no merit in keeping to the rules of accounting if the result is utter penury. Possessions are not the absolutes which should govern life. Despite the stark warning in Luke 16:13, it is impossible to avoid mammon. Nevertheless, divine service must determine one's attitude to it, thus subordinating the standards of the present ages to those of God and ensuring that the unavoidable administration of mammon is carried on according to the divine rules. Entry into the everlasting habitations, as the story of Dives and Lazarus clearly indicates, comes through the use of mammon which recognizes and meets the needs of the outcast.[15]

We should resist seeking to resolve the tensions of Luke–Acts. Mosala's methods offer us a way to explore them. They may well have been provoked by the tension between eschatological existence in Christ and the demands of the overarching political and economic order of the old eon. All this speaks not of growing conformism, in which one may lament a lost narrative of revolution, but it is more the recognition of the constraints imposed upon the practice of religion in circumstances which were hardly auspicious for its particular values. Let me cite a modern parallel. Many Christians who espouse liberation theology understand something of those constraints. In refusing the revolutionary option in El Salvador, for example, Christians have until recently found that the room for maneuver and change has been small. They understand all too well how much discipleship will be hemmed in and how even the smallest opportunity for faithfulness will need to be exploited to the full.

Christian historiography and theology from Luke onwards manifest a greater concern to convince, and perhaps even placate, the influential and important rather than be a mouthpiece for the oppressed. If our major interest is the story of the poor, we shall not find rich pickings in Luke, or, for that matter, elsewhere in the Bible. But history is rarely the memory of the poor and insignificant; their memory is frequently lost forever from our view. Of course, the shape of the story would be different if we sought to write it consistently from the perspective of the poor and voiceless. Its retrieval is often the task of the sympathetic voices of another culture or class. Part of the task of liberation theology has been to engage in that project. The resulting presentation of the "voice of the voiceless" is almost inevitably in an idiom at a significant remove from the story that the poor might tell.

The focus of interest in the Gospels is different from a grassroots story of popular protest. They have christology (albeit in narrative form) at the center of their presentation, and this towers over all other concerns. The poor and outcast are incidental to that dominant concern. But that christological perspective exemplifies the orientation of Christ towards the outcast

---

15. See further Moxnes, *Economy of the Kingdom*.

and rejects. Luke's mediation of the story of Jesus can never fully capture the precise character of the Galilean messianic movement, the voices of those who responded to it, why it was so important for the crowds who followed Jesus (in religious and socio-economic terms), and the character of the liberation that was experienced. But in the process of convincing Theophilus of his version of the story of Jesus, Luke at least ensured that the story was written. In the process it may have been subject to a variety of changes but ensured the continuing interest in the memories and culture of rural Galilee. It is part of the critical task to recognize the shortcomings of all attempts to encapsulate the story, but, as the quest for the historical Jesus indicates, there must be grave reservations about the notion that there is an easy route to a privileged, authentic version of events apart from the extant narrative. The writing of the tradition about Jesus was a formative moment for the way in which the story was appropriated. Whoever took that decisive step set the story in the midst of genres which were largely the prerogative of those who served the interests of the politically powerful. Luke to some extent falls into the category of a book which seeks to set down a story which might hardly merit a record in the annals of the ancient world, and in so doing includes a glimpse of those poor and insignificant people who were the beneficiaries of the Gospel. Luke does not by any means present the story of a Jesus who merely represents the opinions of the groups of people he (Luke) may have been writing for. So, it is hardly surprising that in the modern world basic ecclesial communities have frequently found in reading Luke something of that challenge to the status quo and a voice which in some way expresses their own aspirations and hopes. Whatever its original intention and setting and the distortions which may have taken place in writing, modern readers have been able to retrieve that liberative strand without the difficulty that Mosala suggests.

Theology of a Sectional Interest

One of the major criticisms of liberation theology has been its lack of objectivity, both in terms of the scope of its concern and its theological proposals. Commitment may pose a problem to the ability of a theology to maintain that critical distance from culture so that it avoids ending up as the ideological wrapping for the particular interests. Indeed, many have argued that contextual theology's agenda is being set elsewhere than in the Scriptures, although, despite all the emphasis on the priority of the story of "life," the Christian narrative is by no means an optional extra in the articulation of that primary cry of protest or assertion of hope. Mosala places great emphasis on struggle as an interpretative key. Priority appears to be given to a particular constellation of human strivings which override other considerations. Of course, mere identification with the struggle in an unsubtle and uninformed way is open to criticism. As far as Mosala's approach is concerned, I think a case can be made for seeing his perspective as a useful heuristic device, which may facilitate interpretation provided that "struggle" or "liberation" do not become all-embracing and exclusive hermeneutical keys for the interpretation of Scripture.

In much liberation theology the priority of commitment to the poor is said to be the basic act. The understanding of this can at times be left rather vague, so that there seems to be a large hole at the center of liberation theology which its laudable emphasis on solidarity with the outcast can easily mask.[16] What in fact is motivating its commitment to the poor? Is it really the imperatives of the Christian gospel or a perception of human misery, which owes more to unacknowledged assumptions whose origin lies elsewhere? The commitment which is spoken of as the act prior to theology can seem at times to be a bare act of will in the face of inhumanity and injustice. The role of the Christian tradition in this decisive commitment can at times appear to be peripheral. In Gustavo Gutiérrez's writings,[17] however, I think that we shall find that at the center of his theology is a spirituality based on contemplation of God in the suffering Christ. It is contemplation of the reality of the divine presence hidden in the poor and commitment to the God who summons us to respond. I would prefer to compare that moment of commitment to the final insight of Job when he contrasts past knowledge with present experience which enlivens that knowledge: "I had heard of thee by the hearing of the ear, but now my eye sees thee; therefore, I despise myself and repent in dust and ashes" (Job 42:5-6).

Conclusion

Mosala's frank recognition of his own interests at the starting point of his exegetical work turns the spotlight on an exegesis which claims to be above the struggle of contemporary life. The time is surely past when we can any longer deny that we are engaged in an exegesis which is removed from the messy business of life which is such a dominant concern in Mosala's reading. What is needed is a frank recognition of why it is we prefer to conceal the interests at work in the First World exegetical enterprise. Unmasking

---

16. A good example of this problem is evident in the way in which faith is discussed in Segundo, *Faith and Ideologies*.

17. See particularly Gutiérrez, *Truth Shall Make You Free*.

them will be good for our method and enable us to see more clearly what kind of exercise we are engaged in. But it will make us sensitive to our context, so that the process of learning which is needed within the churches attempts to meet people where they are and empowers them to explore the complexities of modern life in the light of the Scriptures. If Mosala is right about the attitude to the poor in Luke–Acts, for example, there is a sense in which its prominent concern to get the rich to engage with the poor is peculiarly applicable to the concerns of the majority of Christians in the First World. The texts as a whole, though not the individual sayings and stories in them, are more in tune with First World struggles than they are a repository of the cry of the oppressed. In approaching the Scriptures from the perspective of the poor and marginalized, those of us who are protestants are in danger of reinventing the wheel. The Catholic tradition asserts, albeit in muted form, that God has a particular concern for the poor. The contemporary formation of that teaching must be a matter of debate as is the construal of the scope and meaning of the tradition. Nevertheless, the insight, rooted as it is in centuries of teaching, is one that can be a starting point for a biblical study of attitudes to the poor.

Mosala is right to remind us that the Bible is not in any straightforward sense the literary memory of the poor. Merely collecting biblical texts ignores the fact that the Bible continues, as it always has, to be a site of conflict of human interests and in its final form represents an emerging dominant ideology with all its compromises and contradictions which are so typical of such hegemonic discourses. Yet I disagree with Mosala's rejection of a narrative approach to Scripture. The evidence suggests that whatever the origins of texts like Second Isaiah, they have enormous potential for inspiring and determining debates about appropriate responses in situations of injustice. Care needs to be taken with the kind of interpretative method adopted by Mosala. Its concern with what lies behind the text makes the ordinary reader dependent on the skills of the sophisticated interpreter so as to enable a reading that is ideologically aware. More important, it seems to me, than disentangling the ideological struggles in Scripture is the attention to the understanding of the *effect* of a text in a particular context and the way in which that context conditions interpretation: what is it that causes a particular effect and what is it about the situation which conditions its reception?[18] In this the history of interpretation will form a part, but that must be matched by the attempt to understand as much as

---

18. Some recognition of the importance of this is evident in the important commentary on Matthew by Luz, *Das Evangelium nach Matthäus*.

possible the particularity of a context which conditions meaning and the reasons for the particular perspectives which emerge.

Mosala's work is another reminder of the importance of the critique of ideology. With whatever necessary refinements, that is one of the abiding legacies of Marx. But unlike Marx we cannot be so confident that we have that superiority of vantage which can enable a forthright critique of *The German Ideology*. If I understand Theodor Adorno aright, capitalism confronts us like an unassailable cliff. The task of the climber is to discover crevices for handholds. Similarly, the critic is searching for some purchase on the overwhelming reality which surrounds and pervades us. The critique of ideology in such circumstances is a complicated task requiring patience, self-criticism, and resistance to generalization.[19] Mosala reminds us that criticism which is only based in theoretical reflection is insufficient. The perspective of those who find themselves oppressed, vulnerable, and confined to the margins in our world is an essential ingredient for the articulation of the critique. If in Mosala's hands this forms the basis of an imaginative reconstruction of the prehistory of the biblical text, we should not ignore the fact that the primary purpose of exegesis is not ancient history but the prosecution and clarification of the way of God in solidarity with the oppressed. That perspective is not found directly in the pages of Scripture. But even if the Scriptures are the production of an elite, what they produce is not the seamless robe of an all-conquering ideology. Those who produced these texts often found themselves in vulnerable positions on the margins of contemporary culture. The Scriptures are full of traditions which, particularly when illuminated by the awareness of present experience of suffering, indignity, and inhumanity, can facilitate the pursuit of criticism and action which may contribute to a theology which takes seriously the plight of those condemned to the margins of our world.

Bibliography

Adorno, Theodor W. *Minima Moralia: Reflections from Damaged Life*. Translated by E. F. N. Jephcott. London: Verso, 1974.

———. *Negative Dialectics*. Translated by E. B. Ashton. A Continuum Book. London: Verso, 1973.

Coote, Robert B. *Amos among the Prophets: Composition and Theology*. Philadelphia: Fortress, 1981. Reprint, Eugene, OR: Wipf & Stock, 2005.

Esler, Philip Francis. *Community and Gospel in Luke–Acts*. Society for New Testament Studies Monograph Series 57. Cambridge: Cambridge University Press, 1987.

---

19. See, e.g., Adorno, *Negative Dialectics*, 144–45; and Adorno, *Minima Moralia*, 247.

Ford, David. *Barth and God's Story.* Studien zur interkulturellen Geschichte des Christentu 27. Études d'histoire interculturelle du Christianisme. Frankfurt: Lang, 1981.

———. *Barth and God's Story.* 1981. Reprint, Eugene, OR: Wipf & Stock, 2008.

Gottwald, Norman. *The Tribes of Yahweh: A Sociology of the Religion of Liberated Israel, 1250–1050 B.C.E.* Maryknoll, NY: Orbis, 1979.

Graham, Gordon. *The Idea of Christian Charity.* Notre Dame, IN: University of Notre Dame Press, 1990.

Gray, Sherman W. *The Least of My Brothers: Matthew 25.31–46, A History of Interpretation.* Society of Biblical Literature Dissertation Series 114. Atlanta: Scholars, 1989.

Gutiérrez, Gustavo. *The Truth Shall Make You Free.* Translated by Matthew J. O'Connell. Maryknoll, NY: Orbis, 1990.

Jameson, Fredric. *The Political Unconscious: Narrative as a Socially Symbolic Act.* London: Methuen, 1981.

Luz, Ulrich. *Das Evangelium nach Matthäus.* 4 vols. Evangelisch-katholischer Kommentar zum Neuen Testament 1. Zürich: Benziger, 1985–2002.

Mosala, Itumeleng J. *Biblical Hermeneutics and Black Theology in South Africa.* Exeter, UK: Paternoster, 1989.

Moxnes, Halvor. *The Economy of the Kingdom: Social Conflict and Economic Relations in Luke's Gospel.* Overtures to Biblical Theology. Philadelphia: Fortress, 1988. Reprint, Eugene, OR: Wipf & Stock, 2004.

Myers, Ched. *Binding the Strong Man: A Political Reading of Mark's Story of Jesus.* Maryknoll, NY: Orbis, 1988.

Schüssler Fiorenza, Elisabeth. *In Memory of Her: A Feminist Theological Reconstruction of Christian Origins.* New York: Crossroad, 1983.

Segundo, Juan Luis. *Faith and Ideologies.* Translated from the Spanish by John Drury. Maryknoll, NY: Orbis, 1984.

West, Gerald O. *Biblical Hermeneutics of Liberation: Modes of Reading the Bible in a South African Context.* Pietermaritzburg Cluster of Theological Institutions Monograph Series 1. Pietermaritzburg, South Africa: Cluster, 1991.

3

Liberation Theology

Liberation Theology and Contextual Theology

Liberation theology is a form of contextual theology, in which the experience and circumstances of the interpreters are given a prime importance as the first step in seeking to be a disciple of Jesus. It is aptly summarized in the popular education material familiar in Latin American churches, where priority is given to the "text of life" as the key to the approach to the biblical text.

Properly speaking, liberation theology refers to that way of engaging in theological reflection pioneered in Latin America and associated with the work of Gustavo Gutiérrez. It has also come to be linked with other forms of theology with which it is closely related methodologically, namely, feminist theology, black theology, and various other kinds of contextual theology (though from the point of view of historical theology there is no form of theology which is contextless, even the supremely abstract theologizing of the medieval scholastic theological tradition). Feminist theology is much more critical in its use of the Bible, and issues of gender and race were not really part of the political profile of the earliest forms of liberation theology. Nevertheless all these ways of doing theology are characterized by an embracing of experience, broadly defined, as the necessary context and basis for theology.

The theology of liberation arises out of the specific needs and concerns of the poor. For example, in a country like Brazil, where the struggle for access to land is such a potent political issue, especially in rural areas, the story of the Exodus and the promised land has enabled the perception of a direct link between the present circumstances of many peasants and the biblical narrative.[1] In such a correlation, however, there is no expectation of a blueprint from the Bible, the tradition, or contemporary theologians or bishops, which will offer unambiguous guidance, independent of the circumstances in which the people of God find themselves. The basic theological assumption undergirding this approach is that God does not come from outside such a situation but is to be found there, just as much as in the Bible, church, and tradition. The theology of liberation seeks to understand faith from within particular historical contexts. The fundamental hermeneutic starts from humanity, moves thence to God, and then from God back to humanity. Liberation theology is an understanding of the faith from a commitment to the poor and the marginalized, an understanding of the faith from a point of departure in real, effective solidarity with the exploited and the vulnerable.

The first step of the theology of liberation is to grasp the reality of the context in which one finds oneself, assisted by a variety of interpretative tools chosen by the theologian to enable the understanding of injustice. A parallel step is theological in something approaching a traditional sense of theology: it consists in confronting the reality of suffering, which is analyzed and better understood in light of the revelation learned in the heart of the church community. Finally, there is a stage of reflection concerning orientation towards more insightful action. It is important to note, as we shall see below, that the initial step is not reflective but committed and active. The theology of liberation is done by those either directly involved in liberating action or linked with it in some way.

Liberation theology has had an extraordinary influence on theology in the late twentieth century. The *content* of liberation theology is indistinguishable from a variety of types of theological reflection, both ancient and modern, with a political hue. Its contemporary parallels include the writings of Moltmann[2] and Metz,[3] both of whom are often linked to liberation theology. The crucial difference which separates liberation theology, in all its various guises, is its method. Of course, all systematic theology worthy of the name is methodologically self-aware, carefully constructed, and hermeneutically precise. Liberation theology is no exception, but the peculiar form of its theoretical engagement and reflection is what distinguishes it

---

1. Souza, *A Bíblia e a Luta*.
2. Moltmann, *Church and the Power of the Spirit*.
3. Metz, *Theology of the World*; Metz, *Faith in History*.

from much modern theology. The latter, situated as it is in the modern academy, which prizes detachment and the quest for objectivity, is very much at odds with a theology whose very practice demands commitment and involvement, the very opposite from detachment. Both supporters and detractors of liberation theology can give the impression of homogeneity in the outline of its theology, when in fact its genius lies in its very diversity and contingency. Thus, the authors of the collection *Mysterium Liberationis* offer a presentation of the traditional components of systematic theology from a liberation theology perspective.[4] And from opponents, the various statements which emerged from the Vatican during the papacy of John Paul II treat liberation theology as a homogeneous entity. This is misleading. Not only are there a variety of contexts, but many different approaches to them, and very different relationships with the popular movements in church and society which have spawned liberation theology. To lump together the work of Segundo from Uruguay with that of the Boff brothers from Brazil, Gustavo Gutiérrez from Peru, and Jon Sobrino from El Salvador is to create a spurious entity which never exists in quite that "pure" form. Liberation theology is, rather, determined, as its exponents believe it to be, by the very contexts in which they work, and their writings cannot therefore be easily reduced to a single system. There are important distinctions to be made between the various theologians of liberation writing in different contexts, politically and ecclesiastically.

Liberation theology has, then, been a protest at the way theology can be abstracted from ordinary life. Its starting place was not detached reflection on Scripture and tradition but the life of the shanty towns and land struggles: the lack of basic amenities, the carelessness about the welfare of human persons, the death squads, and the shattered lives of refugees in a continent which at the time of its genesis was dominated by military dictatorships and vast discrepancies of wealth and opportunity. It is here in particular that its distinctiveness as compared with the theology of North American and European academies is most marked. Gustavo Gutiérrez characterizes it thus:

> the question in Latin America will not be how to speak of God in a world come of age, but rather how to proclaim God as Father in a world that is inhumane. What can it mean to tell a non-person that he or she is God's child?[5]

---

4. Ellacuría and Sobrino, eds., *Mysterium Liberationis*.
5. Gutiérrez, *Power of the Poor*, 57.

The Historical Context of the Theology of Liberation 1: The Second Vatican Council and the Emergence of the "Basic Christian Communities" (The CEBs: Comunidades Eclesiais de Base)

Liberation theology emerged within the wider context of Catholic social teaching and, in particular, the significant development of Roman Catholic theology based on the Second Vatican Council and the encyclicals associated with it.[6] The decisions taken by the Latin American bishops at their epoch-making meeting at Medellín and reaffirmed at Puebla, with the explicit commitment to take a "preferential option for the poor," were, in addition, crucial in its development.[7]

Despite Latin America having a reputation for a progressive theological tradition, the influence of the theology of liberation is actually quite small. Countries like Mexico, Argentina, and Colombia, which have conservative church hierarchies, show little evidence of the grassroots theology and episcopal support for liberation theology which are evident in Brazil, Peru, and, to a lesser extent, Nicaragua. The power of diocesan bishops is such that attempts to develop grassroots movements without episcopal support find the going very tough indeed, despite the fact that for large numbers of people the social conditions are equally bad as those in dioceses where the theology has taken root. Similarly, in those dioceses where the diocesan bishop is supportive, that power can be used to push a diocese in a progressive direction far more rapidly than would be possible in a more Protestant area. The importance of what has happened in Brazil over the last thirty years makes it the obvious country to focus on to understand further the theology of liberation.

The promotion of "basic ecclesial communities" in encyclicals like *Evangelii Nuntiandi* is one way that liberation theology has come to be rooted in the "Basic Christian Communities" (CEBs). The basic communities are a significant component of both the contemporary political and ecclesiastical scene, especially in Brazil, where, particularly in the 1970s and 1980s, such communities became the typical mode of evangelization. A constant refrain of all the different liberationist approaches is that the perspective of the poor and the marginalized offers another story, an alternative to that told by the wielders of economic power whose story is privileged as the

---

6. Hebblethwaite, "Liberation Theology"; and Dawson, "Ecclesial Community," in Rowland, *Liberation Theology*, 209–28, 139–58.

7. Hennelly, ed., *Liberation Theology*; Walsh and Davies, eds., *Proclaiming Justice and Peace*; Gutiérrez et al., *Santo Domingo and After*.

"normal" account. In the CEBs, hitherto oppressed persons have become the particular means whereby the divine perspective on human existence is offered. They are the "little ones" who are vouchsafed a peculiar insight into the identity of the divine wisdom (Matt 11:25). The vantage point of the poor is particularly and especially the vantage point of the crucified God, and may act as a criterion for theological reflection, biblical exegesis, and the life of the church. The poor are the means by which the church can learn to discern the truth, direction, and content of its mission, and can assure the church of being the place where the Lord is to be found.

Few exponents of the theology of liberation would want a consideration of this distinctive theological approach to start with a story of episcopal decisions or professorial disquisitions. Rather, it is with the "reality" which confronts millions in the continent that it should begin. The contrast between the gross affluence of the tiny minority and the squalor and poverty of the majority has prompted priests and religious to think again about their apostolic task and, in so doing, to learn the importance of living and working with and learning from the poor. The theology of liberation has taken root outside the walls of the seminaries and basilicas, often far away from the nearest priest.

It is the richness of human experience which has helped to promote the theology of liberation in many parts of Latin America. The story of the Roman Catholic Church in São Paulo in the final decades of the twentieth century has revolved around issues linked with the mushrooming of migration within Brazil, particularly from the impoverished northeast to the cities. Conditions in rural Brazil are appalling. As the economy has expanded, those desperate to keep body and soul together have drifted to the big cities, particularly those of the more economically prosperous southeast, drawn by the promise of a better life. As migrants arrived in the city, many with only the possessions they could bring with them, they resorted to making makeshift homes on any piece of spare land available, even under motorway arches. It was this desperation which led to the massive spread of shanty towns where the majority of São Paulo's population lives. Squatters who occupy land and build their rudimentary dwellings are harassed by the police, often provoking violence, while those who have gained title to their land may be evicted by private security firms hired by land speculators. Deaths are all too frequent an occurrence in some areas. Recourse to the courts is often difficult, despite the growth of law surgeries and human rights work. Even with the return to democracy in Brazil, the plight of the urban homeless continues to deteriorate. During the time of the economic boom there was work: men could participate as laborers in building projects—luxury homes for São Paulo's elite, for example, and women could get work as maids for that same group. In times of economic recession, however, work is not so plentiful. Such conditions have made women's work essential for existence. In situations where it is not possible for friends or relatives to look after them, children are left to join the very large number of others in São Paulo who roam the streets, increasing the already alarming problem of "street children."

During the period of military dictatorship in Brazil in the late 1960s and 1970s, close links were forged between the churches and other groups struggling for human rights. This time saw a development of popular movements of which the CEBs are a tangible expression. Grassroots participation during the military dictatorship was focused on church-based bodies, providing an umbrella for individuals from different backgrounds to meet and work for common goals. It was perhaps this experience above all which laid the foundations for the fruitful dialogue and cooperation between the churches and various groups struggling for justice for the majority of São Paulo's population. The community of interest among a wide range of people, many hitherto disenchanted with religion, was galvanized by the shared experience of persecution. This led to a "rainbow alliance" of Christians and trade unionists and politicians on the left for securing a more humane environment for ordinary people. Throughout the period of the military dictatorship, the church in São Paulo was tireless in its defense of human rights; Christians and non-Christians alike suffered torture and even death. There followed a long official campaign of vilification of the leaders of the CEBs, who were indicted as crypto-communist. During the massive influx of migrants into the *favelas* which grew up on the periphery of the city, the archdiocese of São Paulo, in response to Medellín's "preferential option for the poor," devoted significant resources, both human and financial, to support such people. Gradually, a pastoral plan emerged with the following priorities for mission: the defense of human rights; the defense of the right to work and the rights of workers; the defense of the poor on the outskirts of the city; and the organization of the people of God into CEBs.

Historical Context 2: Since 1989, the Vatican Reaction, the Collapse of Communism, and the Future of Liberation Theology

A number of factors have influenced the development of liberation theology since the 1980s.[8] Two "instructions" regarding liberation theology

8. Hebblethwaite, "Liberation Theology"; Petrella *Future of Liberation Theology* and *Latin American Liberation Theology*; Althaus-Reid, *Indecent Theology*; Batstone et al.,

were issued by the Congregation for the Doctrine of Faith in the 1980s: a "more negative" one in 1984, and a "less negative" one in 1986. While the Congregation for the Doctrine of the Faith's earlier instruction contained statements which echo liberation theology, the document's purpose was "to draw ... attention ... to the deviations, and risks of deviations, damaging to the faith and to Christian living, that are brought about by certain forms of liberation theology which use, in an insufficiently critical manner, concepts borrowed from various currents of Marxist thought."[9] This instruction sets out a critique of what are seen as some of liberation theology's Marxist assumptions. The first concerns the relationship between sin and social structures. The instruction simply denies the possibility of making any such distinctions within Marxism. There is a denial that the "analysis" can be separated from the world view. It rejects the way that God and history are identified and the confusion between the poor of the Scripture and the proletariat of Marx. The chief difference between John Paul II and liberation theologians was the systematic "spiritualizing" of the theme of poverty. For example, the Exodus experience, so central to liberation theology, was reinterpreted; the political aspect was subordinated to a spiritual purpose. The second instruction declared, "The Exodus ... has a meaning which is both religious and political. God sets his people free and gives them descendants, a land and a law, but within a covenant and for a covenant."[10] There is acceptance of the basic assumption of liberation theology—God's preferential option for the poor—but this is subtly interpreted as "God's preferential *love* for the poor."[11] Whatever the negative tone of both documents, it was evident that some of the language and commitment at the heart of liberation theology had seeped into the Vatican rhetoric and thence into the theological mainstream of the church.

The fall of the Berlin Wall in 1989 was seen by some as the death knell of liberation theology. This would only have been true if liberation theology were indissolubly linked with the kind of socialist project which had typified the Marxist-Leninist regimes of Eastern Europe. It is true that there have been cordial links with Castro's Cuba, and during the period of the Sandinista regime there was a regular flow of visitors from different parts of the progressive Catholic Church in South America to Nicaragua to offer support to the regime and its Christian supporters, especially at the height of the war with the US-backed Contras in the 1980s. As such,

---

eds., *Liberation Theologies*; Bell, *Liberation Theology*.

9. Sacred Congregation, *Theology of Liberation*, 4.
10. Sacred Congregation, *Christian Freedom and Liberation* (§44), 25.
11. Sacred Congregation, *Christian Freedom and Liberation*, (§68), 40–41.

Nicaragua was a kind of beacon of hope, as Cuba had been for the left a decade or two earlier. The upheavals in Eastern Europe could not fail to have their effects, however, in an era characterized by globalization and the hegemony of US culture, alongside a vibrantly reactionary Roman Catholic Church which sought to check progressive interpretations of the Second Vatican Council. Progressives were replaced in dioceses in Brazil, and the broadening influence of liberation theology was slowly checked. In a memorable phrase, Clodovis Boff compared the situation of the Roman Catholic Church and the CEBs in Brazil with toothpaste which has been squeezed out of a tube and which can never be put back again. At the grass roots, the liberationist perspective still has its effect, less often heard of, but still pervasive. Elsewhere there has been a subtle change in the emphases of those engaging with liberation theology: cultural criticism, ecological issues, compromise with the perspective of radical orthodoxy, and gender politics have become more prominent. Yet the main strands which gave liberation theology its distinctive role have never been completely lost, even if there has been some evidence of a drop in confidence in the particular political project which gave liberation theology its peculiar hue in the last two decades of the twentieth century.

Liberation theology's genius, and the key to its re-emergence, is its commitment to specific contextual projects—not the various theoretical and culturally aware developments that have emerged in the last decade. There is evidence that some regard the post-1989 situation as an opportunity rather than a threat. The old socialism-capitalism dualism has been replaced by a recognition that the all-pervasiveness of capitalism needs to be challenged by an acknowledgement of the complexity of that phenomenon and the myriad opportunities it now offers for social change. When liberation theology loses its commitment to engagement in historical projects to bring life where there is death, it will have lost its soul. Liberation theology put its finger on the pulse of the historical change which is fundamental to the work of the Holy Spirit who makes all things new. Its practitioners have achieved this by realizing that theological understanding comes through commitment to action—and discernment as a complement to that—a commitment to the reading of "the signs of the times" and the changes which they demand in the service of the vulnerable.[12]

---

12. Petrella, *Future of Liberation Theology*.

Praxis and Theory: Epistemology and the Method of Liberation Theology

In liberation theology, faith, reflection, and real life are in dialectical relationship with each other. It is above all a new way of *doing* theology, in that action, rather than detachment and silent reflection by themselves, is deemed to be adequate. It is new in the sense that it contrasts with much of the university or seminary theology of the last two centuries, which prioritizes intellectual discourse and esteems detachment from life and, increasingly, from the practices of prayer and charity. In some ways, liberation theology echoes the theological method of an earlier age when worship, service to humanity, openness to God, and theological reflection were more closely integrated and when the conduct of the Christian life was an indispensable context for theology. What has been rediscovered in liberation theology in particular is the commitment to the poor and marginalized as fundamental for meeting with God. Commitment to, and solidarity with, the poor and vulnerable are therefore the necessary basis for theological activity. So, one first of all *does* liberation theology before learning *about* it. Or, to put it another way, one can only learn about it by embarking on active solidarity with and concern for the amelioration of the suffering of the poor and marginalized. Liberation theology cannot adequately be understood except by commitment in solidarity and action. Because of the deep-rooted connection of this theology with particular contexts and experiences, liberation theology presents peculiar problems for those who seek to write *about* it. A proper understanding of it demands something more than an intellectual appreciation alone. Understanding involves the move from a previous position of detachment, to be open to that transformation of perspective which comes either at the margins of society or in social estrangement. To paraphrase the dialogue of Jesus with Nicodemus in John 3, it is only by changing sides and identifying with the Christ who meets and challenges men and women in the persons of the poor, the hungry, and the naked that one may "see the kingdom of God" (John 3:3).[13]

The basic method of liberation theology has its analogy with Marxist epistemology. The fundamental Marxist insight that consciousness is determined by one's historical context and activity in that context has its echo in liberation theology's method. It is important to see liberation theology as a parallel development to Marxism rather than as a deliberate attempt to insert Marxism into Christian theology. At most, Marxism provided a language for the experience of solidarity with the poor. "Praxis," for Marx,

---

13. Cf. L. Boff, "Epistemology and Method"; Graham, *Transforming Practice*.

is both a tool for changing the course of history and a critical tool. Praxis arises out of, and is determined by, the consciousness-shaping activity undertaken in historical contingencies. Consequently, praxis changes, perhaps even revolutionizes, the understanding of reality through human action. In one of his most famous sentiments, expressed in *The German Ideology*, Marx criticized Ludwig Feuerbach for supposing that all that was needed was a better consciousness of the world when what was actually needed was a comprehension of reality through the activity of changing it. Marx considered the lack of any activist, committed element an Achilles heel in what considered itself a critical philosophy. This is also at the heart of liberation theology's critique of much theology, ancient or modern.

The centrality of a praxis-based epistemology in liberation theology might appear to give weight to the critique of the Vatican, for example, that it is too wedded to an atheistic philosophy. This would be a mistake, however. A glance at Gutiérrez's classic A *Theology of Liberation* will reveal how marginal Marxism is to its theological fabric, even if its sentiments, critical perspective, and focus on the poor are superficially similar. At most we may regard this similarity as evidence of the importance of Marxist hermeneutics as a heuristic device for liberation theology, opening a pathway to the Christian tradition, viewed in its broadest sense. Furthermore, it enables an appreciation of the centrality of praxis as a major determinant of theological reflection. Like Marxism, liberation theology rejects the priority of detached thought in determining the understanding of God, instead prioritizing both the historical activity and the identification of the poor with their privileged position as objects of divine mercy and vehicles of insight into the divine will. The question of God cannot therefore be divorced from questions which arise from practice. Hegel already recognized this, and his criticism of aspects of contemporary theology could well apply:

> It is to be noted that there is a type of theology that wants to adopt *only a historical attitude* towards religion; it even has an abundance of cognition, though only of a historical kind. This cognition is no concern of ours, for if the cognition of religion were merely historical, we would have to compare such theologians with counting-house clerks, who keep the ledgers and accounts of other people's wealth, a wealth that passes through their hands without their retaining any of it, clerks who act only for others without acquiring any assets of their own. They do of course receive a salary, but their merit lies only in keeping records of the assets of other people. In philosophy and religion, however, the essential thing is that one's own spirit itself should

recognize a possession and content, deem itself worthy of cognition, and not keep itself humbly outside.[14]

The indissolubility of knowledge and action is the basis for a concept of education at the heart of liberation theology. Paulo Freire, a crucial figure in the emergence of popular education linked with liberation theology in Brazil, emphasizes the link between knowing and doing. For Freire, the human being should be engaged in active inquiry "with the world, and with each other"—inquiry leading to liberation and transformation, to "mutual humanization."[15] "In Freire's analysis, not only is knowing intimately associated with doing, right education with transformation, but the place where the transformation must first take place is in **the very act of education itself**. The 'how' of education is inseparable from questions of epistemology, ethics, politics, and also theology."[16] Thus the transformation of the learning process into a student-centered or genuinely "humanist" education is not merely a fashion or a learning technique; it is transformative action with the goal of far wider-ranging societal transformation.

Such theological presuppositions reflect crucial issues in the Bible. An oft-quoted passage is Jeremiah 22:15–16 where the prophet asserts that knowing God is doing justice.[17] Even more importantly, the fundamental learning experience in the Gospels is not the teaching Jesus gave his disciples but their activity in walking with Jesus on the way to Jerusalem. To learn what it means that the Son of Man must suffer means taking up the cross (Mark 8:38) and following Jesus by going up to Jerusalem. The reported prophecies of the Passion (e.g., Mark 8–10) are incomprehensible without the learning experience of accompanying Jesus to Jerusalem. This is not just a spiritual journey but, as all the Gospels indicate, a journey to the very teeth of the center of power in Judean society: Jesus becomes the victim of the high priest's decision that "it is better . . . to have one man die for the people" (John 11:50 NRSV).

The importance of the theme of "the way" is now widely recognized in discussions of the Gospel of Mark, for example.[18] Nowhere is it better demonstrated that the contingent basis of theological understanding is in action, rather than contemplation and detachment, than in Matthew 10:20–22. Here the situation is one in which a particular form of demonstration of commitment results in the inspired word of the Spirit in the one bearing witness.

14. Hegel, *Introduction and the Concept*, 128 (italics original).
15. Freire, *Pedagogy of the Oppressed*, 46–49.
16. Moore, "On Copy Clerks," 36–38.
17. Miranda, *Marx and the Bible*, 47–50.
18. Marcus, *Way of the Lord*.

Similarly, in Matthew 18, the *practice* of reconciliation is the prerequisite of the presence of the living Christ: "For where two or three are gathered in my name, I am there among them" (Matt 18:20). Christ's presence turns out to be the consequence of reconciling action. The divine presence, therefore, is to be found in contexts of practical demonstration of forgiveness, just as the meeting with the eschatological judge in this age turns out to be service to "the least of these who are members of my family" (Matt 25:40). What happens in this world, most especially to "the least of these," is theologically fundamental. The understanding of the Christian Scriptures in particular is an activity and a discipline inseparable from that action which is epistemologically fundamental. Such fundamental praxis-orientated epistemology is the foundation for all critical reflection. As in Marxism, it is not one's left-leaning preferences or opinions which lead to a particular perspective, but the commitment to and active involvement with the poor as participants with them in their peculiar role in the divine economy that is the basis of criticism. Liberation theology, therefore, is not to be confused with some kind of armchair radicalism in which the thoughts of a liberal intelligentsia offers an Olympian perspective on the doings of fellow men and women. Indeed, it is precisely those doings, especially of the most vulnerable and the weakest of the earth, which grant a different, critical perspective.

The Bible: The Written Text and the Text of Life

Among the CEBs, the Bible has become a catalyst for the exploration of pressing contemporary issues relevant to the community, offering a language so that the voice of the voiceless may be heard.[19] In the CEBs' engagement with the Bible, there is an immediacy about the way the text is used because resonances are found with the experience set out in the stories of biblical characters. Thus, the Bible offers a means by which the present difficulties can be shown to be surmountable in the life of faith and community commitment. To enable the poor to read the Bible has involved a program of education on the contents of the biblical material, so that it can be a resource for thousands who are illiterate. In such popular education programs, full recognition is taken of the value of the experience of life.[20] The community setting means an avoidance of a narrowly individualist "religious" reading. The experience of poverty and oppression (often termed "life" or "reality") is as important a text as the text of Scripture itself. It represents another text

---

19. Gorgulho, "Biblical Hermeneutics"; Croatto, *Biblical Hermeneutics*.

20. Examples of material produced by the archdiocese of São Paulo may be found in Rowland and Corner, *Liberating Exegesis*, 7–20.

to be studied alongside that contained between the covers of the Bible. God's word is to be found in the dialectic between the memory of the people of God in the Bible and the continuing story to be discerned in the contemporary world, particularly among the people with whom God has chosen to be identified. This twofold aspect is brought out clearly by Carlos Mesters:

> the emphasis is not placed on the text's meaning in itself but rather on the meaning the text has for the people reading it. At the start the people tend to draw any and every sort of meaning, however well or ill founded, from the text. . . . The common people are also eliminating the alleged "neutrality" of scholarly exegesis. . . . The common people are putting the Bible in its proper place, the place where God intended it to be. They are putting it in second place. Life takes first place! In so doing, the people are showing us the enormous importance of the Bible, and at the same time, its relative value—relative to life.[21]

Latin American liberationist hermeneutics is succinctly set out by Clodovis Boff.[22] Boff describes two different kinds of approaches to the Bible. One is more immediate, in which the biblical story becomes a type for the people of God in the modern world. In the other approach, what Boff describes as a "correspondence of relationships" method,[23] the Bible is read through the lens of the experience of the present, thereby enabling it to become a key to understanding that to which the scriptural text bears witness—the life and struggles of the ancestors in the faith. This exploration of Scripture in turn casts light on the present. What is important about Boff's model is that it is not a quest for formulas to copy or techniques to apply from Scripture. Scripture offers orientations, models, types, directives, principles, and inspirations—elements permitting us to acquire, on our own initiative, a "hermeneutic competency." This then offers the capacity to judge, on our own initiative and in our own right, "according to the mind of Christ," or "according to the Spirit," the new, unpredictable situations with which we are continually confronted. The Christian writings offer us not a *what*, but a *how*—a manner, a style, a spirit.[24]

In all of this there is an assumption that the poor are not just objects of pity but subjects in their own right, with a peculiar capacity to understand the ways of God. The poor are blessed because they can read Scripture from a perspective different from that of most of the rich; they find in it a message

---

21. Mesters, "Use of the Bible," 14–15. Cf. Mesters, *Defenseless Flower*.
22. C. Boff, *Theology and Praxis*; Sugirtharajah, *Voices from the Margins*, 9–35.
23. C. Boff, *Theology and Praxis*, 146.
24. Sugirtharajah, ed., *Voices from the Margin*, 30.

which can easily elude those who are not poor. The poor are privileged in the eyes of God and should be the particular concern of all of those who claim to be concerned with the ways of God. Poverty is not glamorized, however. The beatitudes reveal the character of a God who identifies with the poor and marginalized: "the kingdom of God comes first and foremost for those who by virtue of their situation have most need of it: the poor, the afflicted, the hungry of the world."[25] The kingdom is coming because God is humane, because God cannot tolerate the situation of the poor and is coming to make sure that the divine will is done on earth. Jesus' identification with the wretched of the earth, whether in his divine self-emptying (Phil 2:6–11) or in the character of the relationships he established during his mission, demonstrates solidarity with those on the margins.

Liberation theologians would accept Jürgen Moltmann's assertion (on the basis of Matt 25:31–46) that the wretched "are the latent presence of the coming Savior and Judge in the world, the touchstone which determines salvation and damnation."[26] That is a significant role. Because the poor are particularly close to God and the place where one can meet the risen Christ, they constitute the place from which to view the way the world and the tradition are being used. Oppressed persons mediate God because they break down the normal egotism with which human beings approach other human beings. Through them we can begin to engage the question of what "being God" means. Those who deal with the oppressed discern that it is they who are being spoken to, indeed evangelized, not those whom they set out to help. So, to search for God means searching for the poor.[27] This has ecclesiological implications, for the poor become channels for discerning the identity of the church and the direction and content of its mission. It is not the case, as Jon Sobrino has put it, that the church of the poor is "automatically the agent of truth and grace because the poor are in it; rather the poor in the church are the structural source that assures the church of being the real agent of truth and justice."[28] So the church of the poor is not simply a reality alongside mainstream Christianity; rather, the mark of the true church is its acceptance of the perspective of the poor.

Theologians like Leonardo Boff have been at pains to stress the deep roots of the "basic ecclesial communities" in the life of the Catholic Church. Certainly the communities may offer a new perspective and are a sign of hope for the renewal of the Church, but Boff makes it quite plain that he

---

25. Segundo, *Jesus of Nazareth*, 2:62.
26. Moltmann, *Church and the Power of the Spirit*, 127.
27. Sobrino, *True Church*, 222.
28. Sobrino, *True Church*, 93, 95.

does not conceive of them as an embryonic sect, though some critics portray them as such. Rather, Boff argues that they are the leaven in the lump, a remnant within the people of God.[29]

In the writings of liberation theologians the repeated emphasis on Jesus and the Gospels is the central criterion of obedience. Like their European contemporaries, the theologians of liberation have taken up the quest for the historical Jesus as a means of criticizing a preoccupation with the superhuman, remote Christ of ecclesiastical confession. Liberation theologians believe that the historical Jesus was situated, personally involved in a situation that displays structural similarities to that of present-day Latin America.[30] In the christologies of Sobrino and Leonardo Boff, for example, there is a stress on the importance of the historical Jesus as a central criterion by which the theology of the church, particularly its dogmatic explication of Jesus' significance, may be judged.[31] A historical person wrestling with the specific social and political problems posed by his context offers liberation theologians a direct analogy to struggles in their own specific contexts. The various interpretations of liberation theology in Latin America seem to echo the theme: if a christology disregards the historical Jesus, it turns into an abstract christology, one that avoids the responsibility to engage with history in all its particularities, one that is alienating and liable to escapism.

Liberation Theology and Ideological Criticism

One of liberation theology's challenges to theology has come from the recognition of the "ideological" character of all theology and its role within a complex political struggle within the churches of maintaining the ascendancy of certain positions.[32] The emphasis on the contextual nature of all theology has led liberation theologians to question the absolute character of theological pronouncements from the past as well as the present, and to attempt a theological unmasking of reality. Leonardo Boff, for example, challenges theologians to be aware of the socio-economic context in which they practice their theology:

> Theologians do not live in clouds. They are social actors with a particular place in society. They produce knowledge, data, and meanings by using instruments that the situation offers them

---

29. L. Boff, *Jesus Christ Liberator*, 63.
30. Sobrino, *Christology at the Crossroads*, 351–53.
31. Sobrino, *Christology at the Crossroads*; L. Boff, *Jesus Christ Liberator*.
32. Segundo, *Liberation of Theology*.

and permits them to utilize.... The themes and emphases of a given Christology flow from what seems relevant to the theologian on the basis of his or her social standpoint.... In that sense we must maintain that no Christology is or can be neutral.... Willingly or unwillingly Christological discourse is voiced in a given social setting with all the conflicting interests that pervade it. That holds true as well for theological discourse that claims to be a "purely" theological, historical, traditional, ecclesial, and apolitical. Normally such discourse adopts the position of those who hold power in the existing system. If a different kind of Christology with its own commitments appears on the scene and confronts the older "apolitical" Christology, the latter will soon discover its social locale, forget its "apolitical" nature, and reveal itself as a religious reinforcement of the existing status quo.[33]

To view liberation theology as merely a species of the ideological criticism widespread in politically left-leaning academia would be a misjudgment, whatever the similarities or apparent indebtedness to Marxist ideological critique. Use of ideological criticism is the consequence of preexisting commitments to the poor and the disadvantaged on the part of the writers concerned. Indeed, the social engagement of those involved in higher education has become a widespread feature of Brazilian intellectual life, with many university institutions requiring that a significant part of the syllabus in which their students engage and the research their staff undertake should involve social engagement and have relevance to the lives of the communities in which the universities are located. This is a version of the vision of the "organic intellectual" suggested by Antonio Gramsci and often alluded to by liberation theologians who spend a significant part of their working lives oscillating between study, teaching, and engagement with local communities.[34]

Liberation's Contribution to Systematic Theology

Doctrinally, liberation theology departs little from the theological mainstream. Indeed, the claim of its exponents that it is a new way of doing theology indicates that its novelty lies in its method rather than its content. Its character, particularly its situatedness, its concern for improving the lot of the poor, and its emphasis upon protesting on behalf of the vulnerable, makes

---

33. L. Boff, *Jesus Christ Liberator*, 265–66. Cf. Avineri, *Karl Marx*, 135.
34. Gramsci, *Prison Notebooks*, 10–12, 60, 330; West, *Academy of the Poor*.

it particularly important for ecclesiology, pneumatology, and eschatology.[35] The implicit pneumatology of liberation theology stresses the activity of the divine Spirit in the world which does not confine the Spirit's activity either to the church or to its official representatives. The Pauline vision of the body of Christ in which all have their role to play challenges simple hierarchical, ecclesial models. It is that aspect of the theology of liberation which led to the criticism by the Vatican of Leonardo Boff's *Church: Charism and Power*, in which an egalitarian church polity was outlined.[36] Prophecy and reading the signs of the times become key elements in the life of a church committed to the poor and the marginalized through understanding God's will in history.[37] The theological anthropology which is informed by pneumatology questions the fatalism of a view of human sinfulness which despairs of the possibility of change. Not that there is any lack of recognition of the pervasiveness of sin, but, following the emphasis of Catholic social teaching on structural sin, this is not confined to the individual but also involves the critique of the exercise of power in institutions which are themselves pervaded by that which leads to oppression.

Liberation theology has thus given prominence to themes neglected in the mainstream Christian tradition. It has been important to retrieve "alternative stories," whether neglected or buried. This has been a significant component of feminist biblical interpretation.[38] The remarkable "hinterland" of radical themes in the Christian tradition has gradually been accessed,[39] following in the footsteps of an approach to Christian tradition famously pioneered by Ernst Bloch's *The Principle of Hope*.[40] It is its hope for a better world which links liberation theology in general terms with the chiliastic tradition down the centuries.[41] The legacy of Augustine's *City of God* had been so pervasive in Christian doctrine that the view of a this-worldly hope has either been interpreted in other-worldly terms or simply pushed to the margins of the Christian tradition. Joachim of Fiore's interpretation of the book of Revelation and his trinitarian historicism provoked a very different attitude to eschatology.[42] In it there is a decisive

35. The connection with Joachite pneumatology is made explicitly by Comblin, "Holy Spirit," 474–75.

36. Boff, *Charism and Power*.

37. Ellacuría, "Utopia," 289–327; Segundo, "Revelation," 328–49.

38. Grey, "Feminist theology," 105–22; Keller and Ruether, *In Our Own Voices*; Selvidge, *Notorious Voices*; Althaus-Reid, *Indecent Theology*.

39. Bradstock and Rowland, eds., *Radical Christian Writings*.

40. Bloch, *Principle of Hope*.

41. Ellacuría, "Christian Salvation."

42. Reeves, *Influence of Prophecy*.

break with Augustinian eschatology, in that the task of the church is not to prepare people for the world beyond but to be coworkers of God in bringing in the kingdom. This has two aspects: a hope for the coming kingdom in this world,[43] and the conviction that human agency is an important component relating to the establishment of the coming kingdom. Eschatological events ceased to be mysterious, transcendent entities; they became present, historical possibilities. Indeed, in the hands of Joachim's followers, their own contemporary history and their own part in it became the arena for the fulfilment of the eschatological promises.

Both the Joachite tradition and liberation theology echo New Testament texts, and in this very important respect differ markedly from other areas of the Christian tradition. Theirs is a hope for this world rather than for some transcendent realm. The future does not function solely as a regulative ideal which acts as a stimulus to action, for it is also an inner dynamism which acts as a driving force to bring about radical change and to fulfil the hope for a new order in the present. Joachim's strong sense of his own time as of great significance in human history not only reflects New Testament eschatology but also led to an appreciation of the present moment (*kairos*) in human history as an opportunity for historical action of eschatological significance. Indeed, a major contribution of the churches in South Africa, the *Kairos Document*, picked up this language of timely theological and ethical engagement in politics.[44] It would be wrong to see this kind of theology, whether in Joachite tradition or in liberation theology, as a mere byproduct of modern Christian activism, for the implicit pneumatology in both presupposes that human actors have their part to play in preparation for the dawning age.

The influence of liberation theology on systematic theology in general terms reflects its character. The dialectic between social context and theology has become widely acknowledged even if the effects of this acknowledgement have not always led to any significant change in the way systematic theologians have done their work. Nevertheless there has been divergence between North America and Europe in this respect. In the former, contextual theology is a cornerstone of much theological work, and there is a wider recognition of the social context of all theology. The situation is rather different in Europe, where the influence of liberation theology has tended to be more on the fringes of higher education institutions; on the practice of adult theological education, however, its impact has been enormous. Theology is

---

43. About which utopian language can sometimes be used; see Libânio, "Hope, Utopia, Resurrection."

44. Kairos Group, *Kairos Document*.

not just a matter of abstract theorizing, but of reflection on an active faith. The meaning of Scripture and tradition is subordinated to experience as the primary datum; the text of everyday life is given priority over the text of the Bible. Patterns of biblical exegesis which have emerged in parts of Latin America over the last decades offer the most recent example of the way the practical faith of the non-professional reader can be resourced by a mode of reading of the Scriptures which does not need—even if it was often supported by—sympathetic intellectuals.[45]

The dominance of the Roman Catholic Church in Latin America has meant that the character and theological context has been conditioned by the Catholic theological agenda. Nevertheless, some mainline churches in Latin America have supported the outlines of liberation theology. In countries like South Africa, experience of oppression of the majority in the period of the apartheid regime led Protestants to a similar kind of theological method to that which emerged in Latin America. There is an affinity with both the political theology of Europe and North America and the important emphasis on history which emerges in both the work of Pannenberg and Moltmann, both of whom, arguably, reflect a greater distance from the dominance of an Augustinian eschatology in the light of an engagement with the biblical view of history.[46]

Liberation theology forcibly reminds us that the contemporary theological enterprise cannot escape critical reflection on its assumptions and preferences. The preference in liberation exegesis for the teaching of Jesus on the reign of God, rather than the Pauline or Johannine theologies, manifests its own wish to identify the gospel as good news for the poor and as the quest for social justice. The Synoptic Gospels and the book of Revelation have formed the most important part of the liberation process in certain sections of the church in Latin America. Liberation theology has reminded us, if nothing else, that when viewed from the underside of history, from the poor and the marginalized, the message of the kingdom looks rather different from the way in which it has been portrayed by those who have had the power to write the story of the church and formulate its dogmas and its social concerns.

---

45. West, *Academy of the Poor.*
46. Gilbertson, *God and History.*

Bibliography

Althaus-Reid, Marcella. *Indecent Theology: Theological Perversions in Sex, Gender, and Politics*. London: Routledge, 2000.

Avineri, Schlomo. *The Social and Political Thought of Karl Marx*. 8 vols. Cambridge Studies in the History and Theory of Politics. London: Cambridge University Press, 1968.

Batstone, David, et al., eds. *Liberation Theologies, Postmodernity, and the Americas*. London: Routledge, 1997.

Bell, Daniel M., Jr. *Liberation Theology after the End of History: The Refusal to Cease Suffering*. Radical Orthodoxy Series. London: Routledge, 2001.

Bennett-Moore, Zoë. "On Copy Clerks, Transformers, and Spiders: Teachers and Learners in Adult Theological Education." *British Journal of Theological Education* 9.3 (1997) 36–44.

Bloch, Ernst. *The Principle of Hope*. Translated by Neville Plaice et al. 3 vols. Studies in Contemporary German Social Thought. Oxford: Blackwell, 1986.

Boff, Clodovis. *Theology and Praxis: Epistemological Foundations*. Translated by Robert R. Barr. Maryknoll, NY: Orbis, 1987.

———. *Theology and Praxis*. Translated by Robert R. Barr. 1987. Reprint, Eugene, OR: Wipf & Stock, 2009.

Boff, Leonardo. *Church: Charism and Power; Liberation Theology and the Institutional Church*. Translated by John W. Diercksmeier. London: SCM, 1985.

———. *Ecclesiogenesis: The Base Communities Reinvent the Church*. Translated by Robert R. Barr. Maryknoll, NY: Orbis, 1986.

———. "Epistemology and Method of the Theology of Liberation" In *Mysterium Liberationis: Fundamental Concepts of Liberation Theology*, edited by Ignacio Ellacuría and Jon Sobrino, 57–84. Maryknoll, NY: Orbis, 1993.

———. *Jesus Christ Liberator: A Critical Christology for Our Time*. Translated by Patrick Hughes. London: SPCK, 1979.

Bradstock, Andrew, and Christopher Rowland, eds. *Radical Christian Writings: A Reader*. Oxford: Blackwell, 2002.

Comblin, José. "The Holy Spirit." In *Mysterium Liberationis: Fundamental Concepts of Liberation Theology*, edited by Ignacio Ellacuría and Jon Sobrino, 462–82. Maryknoll, NY: Orbis, 1993.

Croatto, J. Severino. *Biblical Hermeneutics: Toward a Theory of Reading as the Production of Meaning*. Translated by Robert R. Barr. Maryknoll, NY: Orbis, 1987.

Ellacuría, Ignacio. "Christian Salvation." In *Mysterium Liberationis: Fundamental Concepts of Liberation Theology*, edited by Ignacio Ellacuría and Jon Sobrino, 251–88. Maryknoll, NY: Orbis, 1993.

———. "Utopia and Prophecy in Latin America." In *Mysterium Liberationis: Fundamental Concepts of Liberation Theology*, edited by Ignacio Ellacuría and Jon Sobrino, 289–328. Maryknoll, NY: Orbis, 1993.

Ellacuría, Ignacio, and Jon Sobrino, eds. *Mysterium Liberationis: Fundamental Concepts of Liberation Theology*. Maryknoll, NY: Orbis, 1993.

Freire, Paulo. *Pedagogy of the Oppressed*. Translated by Myra Bergman Ramos. Penguin Education. London: Penguin, 1972.

Gilbertson, Michael. *God and History in the Book of Revelation: New Testament Studies in Dialogue with Pannenberg and Moltmann*. Society for New Testament Studies Monograph Series 124. Cambridge: Cambridge University Press, 2003.

Gorgulho, Gilberto da Silva. "Biblical Hermeneutics." In *Mysterium Liberationis: Fundamental Concepts of Liberation Theology*, edited by Iganacio Ellacuría and Jon Sobrino, 123-49. Maryknoll, NY: Orbis, 1993.

Gottwald, Norman K., and Richard A. Horsley, eds. *The Bible and Liberation: Political and Social Hermeneutics*. Rev. ed. Bible & Liberation. Maryknoll, NY: Orbis, 1993.

Graham, Elaine L. *Transforming Practice: Pastoral Theology in an Age of Uncertainty*. London: Mowbray, 1996.

Gramsci, Antonio. *Selections from the Prison Notebooks of Antonio Gramsci*. Edited and translated by Quintin Hoare and Geoffrey Nowell Smith. Social Theory. London: Lawrence and Wishart, 1971.

Grey, Mary. "Feminist Theology." In *The Cambridge Companion to Liberation Theology*, edited by Christopher Rowland, 105-22. 2nd ed. Cambridge Companions to Philosophy, Religion, and Culture. Cambridge: Cambridge University Press, 2008.

Gutiérrez, Gustavo. *The Power of the Poor in History: Selected Writings*. Translated by Robert R. Barr. London: SCM, 1983.

———. *A Theology of Liberation: History, Politics, and Salvation*. Rev. ed., with new introduction. Translated and edited by Sister Caridad Inda and John Eagleson. Maryknoll, NY: Orbis, 1988.

Gutiérrez, Gustavo, et al. *Santo Domingo and After: The Challenge for the Latin American Church*. London: Catholic Institute for International Relations, 1993.

Hegel, G. F. W. *Lectures on the Philosophy of Religion*. Vol. 1, *Introduction and the Concept of Religion*. Edited by Peter C. Hodgson. Translated by R. F. Brown et al. 3 vols. Berkeley: University of California Press, 1984-1987.

Hennelly, Alfred T., ed. *Liberation Theology: A Documentary History*. Maryknoll, NY: Orbis, 1990.

Kairos Group. *The Kairos Document: Challenge to the Church; A Theological Comment on the Political Crisis in South Africa*. Grand Rapids: Eerdmans, 1986.

Keller, Rosemary Skinner, and Rosemary Radford Ruether, eds. *In Our Own Voices: Four Centuries of American Women's Religious Writing*. San Francisco: HarperSanFrancisco, 1995.

Libânio, Jâo Batista. "Hope, Utopia, Resurrection." In *Mysterium Liberationis: Fundamental Concepts of Liberation Theology*, edited by Ignacio Ellacuría and Jon Sobrino, 716-28. Maryknoll, NY: Orbis, 1993.

Marcus, Joel. *The Way of the Lord: Christological Exegesis of the Old Testament in the Gospel of Mark*. Studies of the New Testament and Its World. Edinburgh: T. & T. Clark, 1993.

Marx, Karl. *The German Ideology*. London: Lawrence & Wishart, 1965.

Mesters, Carlos. *Defenseless Flower: A New Reading of the Bible*. Translated by Francis McDonagh. Maryknoll, NY: Orbis, 1989.

———. "The Use of the Bible in Christian Communities of the Common People." In *The Bible and Liberation: Political and Social Hermeneutics*, edited by Norman K. Gottwald and Richard A. Horsley, 3-16. Rev. ed. Bible & Liberation. Maryknoll, NY: Orbis, 1993.

Metz, Johannes Baptist. *Faith in History and Society: Towards a Practical Fundamental Theology*. Translated by David Smith. New York: Seabury, 1980.

———. *Theology of the World*. Translated by William Glen-Doepel. New York: Herder & Herder, 1969.

Miranda, Jose Porfirio. *Marx and the Bible: A Critique of the Philosophy of Oppression*. Translated by John Eagleson. 1974. Reprint, Eugene, OR: Wipf & Stock, 2004.

Moltmann, Jürgen. *The Church in the Power of the Spirit*. Translated by Margaret Kohl. London: SCM, 1977.

Paul VI, Pope. *On Evangelization in the Modern World: Apostolic Exhortation Evangelii nuntiandi, Dec. 8, 1975*. Washington, DC: Publications Office, United States Catholic Conference, 1976. https://www.vatican.va/content/paul-vi/en/apost_exhortations/documents/hf_p-vi_exh_19751208_evangelii-nuntiandi.html/.

Petrella, Ivan. *The Future of Liberation Theology: An Argument and a Manifesto*. Aldershot, UK: Ashgate, 2004.

———, ed. *Latin American Liberation Theology: The Next Generation*. Maryknoll, NY: Orbis, 2005.

Reeves, Marjorie. *The Influence of Prophecy in the Later Middle Ages*. Oxford: Clarendon, 1969.

Rowland, Christopher, ed. *The Cambridge Companion to Liberation Theology*. Cambridge Companions to Philosophy, Religion, and Culture. 2nd ed. Cambridge: Cambridge University Press, 2008.

Rowland, Christopher, and Mark Corner. *Liberating Exegesis: The Challenge of Liberation Theology to Biblical Studies*. Biblical Foundations in Theology. London: SPCK, 1990.

Sacred Congregation for the Doctrine of the Faith. *Instruction on Certain Aspects of the Theology of Liberation*. Boston: St. Paul, 1984.

———. *Instruction on Christian Freedom and Liberation*. Washington, DC: United States Catholic Conference, 1986.

Segundo, Juan Luis. *Jesus of Nazareth Yesterday and Today*. Vol. 2, *The Historical Jesus of the Synoptics*. Translated by John Drury. 5 vols. London: Sheed & Ward, 1985.

———. *The Liberation of Theology*. Translated by John Drury. Maryknoll, NY: Orbis, 1976.

———. "Revelation, Faith, Signs of the Times." In *Mysterium Liberationis: Fundamental Concepts of Liberation Theology*, edited by Ignacio Ellacuría and Jon Sobrino, 328–49. Maryknoll, NY: Orbis, 1993.

Selvidge, Marla J. *Notorious Voices: Feminist Biblical Interpretation, 1500–1920*. London: SCM, 1996.

Sobrino, Jon. *Christology at the Crossroads: A Latin American Approach*. Translated by John Drury. London: SCM, 1978.

———. *The True Church and the Poor*. Translated by Matthew J. O'Connell. London: SCM, 1984.

Souza, Marcelo de Barros. *A Bíblia e a Luta pela Terra*. Coleção Da base para a base 11. Petropolis, Brazil: Comissão Pastoral da Terra, 1983.

Sugirtharajah, R. S. *Voices from the Margin*. London: SPCK, 1991.

Tombs, David. *Latin American Liberation Theology*. Brill Book Archive, Part 1. Religion in the Americas 1. Leiden: Brill, 2002.

Walsh, Michael, and Brian Davies, eds. *Proclaiming Justice and Peace*. London: CIIR and CAFOD, 1984.

West, Gerald O. *The Academy of the Poor: Towards a Dialogical Reading of the Bible*. Interventions 2. Sheffield: Sheffield Academic, 1999.

4

Liberation Theology and Politics

I RECALL THREE CONVERSATIONS I had on my first visit to Latin America in 1983. When I was in Mexico City I met Jose Portfirio Miranda, author of *Marx and the Bible* and an exponent of the theology of liberation whose writing had secured him a wide audience in Europe and North America. I was treated to a very gloomy set of predictions about the future of the theology of liberation: "all that will be left of it in a few years' time will be our books," he said. It has to be said that he was speaking in a country where the theology of liberation has never gained a firm foothold, and as a result the distinctive features of its theological and pastoral method are not much in evidence. The second conversation echoed some of these fears. I was at a celebration of one of the few "middle-class" Basic Ecclesial Communities (CEBs) in São Paulo. During it one of the theological advisers of the group, who taught at the pontifical seminary, spoke of her fears about the crackdown on the theology of liberation which would precede the celebrations of the evangelization of the Americas in 1992. She pinned her fears then on Lopez Trujillo of the Latin American Conference of Bishops and talked of the desire to present "a pure church," unsullied by politics, to the pope in time for the next conference at Santo Domingo in 1992. That meant, she suggested, breaking the power of the then progressive Brazilian Bishops' Conference. The third conversation was in contrast with both of these. In it Clodovis Boff, brother of the more famous Leonardo, himself a member of a religious community, spoke of the Basic Ecclesial Communities as a force in Brazilian life which could not be stopped. He said that whatever the attempts by forces of reaction to put a stop to the process of change and renewal in the Church leading to involvement in action for social change there could be no putting the clock back. Or as he more graphically put it, "once the toothpaste has been squeezed from the tube there can be no putting it back in again."

I mention these conversations at the beginning of this lecture because, seven years later, there are elements of truth in what all three said. Over recent years in many countries of Latin America, particularly Brazil, there has been a spate of appointments at the episcopal level which has seen the progressive bishops replaced with conservatives or moved to peripheral dioceses. This has meant a clear shift in the balance of power in the powerful Brazilian Bishops' Conference away from the progressive and often controversial style of recent years. Observers in Brazil suggest that the Church is everywhere on the retreat back to altar and presbytery. Yet despite all that, at the grassroots the Church as the people of God is as involved as ever. Millions of ordinary men and women whose names will never make the theological libraries of Europe and North America are struggling in the midst of hardship and injustice. They are convinced that their faith emboldens and enables them to engage in activity which confronts the powerful and struggles for better conditions for themselves and the poor here and now. They may have less recognition from official ecclesiastical organs, but the extent of their faith and their commitment cannot be in doubt. The next few years promise to be tougher for them. Some will become disillusioned. But many will carry on, confident that their faith in Jesus demands it of them. Are they misguided, the dupes of the widely discredited secular theologies of the sixties or have they in fact got insights into the nature of the gospel which we do well to learn from and take to our hearts? My concern in this lecture will be to explore something of that interpretation of Christianity and suggest reasons why it is not only a valid reading of the Christian tradition but one which has grasped a central insight which we ignore at our peril.

The theology of liberation has taken different forms throughout the world. In all of its manifestations, however, there are two basic features. First of all, God is to be understood in the experience of oppression and poverty as a God who identifies with those who experience injustice. Second, no theology can be done without an account about that experience of God as well as attention to the language of theology built up over the centuries. Even though the best-known example of the theology of liberation is from Latin America, many related types of theology have emerged from various parts of the Third World. The extent of their convergence may be gauged by the proceedings of the Ecumenical Association of Third World Theologians (EATWOT). My knowledge is such that I cannot begin to do justice to the various characteristics of Minjung, Black, and feminist theologies.

What I shall do in this lecture is concentrate on Latin American theology of liberation. My main focus will be on Brazil, partly because it is the form I have seen firsthand and partly because in terms of importance, theologically and institutionally, Brazil can legitimately be considered the crucible of the Church's experience of the theology of liberation.

The Basic Ecclesial Communities (CEBs)

Throughout Brazil tens of thousands of small groups meet regularly in *favelas* or rural villages for worship, Bible study, and reflection on the everyday realities of poverty and injustice which confront them. For thousands of ordinary Brazilians, the dialogue between the reality of poverty and the hope and inspiration offered by the Scriptures has engendered a commitment to social change at local and national levels based on popular participation and insight. These small groups, known as Basic (because they are rooted in the lives of ordinary people and communities) Ecclesial Communities, are a significant component of the contemporary political as well as ecclesiastical scene. They are made up and run by laypeople. There is little suggestion of edicts being passed down from on high, though, equally, there is a recognition that priests and religious have a legitimate contribution to make to the development of understandings of contemporary discipleship. It has until recently been difficult to drive a wedge between the so-called "popular church" and mainstream Catholicism in Brazil. Certainly there are tensions, particularly in those dioceses where there is less sympathy towards the CEBs. But Brazilian Catholicism is characterized by a widespread acceptance of the CEBs and their central role in being the church in contemporary Brazil, a fact which is evident from the episcopal support of the CEBs' assembly in 1986 and equally evident in the most recent conference in Caxias in 1989.

The CEBs have over the years enabled the pursuit of a variety of different interests from many groups: trade unions, political parties, neighborhood groups, the landless movement (where they have taken important initiatives in land reform over the years), slumdwellers, marginalized women, fishers, the aged, the physically handicapped, children, blacks, and the Indian nations. Its concerns include women's participation in church life; the cause of the oppressed; commitments to political parties; and land reform. The land is a pressing issue in contemporary Brazilian politics. Hundreds of thousands of peasants have found themselves ejected from land they have farmed for generations in the interests of the growing agro-business, so important is this for economic growth and the servicing of the foreign debt. Even if land reform legislation were enacted, the problem for many poor people is how to obtain redress from the courts without adequate legal support. Fine-sounding words and phrases in state legislation are no substitute for the ability to implement that legislation on the ground. In the latter particularly we may glimpse something of the controversial activities in which CEBs have been engaged. They pursue the struggle for land reform, participating peacefully in actions such as resisting land expulsions, occupying unused land, communally organizing occupied lands, pressuring government agencies, accompanying landless workers, and encouraging the Church to set an example of land reform.

There is a growing concern for the rights of indigenous peoples, particularly on the occasion of the celebration of 500 years of evangelization in Latin America. The memory of the victims of colonization should be recovered, be they Indian, Black, or other oppressed peoples, to allow for, as they put it, "a new and courageous liberating evangelization of the whole continent." The problem of the indigenous people is particularly sensitive. Nowhere is the tension between justice for the possessors of land and the economic needs of contemporary Brazil so starkly put as here. They were the first to experience eviction from their land when it was despoiled by the Spanish and Portuguese conquests. The concept of liberation itself in its more obvious Hebrew Bible guise of the liberation or deliverance of the people of God from oppression and their journey to a promised land is a potent story. It relates directly to the experience of the people, particularly when many of them have engaged in their own exodus and wanderings seeking better things in Brazil in waves of emigration from the poor northeast to the big cities of the south.

The growth of internal immigration within Brazil, particularly from the impoverished northeast to cities like São Paulo during the period of the so-called economic boom in the late sixties and early seventies, and more recently from the south to Amazonia, caused severe social dislocation. The conditions facing those uprooted from rural Brazil were awful. Drawn by the promise of a better life as the economy expanded, those who were desperately trying to keep body and soul together drifted to the big cities, particularly in the prosperous southeast of the country. Those who arrived at the bus station with only those possessions they could bring with them resorted to building makeshift homes on any piece of spare land available or under motorway arches. It was this desperation which led to the mushrooming shantytowns (*favelas*). Even in the *favelas* rents are extortionate. Those who do occupy land and build their rudimentary dwellings are harassed. Private security firms are hired by land speculators to evict even those who have gained title to the land; those who are squatting are harassed by police which provokes violence, and deaths are all too frequent an occurrence in some areas. Recourse to the courts is often difficult. Even with the return to democracy in Brazil the plight of the homeless in cities like São Paulo continues to deteriorate. Now immigration from the countryside has slowed down, even though the plight of millions in the countryside has not improved. During the time of the economic boom there was work: men could participate as laborers in building projects, luxury homes for the urban elite, for example, while the women could get work as maids for that same group. In a time of economic recession work is not so plentiful, but that has made women's work essential for existence. In situations where it is not possible for friends and relatives to look after children, thousands of children are left to join hundreds of thousands more children in Brazil's cities to roam the streets and increase the already alarming problem of "the street children." Estimates are difficult but some have suggested that as many as twenty million children are left in various forms of abandonment. There is a problem of cataclysmic proportions for Brazil when one considers that three-fifths of Brazil's population is under the age of twenty-five.

Close links were forged between the churches and other groups struggling for human rights during the dictatorship of the late sixties and seventies. The Church was instrumental in setting up commissions on human rights and later the CEBs have played a prominent part in the left-of-center Workers Party (PT). The development of popular movements covers a wide range of positions and the CEBs offer one expression of it. Grassroots participation during the period of the military dictatorship (1964–1985) was focused on church-based bodies which provided an umbrella for individuals from different backgrounds to meet and work for common goals. It was perhaps that experience above all which laid the foundations for the fruitful dialogue and cooperation between the churches and various groups struggling for justice for the majority. The common interest in this goal, the shared experience of persecution led Christians and politicians and trade unionists on the left to sink their differences in search of a more humane environment for ordinary people to live in. Throughout the period of the military dictatorship the Church, particularly in cities like São Paulo, was tireless in defense of human rights, and Christian people themselves suffered torture and even death. This led to a long official campaign of vilification of leaders and basic communities as crypto-communist.

In the last decade or so, pastoral programs have been consolidated with programs of development in education, health, and human rights in which the political dimension of Christian mission is very much to the fore, evident in a variety of educational projects. The consequence of all this is that the activity of the Church is often focused on the CEBs. In them the capacity of the people to unite and promote justice and human rights has probably had a not insignificant role to play within the gradual return of Brazil to a more democratic form of government. Still there are pressing problems stemming from the appalling economic conditions in the country. Economic conditions there have deteriorated markedly in the last year since the election of the Collar government. Meanwhile there is evidence that the Church has retreated from the advanced political positions that it held in the seventies and early eighties. This is in part because of the greater freedom for political activity in the restored democracy but also in part because of the greater reluctance of a more conservative church hierarchy to be involved in more controversial kinds of political activity. Despite this, there is widespread support among grassroots Christians for the Workers' Party and its charismatic leader, Lula, who came so close to winning the presidential elections in Brazil last year on a platform of justice for the poor and the repudiation of the foreign debt.

The CEBs offer a space for hope in a situation which seems devoid of it. Also, they offer an opportunity for a different perspective on the reality of life. How often have I heard men and women saying that through their involvement in the CEBs "their eyes were opened" to injustice and the possibility that things might be different. Confidence is gained for the powerless to act and have a sense of their own worth. Being involved in the CEBs leads to involvement in rural unions and grassroots political activity. Members of the CEBs do not wait for structural change globally or in society but start making changes at the grassroots, attempting to construct new ways of living together which they hope to see implemented in society as a whole.

The influence of priests and religious touched by European political theology has rubbed off on these groups, particularly in those dioceses where there has been a well-organized pastoral program. But it is not just a matter of the influence of a modern political theology. The understanding of evangelization rooted in the Second Vatican Council, which highlights bringing good news into all strata of humanity and making it new, has had its part to play in the understanding of mission in today's world. Sometimes the ethos of the CEBs can be narrowly religious. Pentecostalism has its attractions in Latin America and is a rapidly growing social force in the sub-continent. This has sometimes led to a loss of support from the Basic Christian Communities to pentecostalist and other protestant groups with grassroots involvement (though some of the members have chosen to exercise their political involvement through the trade unions and the PT). The rapidly growing influence of Pentecostalism and its appeal because of its apparently "supernatural" character is a matter which is disturbing leaders of the Church as also are the steady inroads made by US-backed fundamentalist Christian groups with their allegedly "apolitical" stance. Such developments are a reminder that the story of Christianity in contemporary Latin America is incomplete without reference to the surge of support for fundamentalist groups, often supported from North America.

Explaining Liberation Theology

While liberation theology takes its start from the experience of exploitation and poverty which is the lot of the vast majority of the population of Latin America, the approaches to the Christian tradition manifest in the writings of its various exponents cannot easily be reduced to a single system. Of course, there are recurrent patterns which can be discerned in much liberation theology (stemming from the option for the poor taken by the Latin American bishops at their conference at Medellín), and some of these common elements we shall examine in a moment. But liberation theology is being carried out in many different situations varying from war-torn countries like El Salvador and dictatorships like Chile via emerging democracies of Brazil and Uruguay to the post-revolutionary situation of Nicaragua. Thus, there are important distinctions to be made between the various theologians of liberation.

Liberation theology can be briefly described as a form of contextual theology in which the experience and circumstances of the interpreters are given a prime importance as the first step in seeking to be a disciple of Jesus. Thus there is no blueprint from the tradition, the theologians, or, for that matter, from the bishops which is going to offer unambiguous guidance independent of the circumstances in which the people of God find themselves, struggling for justice amidst oppression and want. A theological assumption undergirding this approach is that Christ is be found there as well as in the tradition and the community of the faithful gathered for worship. Action for justice in the face of a reality of oppression is the prime step in theology. The poignant words of the Son of Man in the story of the Last Judgement in Matthew 25:31–46 provide a clue to the first step of this theology: "Inasmuch as you have done it to one of the least of these you have done it to me" (my translation).

We may understand something of what this may mean if we look at the outline of the liberation theology perspective sketched by Gustavo Gutiérrez, the founding father of liberation theology. Gutiérrez has contrasted the approach of the theology of liberation with some of the concerns of European and North American theology in the following way:

> The question in Latin America will not be how to speak of God
> in a world come of age, but rather how to proclaim God as father

in a world that is inhumane. What can it mean to tell a nonperson that he or she is God's child? These were questions asked after their own fashion by Bartolomé de las Casas and so many others in their encounters with native Americans. The discovery of the "Other," the exploited one, led them to reflect on the demands of faith in an altogether different way from the approach taken by those on the side of dominators.[1]

The emphasis on the prior commitment which is the result of identification and action with and on behalf of the poor is a distinctive mark of the theology of liberation. Theology is not the articulation of a set of ideas worked out in isolation from the pressing realities which confront millions in Latin America. Rather theology emerges from the experience, the reflection on, and action to change that reality of oppression and injustice which is the daily lot of millions. The discovery of truth is something found on the journey of life (a metaphor which is very popular in liberation theology). Liberation theology marks a different theological method. The way one will ascertain the voice of God is by starting where people are, because it is where poor and particularly oppressed people are that one will find God. It is with those people that the Bible is particularly concerned: the dispossessed, the widow, the orphan, the stranger, the prostitute, and the tax-collector. As Charles Elliott has put it, "the liberation theologian will say very simply 'the test for truth is the effect it has on people's lives. Is this proposition . . . actually liberating people or enslaving them?'"[2]

At the heart of the theology of liberation is the belief that in the experience of oppression, poverty, hunger, and death God is speaking to all people today and that God's presence among the millions unknown and unloved by humanity but blessed in the eyes of God is confirmed by the witness of the Christian tradition, particularly the Scriptures themselves. It is this conviction, nurtured by the thousands of Basic Ecclesial Communities, which is the dynamic behind liberation theology, which would not exist in any meaningful sense without it and the preferential option for the poor. It is, as Derek Winter has remarked, "theological reflection that rises at sundown, after the heat of the day when Christians have dirtied their hands and their reputations in the struggle of the poor for justice, for land, for bread, for very survival." The understanding of theology as a secondary task, namely, one of critical reflection on life and practice, is not new to Christian theology. That subtle dialectic between the "text" of life, viewed in the light of recognition and non-acceptance of unjust social arrangements and the

---

1. Gutiérrez, *Power of the Poor*, 60.
2. Elliott, "Liberation Theology for the UK?"

other "text" of Scripture and tradition is the kernel of a lively theological or, for that matter, any interpretative enterprise. The world of the poor as well as their imagination provides shafts of light which can often throw into the sharpest possible relief the poverty of much First World interpretation.

It is a theology which places the victims of violence, injustice, and oppression at the center because the cross of Christ stands at the center. Of course, the cross has always been at the center of Christian theology. In liberation theology the cross stands as a challenge to the wisdom of the world which claims rationality and justice while leaving millions impoverished. The dying Jesus is not a reason for fatalistic acceptance of one's lot but a reason for living, struggling, and if necessary, dying for the justice of God and a glimpse of the good news in the everyday lives of the poor. Jesus is a martyr for the gospel. Leonardo Boff speaks of him thus:

> Jesus did not go unsuspectingly to his death. He courageously took on that risk; in his final period he hid himself from the Temple police, but he made no concessions to the danger of his situation; he remained radically faithful to his message.... He did not avoid his adversaries ... but resolutely took the road for Jerusalem (Luke 9:51) for the final confrontation.... [Jesus' martyrdom] was the result of the rejection of his message and person by those who refused to be converted to the kingdom of God. If Jesus was to be faithful to himself and to his mission, he had to accept persecution and martyrdom The martyr defends not his life, but his cause ... and he defends this cause by dying.... The resurrection of the martyr Jesus Christ has ... this theological significance: who loses his life in this way receives it in fullness.[3]

Mention of the story of Jesus brings us to biblical interpretation. The Bible is being used as part of the reflection by the poor on their circumstances as they seek to work out appropriate forms of response and action. There is often a direct identification of the poor with biblical characters and their circumstances, with little concern for the interpretative niceties which are invoked in applying the text to our own circumstances. In their use of Scripture, the resources of the text are used from their perspective of poverty and oppression, and a variety of meanings are conjured up in a way reminiscent of early Christian and ancient Jewish interpretation. The situation of the people of God reflected in many of its pages is their situation. That aspect is well brought out by Carlos Mesters:

> the emphasis is not placed on the text's meaning in itself but rather on the meaning the text has for the people reading it....

3. Boff, "Martyrdom."

> The common people are putting the Bible in its proper place, the place where God intended it to be. They are putting it in second place. Life takes first place! In so doing, the people are showing us the enormous importance of the Bible, and at the same time, its relative value—relative to life.[4]

In its rootedness in the Basic Ecclesial Communities an agenda is being set for the interpretative enterprise which is firmly based in the struggles of millions for recognition and justice. The text becomes a catalyst in the exploration of pressing contemporary issues relevant to the community; it offers a language, so that the voice of the voiceless may be heard. There is an immediacy in the way in which the text is used because resonances are found with the experience set out in the stories of biblical characters which seem remote from the world of affluent Europe and North America. The Bible offers a typology which can be identified with and at the same time a means by which the present difficulties can be shown to be surmountable in the life of faith and community commitment. To enable the poor to read the Bible has involved a program of education of the contents of the biblical material so that it can be a resource for thousands who are illiterate. In such programs full recognition is taken of the value of the primary text, experience of life. Therefore, the poor are shown that they have riches in plenty to equip them for interpretation. This is balanced with the basic need to communicate solid information about the stories within the Bible, of which many remain ignorant.

Most exponents of liberation theology would not want to claim that they have the key to the proper reading of Scripture (though there *are* some who think the perspective of the poor is the criterion for a true reading of Scripture). The evangelical and popular roots of liberation theology need to be recognized. It is known in this country as a result of the translations which have been made of many of the writings of the leading liberation theologians from Latin America. The form which that theology takes is normally not unfamiliar to the sophisticated theological readership of the First World. That should not surprise us as most have experienced the theological formation of Europe or North America. Nevertheless it is a facade which needs to be pierced in order to understand more clearly what precisely energizes these writers. In a very important sense they have broken with that tradition in the perspective from which they have chosen to do their theology.

Those involved in liberation theology stress the importance of the wisdom and insight of the poor as the focal point of theology (something also noted by the Latin American bishops at their conference at Puebla). Both

---

4. Mesters, "Use of the Bible," 14–15.

gain insights from listening to the poor reading and using Scripture in the whole process of development and social change. The theologians find that this process of listening, and learning has given a stimulus to their theology. This grassroots biblical interpretation provides a basis for the more sophisticated theological edifices they wish to build. Yet it is clear that the different experiences and worldview of the poor offer an unusually direct connection with the biblical text, which, whatever its shortcomings, has reminded Christians that there is another form of Christian reflection in which the insight of the apparently less sophisticated can inform the sophistication of the wise. The words of Jesus encapsulate the point: "I thank you Father, lord of heaven and earth, for hiding these things from the learned and wise, and revealing them to the simple" (Luke 10:21 REB).

The memory of the poor and outcast is frequently lost forever from our view. Its retrieval is often the task of the sympathetic voices of another culture or class. Luke falls into this category. After all, Luke preserves the memory of a Jesus who represents an option which contrasts with that of the class of people he may be writing for. It is a mark of Christian historiography and theology from Luke onwards that there is greater concern to placate the mighty than to represent the cry of the oppressed. The shape of the story would be different if we sought to write it consistently from the perspective of the poor and voiceless. As the history of liberation theology itself indicates, the presentation of the "voice of the voiceless" is almost inevitably in an idiom which is at once both more familiar and at a significant remove from the story that the poor might tell. There is a mediation involved in this which is inevitable and necessary. Like Luke's mediation of the story of Jesus, however, it can never fully capture the authentic voice of the cry of the oppressed and the reality of the liberation they hope to experience.

The perspective of the poor and the marginalized offers another story, an alternative to that told by the wielders of economic power whose story becomes the "normal" account. The story of Latin America is a story of conquest. It is *Latin* America, a continent whose story begins only with the arrival of the Europeans. Liberation theology has its contribution to make to these projects. Of course, its complicity as part of the ideology imposed on the indigenous peoples of the sub-continent as the European conquerors swept previous cultures aside puts Christianity, in however progressive a form, in a rather difficult position. Yet its encouragement of the study of popular religion, whether Christian, Indian, or African American, must be part of its project to enable the story of the "little people" of the sub-continent. In addition, it has championed the recovery of the religion of those with the Christian tradition who resisted the practice of conquest and despoliation, like Bartolomé de las Casas and Antonio Valdivieso, whose ministry takes its part alongside those whom the conquerors would prefer to forget. The familiar story of the wars of kings and princes which all too easily becomes the staple fare of a normal view of life is challenged as the horizons are expanded by attention to the voices drowned out by the noise of the mighty. It is part of the task suggested in Walter Benjamin's words, "In every era the attempt must be made anew to wrest tradition away from a conformism that is about to overpower it."[5]

A question remains. Is the theology of liberation merely a passing phase in the history of Christian doctrine, to join that long list of contextual attempts to make Christianity relevant?

A mere appeal to the emotions is unlikely to convince those who think that Christianity has little to say about change in this world save to hang on for the next. Indeed, there have been several questions raised about its propriety as a Christian theology from within the Roman Catholic Church itself, particularly in the First Vatican Instruction published in 1984. Many of the assumptions of that document were convincingly answered by various exponents of the theology of liberation themselves, and it was significant that a much softer line has emerged on the theology of liberation in general since (even though individual exponents have continued to be under a cloud).

Doubts may be raised whether Christian tradition sanctions a privileged epistemological stance for the poor. Clearly the Bible excludes the identification with the rich and powerful as being that of the perspective of God. Even if we might not want to identify the perspective of God solely with the perspective of the poor, we must accept that some balance is needed in the ways in which we view the world, and the continuous exclusion of the perspective of the poor from our decision-making and our values cannot be tolerated. It is not just a matter of equality of perspective but also of seeking to do justice to the thrust of the Christian tradition's perspective which in the words of a recent papal encyclical:

> the option or love of preference for the poor . . . is one . . . to which the whole tradition of the Church bears witness. It affects the life of each Christian inasmuch as he or she seeks to imitate the life of Christ, but it applies equally to our social responsibilities and hence to our manner of living, and to the logical decisions to be made concerning the ownership and use of goods . . . [this] cannot but embrace the immense multitudes of the hungry, the needy, the homeless, those without medical care, and above all, those without hope of a better future. It is

---

5. Benjamin, *Illuminations:* "Theses on the Philosophy of History," thesis 6.

impossible not to take account of the existence of these realities. To ignore them would mean becoming like the "rich man" who pretended not to know the beggar Lazarus lying at his gate.[6]

That view may command wide support. Where the theology of liberation has parted company from conventional Christian wisdom is in its argument that charity is not enough. That point was put with characteristic acuteness by Dom Helder Camara, former Archbishop of Recife and Olinda when he said: "If I give food to the poor, they call me a saint; if I ask why the poor have no food, they call me a communist." It is a mark of the theology of liberation that it has not been ready to accept things as they are as the moral and social order ordained by God.

If the theology of liberation had contented itself merely with discussion of the reasons for poverty, it might legitimately be criticized as a theological talking-shop for the progressive wing of the churches. But, in addition to asking why things are as they are, it has sought means of putting them right by demanding that the structures of society should be changed in conformity with the reign of God. Throughout Latin America there are numerous examples of small-scale activities in which the poor are being empowered to challenge the inevitability of their poverty and work for something which contributes to their dignity. So it is not a matter of theological rhetoric only, but of the exploration of realistic possibilities to enable the promotion of human dignity rooted in the inspiration of the Scriptures and sustained by the fellowship of the people of God. My contact with Christian Aid over the last decade has enabled me to see the way in which the values of the theology of liberation have formed small-scale projects which have empowered the poor and been a practical demonstration of humanity and hope.

The theological assumptions upon which the theology of liberation and the social action of the CEBs are based have been widely contested. It is said that changing the world into the pattern of the kingdom of God is a human activity; that the kingdom can be built and can in some sense be realizable in this world; and that it is part of the task of evangelization to bring about societal as well as human change. There is in my view a long and honorable pedigree for these assumptions rooted in the story the Church tells of Jesus of Nazareth. Indeed, it is no coincidence that the theologians of liberation are frequently to be found going back to this story as the foundation of their task. We have in the Gospels not the story of charitable action or even of the wise teacher. Rather it is a life of activity rooted in the conviction that the reign of God when sorrow and sighing would flee away was not some pious hope but a present possibility. In

6. Pope John Paul II, *Sollicitudo Rei Socialis*, 85.

this the powers of evil which afflicted individuals and society were being overthrown. The consummate challenge to the structures of the day came when, for whatever reason, Jesus set his face to go up to Jerusalem and met the powers that ran the political system of his nation.

The confrontation cost him his life, but in it we see the seeds of the conflict/struggle with the powers which was to find its theological expression in the *Christus Victor* doctrine of the atonement. The resurrection of Jesus is both a sign that things need not remain always so and a demonstration of the rectitude of Jesus' message and a pledge of the transformation that still awaited. Christian faith means identification with that hope and empowerment with the life of a God who makes *all* things new. It is a mark of Christianity's tenuous links with its Jewish past that it has so often lost its grip on the realm of history as the arena of God's saving purposes, so that it can despise the material character of Jewish hope by juxtaposing it with its own, supposedly superior, spiritual salvation. In so doing, we not only diminish Judaism but also the character of salvation as set out in the biblical documents which are the foundation of faith.

To the charge that they have sold out to atheistic communism, many liberation theologians would echo the words of the Peruvian bishop at the meeting of Latin American bishops at Puebla. When conservatives accused liberation theologians of being Marxists thinly disguised as Christians he responded: "Let him who is without ideology cast the first stone." It is precisely that challenge which is at the heart of its most pungent challenges to theology. Liberation theologians question the use made of certain doctrines and ask in whose interests they have been utilized: for those with power in society or the poor? It becomes important, therefore, to challenge the dominance of the theological agenda set by First World theology when the pressing concerns of the poor in the Third World demand very different priorities.

The situation of Latin America and the poor in our world will not go away. In a recent article the Latin American writer Carlos Fuentes has written:

> Latin America . . . now faces the obligation to promote and defend social justice in a continent where the absolute number of poor people is continuously growing while income distribution becomes daily less equitable. It is a continent where wages decrease, jobs disappear, food becomes scarce, public services deteriorate, crime and insecurity grow, repressive bodies become

autonomous in the name of the anti-drug campaign, malnutrition, and infant mortality increase . . .[7]

Confronted with the reality of the world's poor, can Christians, too, remain silent? Even if we decide that the theology of liberation is an appropriate response to injustice at a particular time and a particular place which are different from our own, as part of the *oikoumenē*, may we ignore the plight of other peoples because they are not our own? Are they not after all "our poor" (to use Leonardo Boff's words) whose poverty and situation are in many ways the result of our own prosperity and well-being?

Any theology we do, any evangelization we embark upon in this country cannot ignore the plight of our sisters and brothers in the so-called Third World, whether it be death squads in El Salvador, the brutal treatment of children in Guatemala so recently seen on our TV screens, or the terrible plight of the street children of Brazil banished from our television screens two weeks ago to be replaced by further analysis of the Gulf War. All Christians can understand the solidarity with the poor and oppressed. Indeed, it is part of our understanding of what discipleship is to do exactly that.

Something of that was well appreciated by Paul when he commended the "collection" for the poor in Jerusalem. What is remarkable is the evidence of Paul's persistent concern to engage the relatively well-to-do members of his churches in an enterprise to deal with need. Whatever the motivation for this activity, Paul clearly sees it as a significant contribution to the service of God, using language in 2 Corinthians 2:9 which he uses elsewhere for this apostolic ministry in Colossians 1:24. It was a relief operation with few parallels in the contemporary world. That need is dealt with not in terms of the dependence of the needy on those who have plenty but by means of stressing mutual responsibility and the sharing of resources. It is very easy to get into a way of thinking that we can do something for the poor and share our material resources, but we can be recipients of their wealth of insight. Their struggles for justice and recognition put them in touch with truths so easily drowned by our stampede for material wealth: a sense of community, care of the earth, and the worship of a God who is concerned for the whole of life, not merely the salvation of souls.

There is a legitimate question about the appropriate means of enabling the poor to have a better life. There is a clear concern on the part of those avid exponents of the North American spirit like Michael Novak that the poor of the world deserve our concern. He is convinced that the application of the American ideal to the situation of the poor will bring about their betterment (as it has, he would argue, in Southeast Asia). Fuentes speaks for

---

7. Fuentes, "Changing World," 10.

many of the theologians of liberation when he questions whether the economic experiments of the last twenty years have really benefited the poor:

> We are told that unfettered development of private industry will bring us prosperity, as it did in Germany, France, or the US. All this... is to forget that the US is experiencing the worst financial crisis of the century [with] millions living below the poverty line in the land of conspicuous consumption of superfluous goods. ... All this so undervalues the experience of 200 years of Latin American existence.... Since 1820 we have been subjected to the will of private industry both internally and externally, and our problems have not been solved.[8]

The challenge that Fuentes says is posed for humanity is that of "the Other" (a word used by Gutiérrez in the passage quoted earlier). That challenge is one that Christians can recognize, for it is at the heart of the story they tell: strangers, pilgrims, peripheral people, those who, in the words of the Letter to the Hebrews, are "the deprived, oppressed and ill-treated of whom the world was not worthy" (Heb 11:37–38 my translation). We see in the poor features of the suffering of Christ himself.[9]

The theology of liberation may not always get right the balance between evangelical commitment and political action. But it surely is seeking to be true to the story which the Church exists to proclaim in word and deed, in identification with the poor and outcast. There is in the articulation of an appropriate response to their struggle for justice an understanding of the gospel which is faithful to the way of Jesus and the prophets. It is a response whose starting point is contemplation and attention to the needs of the poor and outcast, not the blueprints of the political theorist. As Gustavo Gutiérrez has put it:

> Contemplation and commitment combine to form what may be called the phase of *silence* before God.... Silence is a condition for any loving encounter with God in prayer and commitment.... Theology is talk that is constantly enriched by silence. In our dealings with the poor we encounter the Lord (see Matt 25:31–46), but this encounter in turn makes our solidarity with the poor more radical and more authentic. Contemplation and commitment within history are fundamental dimensions of Christian practice.... The mystery reveals itself through prayer and solidarity with the poor. I call Christian

---

8. Fuentes, "Changing World," 10.
9. Cf. Pope John Paul II, *Salvifici Doloris*.

life the "first act"; only then can this life inspire a process of reflection, which is the "second act."[10]

To me that sounds like a theology which is rooted in the heart of the gospel of a person to whom injustice and violence were done, for it seeks to take seriously the reality of the suffering of the majority of our world.

Bibliography

Benjamin, Walter. *Illuminations*. Edited and with an introduction by Hannah Arendt. Translated by Harry Zohn. New York: Harcourt, Brace & World, 1968.

Boff, Leonardo. "Martyrdom: An Attempt at Systematic Reflection." In *Martyrdom Today*, edited by Johann Baptist Metz and Edward Schillebeeckx, 12–17. English-language editor, Marcus Lefébure. Edinburgh: T. & T. Clark, 1983.

Elliott, Charles. "Is There a Liberation Theology for the UK?" Heslington Lecture, University of York, 1985.

Fuentes, Carlos. "The Changing World: Too Soon to Hail Capitalism's Triumph—as Old-Style Ideology Loses Its Sway, Encounters between People of Different Races and Cultures Will Define the 21st century." *The Guardian*, December 27, 1990, 10.

Gutiérrez, Gustavo. *The Power of the Poor in History: Selected Writings*. Translated by Robert R. Barr. Maryknoll, NY: Orbis, 1983.

———. *The Truth Shall Make You Free: Confrontations*. Translated by Matthew J. O'Connell. Maryknoll, NY: Orbis, 1990.

John Paul II, Pope. *Salvifici Doloris*. Apostolic Letter (Rome, St. Peter's Basilica: February 11, 1984). https://www.vatican.va/content/john-paul-ii/en/apost_letters/1984/documents/hf_jp-ii_apl_11021984_salvifici-doloris.html/.

———. *Sollicitudo Rei Socialis*. Encyclical (Rome, St. Peter's Basilica: December 30, 1987). https://www.vatican.va/content/john-paul-ii/en/encyclicals/documents/hf_jp-ii_enc_30121987_sollicitudo-rei-socialis.html/.

Mesters, Carlos. "The Use of the Bible in Christian Communities of the Common People." In *The Bible and Liberation: Political and Social Hermeneutics*, edited by Norman K. Gottwald and Richard A. Horsley, 3–16. Rev. ed. Bible & Liberation. Maryknoll, NY: Orbis, 1993.

---

10. Gutiérrez, *Truth Shall Make You Free*, 3.

5

The Bible and Politics

THE STUDENT WHO IS beginning academic study of the Bible may wonder what the Bible has to do with politics. Politics is about the organization of society and public affairs. It concerns the nature and power of the state, but it also relates as much to a church or other religious body and its operations as to a national or local government. The political dimensions of how people relate to one another and function together are just as much a way of understanding religious groups as any other group.

Basically, then, politics is about how groups of people organize themselves. There are different examples of such organization. So the word "political" can be used to describe organizations and the dynamics of relationships of groups, as well as the power relations in the group and the patterns of authority which emerge. That is an important point. In our modern world it is assumed that in some ways the political is different from the religious. But this is to misunderstand the role of the political, which offers a perspective on human interaction and organization rather than asking questions about the nature of the theological dimensions of such a group. Thus, the political and the religious complement each other in what they offer to anyone seeking to reflect on and analyze what is going on within a body of people. Reading the Bible therefore involves thinking about both theology *and* politics.

Politics and the Bible: Uses and Abuses

The Bible is full of texts from different times and different places reflecting the culture and the political concerns and pressures of each particular age. From the most ancient traditions in the Hebrew Bible, or Christian Old Testament (OT), to the writings of the New Testament (NT), the texts evince first the world of tribal leadership, including its religion and organization, and eventually, with the growing imperial power which over several centuries dominated the life of the Middle East, the sort of world that culminated in the hegemony of Rome in Judea in the first century CE. We cannot always reconstruct the details of the backgrounds of texts with certainty. Nevertheless, it is clear that from the perspective of modernity there are many practices, beliefs, and cultural arrangements which sit uneasy with our assumptions and prejudices on a variety of issues.

It is tempting to go back to the Bible and suppose that we are going to find values that support our modern prejudices, but it is not as easy as that. On a range of issues, the Bible demonstrates not only its cultural and political contextualization but also how different the assumptions are when compared with our own. Take the issues of slavery and race, for example. There are few in the modern world who would argue for slavery. Nevertheless, with the exception of a few verses which may suggest support for the abolition of slavery, the Bible says little about slaves that is anything other than supportive of an institution which is abhorrent to modern sensibilities.

The story of the exodus from Egypt has been used to support the ideology of a powerful group having the right to inhabit land at the expense of the people already dwelling there. The stories of the birth of the Jewish people are tied up not only with belief in God, but also with a promise made to Abraham and his descendants (e.g., Gen 12) to inherit the land. The account of the conquest of this land, where Abraham was said to sojourn, by the nascent Jewish (Israelite) nation under Joshua, is as much a part of historical and contemporary *Realpolitik* as any item of the Bible.[1] Historically, there have been several examples of construing one's right to travel, like Israel out of Egypt, to displace indigenous peoples before taking possession of their land. For instance, the promise of the land to a group who regarded themselves an elect nation, a "city set on a hill" (cf. Matt 5:14), fired the European expeditions of exploration, expansion, and colonization by the Boers in South Africa, and before that the journeys to the "New World" that led to the conquest of the Americas. It is important to recognize that contemporary liberation theology uses the innage of liberation from bondage in Egypt, while avoiding the rest of the story and thus the displacement—and indeed slaughter—of the indigenous Canaanites, in espousing its rhetoric of liberation.

---

1. *Realpolitik* refers to pragmatic politics with little or no ethical concerns.

The same sort of interpretive challenge is true for issues as diverse as race, gender, and sexuality. That is not to say that we do not find ways in which we can see in the Bible deep-seated support for struggling with received wisdom and the task of finding ways of being more loving, just, and fair in our interpersonal and political arrangements, but there is no blueprint for that which we can read from the pages of the Bible. A glance at history confirms this claim.

A Window on Monarchy, Power, and the Politics of Holiness

Much of the account of the origins of the Jewish nation is a story of their monarchy in the period up to the sixth century BCE, and then narratives of how the people related to the imperial rulers of the world empires of the day. The biblical accounts of kingship are full of ambivalence about monarchy as an institution and its effects, nowhere better exemplified than by 1 Samuel 8 and 10 and the rules for the exercise of kingship in Deuteronomy 17.

The Hebrew Bible accounts of monarchy have provided a blueprint for later political arrangements in different ways. The sixteenth and seventeenth centuries in England are only one example of the way in which opposing sides have appealed to the Bible to endorse their political preferences. Thus, the monarchists could see the way kings like David and Josiah were models of kingship and how the "Lord's anointed" was one whose authority was absolute since he reigned with the authority of God. The "good king" (for example, Josiah, according to 2 Kings) was a paradigm for the first Protestant monarch in England, Edward VI. Like Josiah, Edward was monarch of a reforming kingdom, which looked back to the law of God to remove the abuses which had built up over the years in the practice of religion. But there were contemporaries of Edward who appealed to the ambivalence toward monarchy found in Deuteronomy 17:14–20 and especially in the dire warning that the prophet Samuel gave to the people about the effects of monarchy (1 Sam 8:7–9).

There is a critique of monarchy in the portrayals of Jesus in the Gospels, where Jesus (as Messiah/king) contrasts markedly with royal behavior of the conventional kind. In the Gospel of John, the understanding of Jesus as a king is of one crowned with thorns (John 19:5), whose followers do not wage war (John 18:36). Throughout the Gospels, Jesus behaves as one who is lowly and humble (e.g., Matt 21:1–11). There is a pattern of leadership and an example for others which are based not on superiority or mighty acts of military power, but on service (e.g., Mark 10:42–45). Nowhere is this seen more clearly than in the juxtaposition in Revelation 5:5–6, where the Lion of the tribe of Judah, the descendant of king David, is a slaughtered lamb, not a warrior king like David (e.g., 2 Sam 5:25).

Before Constantine, Christianity was a fringe movement which often attracted hostile interests of contemporaries and those in authority. Once Christianity became part of the fabric of political power, biblical imagery provided the ideological justification of the emperor. The image of Pantocrator (Greek *Christos Pantokratōr*, "Ruler of All") enthroned in glory offered a pattern for the imperial rule. Mainstream Christianity was content with an ordered status quo in this life, preferring to worship Jesus as Lord, the guarantor of earthly potentates, rather than the humble Son of Man who had nowhere to lay his head (Matt 8:20).

Consistently pervasive in Scripture, however, is that tradition of which runs like a thread from the command to love one's neighbor in Leviticus 19 to the ethics of the Pauline communities. Throughout the Bible, priority is given to this ethic, above "burnt offerings and sacrifices" (Matt 9:13; 12:7; Mark 12:33; cf. Hos 6:6). For Paul, the exercise of power through the Spirit cannot be the true mark of the nascent community. In the famous passage 1 Corinthians 13, prophecies and tongues of ecstasy must take second place to that which will always be the hallmark of life in Christ: love. It is this theme which typifies the practical advice Paul gives to the Christians in Corinth as they struggle to find ways of being community.

The authority and demand for exclusive devotion to the God of Israel is a constant theme in the Hebrew Bible, and not unrelated to the love command (Lev 19:18b; Deut 6:5). The exclusive devotion demanded of the people of God in the Bible is encapsulated in the word "holiness." God is holy; therefore, the people are expected to be holy (Lev 19:2). That sense of separation and distinctiveness is epitomized by Sabbath observance, which, according to the creation narrative, reflects the rest that the Deity enjoyed after the six days of creation (Gen 2:1–3; cf. Exod 20:8–11). The distinctiveness of Jewish life finds its focus in Sabbath observance and the attention it attracted. In lives lived in the middle of other cultures, this kind of practice, matched by obedience to the rest of the law of Moses, is the bedrock of the pattern of life which distinguished the life of a holy nation. The service of God by keeping the divine commands involved a polity which protected the vulnerable and maintained justice. Early Christianity before Constantine paralleled this pattern to a large extent. The politics of holiness in the Bible, which also pervades the language and ideology of the New Testament (e.g., 1 Pet 1:16; 2:9), cannot be overestimated.

Two Principles of Interpretation

The previous discussion raises questions about an appropriate hermeneutic, or interpretive strategy, when it comes to politics. There are two principles of interpretation which I want to stress.

First, there is the christological criterion: how does a political arrangement or practice look in the light of the Jesus story as we find it in the canonical Gospels? As we have seen, a Christian reading of the Apocalypse (Revelation) has its key in the person of Christ, the Lamb in the midst of the divine throne, standing as if it had been slaughtered (Rev 5). The orientation is toward Christ the faithful witness (Rev 3:14). The fundamental story which shapes the community's life is of a crucified messiah who refused armed struggle as a way of inaugurating the kingdom of God (Matt 26:53; John 18:36). This christological criterion is not the reconstruction of scholars, nor does it emerge from noncanonical texts. It evinces a clear preference for the fact that the canonical Gospels witness to Jesus in life and death, and this must pervade interpretations of the Bible and indeed of experience itself. Therein lies a crucial aspect of criticism. The story of the Lamb who is slain offers a critique of human history and of our delusions, of the violence we use to maintain the status quo and the lies with which we disguise the oppression of the victim.

The second principle comes from Latin American liberationist biblical hermeneutics. Clodovis Boff, in his *Theology and Praxis*, contrasts two ways of engaging with the Bible in liberationist hermeneutics. One of these he terms "correspondence of terms" and the other "correspondence of relationships." Correspondence of terms is a *direct, immediate* engagement in which the modern reader identifies with a biblical story; the person or event depicted in the Bible offers an imaginative frame for viewing the modern world. In this kind of engagement with the Bible, biblical words become the tool for discernment in the present. The Bible functions less as a window onto antiquity and more as a way of understanding oneself that is socially and contextually meaningful.

Correspondence of relationships complements correspondence of terms, according to Boff. In this approach, one looks at the similarities between the biblical text, which bears witness to the life and struggles of the people of God at a particular time and place in the past, and the contemporary situation and experience of a reader or community of readers. The contemporary state of affairs is understood as *analogous* to that to which the Bible bears witness, and it may inform, inspire, and challenge readers of the Bible. This method is not about applying a set of principles from a theological program, however, but offering orientations, models, types, and inspirations to the biblical interpreter.

We return now to the text of Scripture itself, having already briefly noted its political character and considered two basic principles of interpretation: the christological criterion and the principle(s) of correspondence. What are some of the ways in which we see politics at work in each of the Testaments?

Politics in the Bible

Politics in the Hebrew Bible

As noted above, the story of the Hebrew Bible is itself a story of politics, of a nation's culture, its fortunes, and the evolution of its political arrangements over centuries, as well as its relationship with dominant imperial forces in the region. It is a mix of stories of migration, of enslavement and liberation, of settlement and the relationship with indigenous peoples and cultures, and of the consequences of being caught up in wider global forces. Large parts of the Hebrew Bible are the product and consequence of one episode of these larger forces, as the Jerusalem elite was transported to exile in Babylon in the sixth century BCE. This crisis, at once religious and political, led to a time of reappraisal and self-understanding, which was as remarkable for its depth and productivity as for its later effects. The memories and legends, the laws, and the analysis of what went wrong—all of which led to the debacle of exile—are mirrored in the pages of the Hebrew Bible.

The distinctive sociopolitical arrangements and the consequence of their accommodation to the settled life in and around Jerusalem occupy much of the Hebrew Bible. The politics of identity and of difference, and the ability to offer a critique of the shortcomings of those who were at ease in Zion, constitute one of the most remarkable political stories in history. The foundation of it all is a discomfort with ease and complacency, and thus the necessity for the maintenance of a different perspective on social arrangements. During the heyday of King Solomon's reign, the triumph of Judea, its incipient hegemony in the Middle East, and its prestige were the start of a movement of criticism, which resulted in the prophetic writings of the Hebrew Bible. Whether through vision or social isolation or marginality, the prophets forged another perspective on the myths and the confidence of the political settlement in what became a divided state. They catalogued its shortcomings, perhaps inspired by the alternative vision of society which finally saw the light of day in biblical books like Deuteronomy and Exodus.

It is all too easy to be so caught up with the religious texture of these texts (and the way in which they have inspired Judaism, Christianity, and Islam) that we miss the extent of their political character. Throughout, the Hebrew Bible tells a thoroughly political story. Incipient social arrangements were transformed into the monarchy and its attendant cultic arrangements, as the temple in Jerusalem, and also in Samaria on Mount Gerizim, became an institutional vehicle for the politics of identity and offered an ideology for the political arrangements which accompanied them. The genius of the Hebrew Bible, however, was that political critique accompanied these developments. One cannot read Amos or sections of Isaiah without being struck by the way in which a nation's ability to offer a critique of its political and institutional arrangements had emerged, and in the form in which they presented what turned out to be a necessary counterpoint to the story of settlement and consolidation. There is grit in the shoe of the political story told. "You were once slaves in Egypt" acts as a constant refrain, bringing a people back to their origins as migrants and as an oppressed people, who needed always to be aware of another dimension to the politics of their day which relativized—and indeed tempered—self-satisfaction about the present.

The Political Character of Early Christianity (The New Testament)

Christianity began life as a thoroughly political movement, in which the relationship with the political is endemic to what it is about. The fact that this should have become attenuated is itself a cause of puzzlement, but it is a dimension of the Gospels which has been recovered in recent years. Christianity had its beginnings in, and was originally confused with, Judaism, because of its countercultural aspects. The ongoing input of Jewish sources into emerging Christianity meant that it inherited the political characteristics of Judaism. Sociological approaches to the Bible have been highly illuminating in drawing out the political character of much early Christian identity, with its countercultural attitudes and practice.[2] When Paul set up communities in different places, there was an immediate political impact, in varying ways, both internally within those groups and externally in how they related to the wider society. Paul never set out to write a systematic set of instructions on how these communities should function, but it is significant that the Greek word he used to describe them, *ekklēsia* (assembly), is very political in its character and harks back to the Hebrew Bible's notion of

2. See Green, "Modern and Postmodern Methods."

the public assembly of Israel. Similarly, Paul's notion of the body of Christ resembles the ancient understanding of the body politic.

Rembrandt van Rijn, *Christ Driving Out the Money Changers from the Temple*, 1635, print of an etching on laid paper. In the public domain. Image courtesy of the National Gallery of Art, Washington, DC (CC0)

John the Baptist and Jesus

This political character of Christianity is built into it from the very start. According to the Gospels, Jesus was linked with John the Baptist, who was executed for subversion by Herod Antipas (Josephus, *Jew. Ant.* 18.116). John's message of a decisive moment in God's purposes provided the context for Jesus' own activity. Jesus was in conflict with scribal religion, and the volatile atmosphere of Jerusalem at Passover time, a festival particularly linked with political liberation, also led to attempts by the priestly hierarchy in Jerusalem (the local elite which managed the Roman colony) to take action against him. According to the Gospels, Jesus was executed with the connivance of the Roman colonial governor of Judea, Pontius

Pilate, yet with the active involvement of the Jerusalem priestly elite. Jesus preached against the temple, something which had attracted intense opposition when Jesus' prophetic predecessors embarked on the same activity (Jer 7; Matt 23; Luke 11:42–52). In addition, from the perspective of the authorities (in Jerusalem in particular), this made Jesus a threat to public order. When he neared Jerusalem, his position became untenable. Jesus resembled other prophetic figures described by the first-century Jewish writer Josephus (e.g., *Jew. Ant.* 20.97–99, 167–72, 185–88), figures who looked back to God's deliverance of old and promised a new era of deliverance. In Jesus we have a nonconformist with eschatological beliefs, which put him in a different position from that of a mere prophet of doom and made him to be more of a harbinger of the messianic age.

Paul

What about Paul? There is no explicit attempt to confront the might of Rome in the Pauline Letters. Instead there is an attempt to negotiate a *modus vivendi* (way of life) and wherever possible to keep one's head down (e.g., 1 Thess 4:10–11), thus offering a better outcome than a deliberate confrontation with the religion of empire. By contrast, the early Christian martyr narratives of the second to fourth centuries present a more heroic, but probably partial, picture of early Christian experience. Such public profession was the exception rather than the rule, however paradigmatic the martyr narratives were intended to be. Many Christians functioned "below the radar," carving out patterns of life which contrasted with dominant culture, thereby attracting new adherents to what was as much a political as a religious movement. The politics of Paul is to be found in the complex negotiation of community formation, in which the boundaries of a new political entity (the body of Christ), based on the convictions about the coming of the Messiah, create ambiguous relationships with those outside it (cf. 1 Cor 8).

The service of the practical politics of community formation and maintenance is what pervades the Pauline Letters. Paul was actively engaged in shaping and holding together embryonic communities, so that social cohesion takes precedence over human freedom, a theme particularly explored in 1 Corinthians 8–9 (cf. Rom 14, esp. 14:19). The character of life in the messianic community, waiting for the consummation of the messianic times, emerges as *the* crucial issue in the Pauline corpus, even if Paul paradoxically resorts to law as the means of enabling the social cohesion that he regards as crucial. The messianic impulse and community cohesion are a constant dialectic in the Pauline Letters.

What distinguishes the messianic life is, according to Paul, above all social rather than aesthetic or spiritual. As with Jews, there was the necessity among Christian communities for distance and nonconformity in belief and practice, which Paul also explores in 1 Corinthians 8–10. Messianic life may seem to be socially conservative, but that initial assessment conceals the complex mix of negotiating the time while waiting for the "impending crisis" (1 Cor 7:26), which required the implementation of certain patterns of living which characterize life as the "temple of the Holy Spirit" (1 Cor 6:19). Being *in* the world means inhabiting the present age; not being *of* the world indicates that "our citizenship is in heaven, and it is from there that we are expecting a Savior" (Phil 3:20). It is that pattern of messianic life in this age—a politics of holiness—which is explored in the pages of the NT. The Letters of Paul indicate the difficulties posed by the improvisation necessary for the communities living "as if" a new age has come but recognizing the culture of the old age as still very much something to be reckoned with.

Apocalypticism

Apocalypticism—the term comes from the Greek word *apokalypsis*, meaning "revelation"—was important to early Christianity, *not* because it is a form of cataclysmic eschatology (as is often thought), but because it offered a different mode of understanding, based on experience of the divine through vision, audition, or dream, which could bypass conventional channels of authority based on tradition. *The* apocalyptic text in the Bible, the book of Revelation (the *apocalypse* [= "revelation"] of Jesus Christ, according to Rev 1:1), typifies Christian hope and its political outlook. This is nowhere better seen than in its unmasking of the pretensions of the Beast and Babylon (Rev 13 and 17) and in the hope for the transformation of this world and its structures. The book of Revelation offers the most sustained political discourse in the NT. The Apocalypse enables an enhanced vision of the reality that confronts people living in a particular moment of time and does not offer a timetable about the end of the world. Central to early Christian hope was the expectation of a new age *on earth* (see Rev 21:1–4), a belief which was still widely held, at least to the end of the second century, as is evident in the writings of Justin Martyr, Irenaeus, Hippolytus, and Tertullian (see, e.g., Irenaeus, *Against Heresies* 5.33.3–4).[3] This is the type of belief presupposed in the Matthean version of the Lord's Prayer, where there is an earnest longing for God's kingdom to "come on earth as it is in heaven" (Matt 6:10).

---

3. This belief appears as well in later writers such as Lactantius (240–320 CE).

Conclusion

In Martin Luther's influential two-kingdoms theology, the religious and the political are the means of effecting the ordering of the world for human flourishing. The divinely appointed rulers are agents of God, leaving the church to attend to spiritual matters. Such a division can seem to be underpinned by Jesus' enigmatic words, "Render to Caesar the things that are Caesar's, and to God the things that are God's" (Mark 12:17 RSV). But in all likelihood, given the context in which the saying is found, this tantalizing comment tells us little about a worked-out political theology and more about the need for circumspection in responding to those who would question. Indeed, the very ambiguity of the saying is suggested by the charge leveled against Jesus, according to Luke's Gospel: "We found this man perverting our nation, forbidding us to pay taxes to the emperor, and saying that he himself is the Messiah, a king" (Luke 23:2). It is a comment which aptly indicates the political character of the stories told in the Bible and the effects of those images on ancient and modern readers alike.

Bibliography

Boff, Clodovis. *Theology and Praxis*. Translated by Robert R. Barr. 1987. Reprint, Eugene, OR: Wipf & Stock, 2009.

Green, Joel B. "Modern and Postmodern Methods of Biblical Interpretations." In *Scripture and Interpretation: A Global Ecumenical Introduction to the Bible*, edited by Michael J. Gorman, 187–204. Grand Rapids: Baker Academic, 2017.

6

How the Poor Can Liberate the Bible

MANY OF US OVER the last decade have spoken warmly of all that we have learned from liberation theology about the way in which we read the Bible. It is appropriate in the year that we remember the invasion of the "Americas" by appreciating how much has been received by Europe and North America from the suffering people of the Americas. To paraphrase Paul's words, "we are in debt to them, for we have come to share in their spiritual blessings and ought also to be of service to them in a material way" (Rom 15:27 my paraphrase).

We have indeed benefited so much. Yet there is at times a rather romantic aura about liberation theology and the Basic Ecclesial Communities which are such an important feature of its practice. There is a romantic illusion that a theological response is so much less complicated.

So runs a typical response to liberation theology—and an implicit rejection of its relevance. We can find ourselves locked into patterns of thinking which admire what goes on four thousand miles away provided that we do not have to engage with it ourselves.

However strong our commitment and activism, liberation theology is appropriate to circumstances different from our own. Giving our money to the Catholic Agency for Overseas Development (CAFOD) and Christian Aid is necessary, but it must not be at the expense of allowing what fellow Christians are suffering as a spiritual blessing which probes our prejudices. There is a lot of probing to be done. Of course, no one can deny the terrible impact of the squalor of the slums of the big cities and the horrendously callous attitude to the homeless children. But we need to be reminded that we are part of the one world, not to mention one Church. Equally importantly, our islands are the home of a bitter guerrilla war and rising injustice, masked by the affluence and political complacency of the majority. When we find out more about liberation theology, we can write it off as too political or even manipulative of the text of Scripture, for contemporary ends. We need to own these negative reactions and not be ashamed of them. It is only by owning up to them that we shall fully allow the different approach of liberation theology to search out our prejudices.

Preoccupation with the Past

What is it that makes Scripture come alive? Many of us will reply that it is the moment of insight which enables us to see the way a passage can illuminate our present circumstances. But there is another important dimension of Scripture study which has been dominant in our seminaries and colleges. An enormous amount of intellectual endeavor has been devoted to illuminating the original context and purpose of the biblical texts in the ancient world. That has been in many ways a beneficial enterprise.

Yet the preoccupation with the past has had its "down" side. We can see these texts as part of a strange and perhaps alien culture irrelevant to our modern age. Of course, the narrow concern with the past may excite our curiosity. Sensational exposés of the *real* Jesus or whatever will always attract attention. An approach to the Bible which concentrates on its historical context or lack of historical credibility will attract much attention. The danger is that this becomes an end in itself. One of the many things that liberation theology has done is to insist that as readers we inevitably bring something of ourselves to what we read. The Bible is not just an ancient text; it is a Christian Scripture which has informed the lives of men and women down the centuries.

See—Judge—Act

Carlos Mesters writes from the perspective of one whose work has involved him in interpreting the Bible with the poor of Brazil. He regrets the way in which the "scientific" study of Scripture has had the effect of distancing the Bible from the lives of ordinary people, so that its study has become an arcane enterprise reserved for a properly equipped academic elite. There has been little encouragement of methods of reading which would enable the people of God to respond to the needs which the life of faith in a changing world is placing upon them. Learned works on exegesis have little appeal or relevance for the millions seeking to survive in situations of injustice and poverty.

In that situation, however, a new way of reading the text has arisen, not among the exegetical elite of the seminaries and universities, but at the grassroots. Its emphasis is on the method: *see* (starting where one is with one's experience, which for the majority in Latin America means an experience of poverty), *judge* (understanding the reasons for that kind of existence and relating them to the story of the deliverance from oppression in the Bible), and *act*. Ordinary people have taken the Bible into their own hands and begun to read the word of God in the circumstances of their existence but also in comparison with the stories of the people of God in other times and other places. Millions of men and women, abandoned by government and church, have discovered an ally in the story of the people of God in the Scriptures.

Oral Theology

This different way of doing theology in the Basic Christian Communities is an oral theology in which story, experience, and biblical reflection are intertwined with the community's life of sorrow and joy. That experience of celebration, worship, varied stories, and recollection, in drama and festival is, according to Mesters, exactly what lies behind the written words of Scripture itself. That is the written deposit which bears witness to the story of a people, oppressed, bewildered, and longing for deliverance. While exegete, priest, and religious may have their part to play in the life of the community, the reading is basically uninfluenced by excessive clericalism and individualistic piety. Revelation is very much a present phenomenon: "God speaks in the midst of the circumstances of today."[1] It contrasts with an approach which sees revelation as something entirely past, in the deposit of faith, something to be preserved, defended, transmitted to the people by its guardians.

So the Bible is not just about past history only. It is also a mirror to be held up to reflect the story of today and lend it a new perspective. Mesters argues that what is happening in this new way of reading the Bible is in fact a rediscovery of the patristic method of interpretation which stresses the priority of the spirit of the word rather than its letter.

God speaks through life; but that word is one that is illuminated by the Bible: "the principal objective of reading the Bible is not to interpret

---

1. Mesters, *Defenseless Flower*, 160.

the Bible, but to interpret life with the help of the Bible."[2] The major preoccupation is not the quest for the meaning of the text in itself but the direction which the Bible is suggesting to the people of God within the specific circumstances in which they find themselves. That situation permits the poor to discover meaning which can so easily elude the technically better equipped exegete. So, where one is determines to a large extent how a book is read. This is a reading which does not pretend to be neutral and questions whether any other reading can claim that either. Of course, there are difficulties with this approach.

Mesters asks us to judge the effectiveness of the reading by its fruits: is it "a sign of the arrival of the reign of God . . . when the blind see, lepers are clean, the dead rise and the poor have the good new preached to them"?[3]

The experience of poverty and oppression is for the liberation exegete as important a text as the text of Scripture itself. The poor are blessed because they can read Scripture from a perspective different from most of the rich and find in it a message which can so easily elude those of us who are not poor. The God who identified with the slaves in Egypt and promised that he would be found among the poor, sick, and suffering demands that there is another text to be read as well as that contained between the covers of the Bible:

> . . . the emphasis is not placed on the text's meaning in itself but rather on the meaning the text has for the people reading it. [The poor] are putting the Bible in second place. Life takes first place! In so doing, the people are showing us the enormous importance of the Bible, and at the same time, its relative value—relative to life.[4]

Political Struggle

The interpretation of life by means of the Bible is one that may elicit sympathy. Yet there are important consequences which flow from this. The Bible becomes an instrument in political struggle. It ceases to be confined to the sanctuary or the solitary religious life.

Take the way in which the book of Exodus is read by those involved in the struggle for land.[5] The struggle for basic rights to land and sustenance

2. Mesters, *Defenseless Flower*, 160.
3. Mesters, *Defenseless Flower*, 163.
4. Mesters, *Defenseless Flower*, 160–61.
5. Some of which of which are graphically illuminated in Paul Vallely, *Promised Lands*.

resonates with a story of a land promised to an enslaved people who are delivered and formed into a community with a different vision of society as compared with that which they knew in Egypt. Liberation theology has reminded us that, in its complex formation, and in its use down the ages, the Bible has been part and parcel of politics. It is no less political for being the means of encouraging subordination and conformity as it has been in many parts of Christendom. The Bible is not a textbook of an otherworldly religion. Millions find in it an inspiration which sustains and informs their experience.

The experience of Latin American Christians seems remote from our own. We do not have to struggle to survive; we are rarely threatened by violence or excessive human rights abuses. Yet it would be a mistake to think that there is no struggle in our lives. One way in which we avoid it is by choosing to understand our faith as minimally at odds with contemporary culture. There is a long tradition in Scripture and in the teaching of the Church over the danger and delusions of wealth. Most of us make our compromises with the witness of Christ and avoid the struggle involved in refusing to capitulate to the dominant Mammon-orientated society. We think that if we struggle against sexual desire and maintain relatively blameless individual lives we have done our Christian duty. The reality is different, if only we have eyes to see the poverty and injustice around us. There is a personal and communal struggle to avoid collusion with them and to seek to be agents of God's spirit in convicting the world of sin, justice, and judgement. Fellowship with the poor and oppressed in the Body of Christ makes that task an essential part of the gospel, not some optional extra which we may take or leave according to taste. This is at the heart of our evangelical task. In so far as we begin to share that struggle we shall, like them, begin to read Scripture with different eyes.

Of all the texts of the New Testament it is the Gospel of Mark which has been the subject of closest study from the perspective of liberation theology. It is impossible to do justice to the richness of the treatment, though further reading is included at the end of this chapter.

The novelty of the message of Mark is enunciated right at the start of the Gospel. Here is a text which sets out to offer a contrast with the propaganda of the Roman empire where "good news" revolved around the military achievement. This good news is very different. John appears on the scene, *not* in the palaces of kings and princes, who are the ones to destroy John. It is in the wilderness on the very margins of society that John makes his appearance, and it is there that God meets Jesus at the moment of his identification with the Baptist and his message of God's judgment and the promise for a better future. Like the prophet Ezekiel, who saw God's glory in a foreign land far away from the glory of the Temple of Jerusalem, Jesus saw the heavens opened and God's spirit descending upon him, not in the Temple but far away from the center, on the margins, in the life and work of a tortured prophet.

Macho Image

Jesus' end is hardly the death of a typical male hero. Not only can he not carry his own cross (Mark 15:21), but he seems to deny God's presence at the very last (15:34). In an age when the macho image of powerful men abounds, this picture is a salutary reminder that at the heart of the Christian gospel is a fragile human being, alone and impotent. No more telling reminder could be found that the God whom we worship at the moment of crucifixion for all eternity is identified with the poor and wretched of our world, for that is how he ended his life on earth. The moment of his death marks the destruction of the veil in the temple, the means of preserving the mystery which guarantees the power of this institution over people's lives. The temple is shown to be an empty shell, a pretentious but powerless institution. Mark's Gospel comes to its climax with a proclamation of the bankruptcy of the old political order and the articulation of something different: "those who are supposed to rule over the nations lord it over them, and their great men exercise authority over them. But it shall not be so among you . . ." (Mark 10:42 my translation).

So Mark presents a message with a definite political hue. The climax of Jesus' life is the journey to Jerusalem and the challenge to the religio-political complex focused on the temple. Where then does the famous passage about the tribute money fit into all this?

The Coin

The context of the saying is one where Jesus is being put to the test by his opponents. In such a situation it is unlikely that Jesus would have given an answer that would have implicated himself either with the rejection of Roman power by the Jewish freedom-fighters, the Zealots, or those collaborators who had come to some accommodation with the occupying power. Jesus makes his opponents show him a coin. He himself does not appear to possess one. After being presented with a coin bearing the image of the Roman emperor, he asks whose image and superscription it is. Perhaps he wishes to point out that the possession of the coin by Jews is evidence that the possessors are already contaminated by an alien ideology which, in direct contradiction to Jewish law, allowed images of human beings to be engraved (Deut 5:8). Those who possess such objects of an alien system might expect, therefore, to have to abide by the rules of that system. Jesus' response may indicate that participants in the Roman economic system, based as it was on slavery and conquest, were bound to pay the tax. But those who recognized the supremacy of God over the universe maintain their distance from Rome and its exploitative and idolatrous practice.

This point is made by a peasant in a well-known collection of biblical interpretation by the poor of Latin America in a series of reflections on the Gospels collected by Ernesto Cardenal. In the place of the sermon each Sunday there would be a dialogue between Ernesto and the *compesinos* who attended the Sunday Mass on the Island of Solentiname in Lake Nicaragua. As the following extract (which is the comment of a young Nicaraguan, Laureano) indicates, it reflects the situation in Nicaragua before the Sandinista revolution in 1979, where the links between the oppressive conditions in twentieth-century Central America resonate with the colonial oppression of first-century Judea:

> It isn't that the money belonged to the emperor; the money belonged to the people, but Jesus tells them to notice the coin, so they can see what imperialism is: a coin with the face of a man there. He wanted them to see that from the time when the emperor puts his name and face on a coin he is making himself boss of everything in the country, of everybody, of the money that belongs to everybody. And Jesus is showing them that Caesar is a complete dictator because he is putting his portrait on the coin and taking for himself what belongs to the people. He is telling them that he is grabbing the money, because he is pictured there as owner and lord of everything; then he wants to make himself owner even of the people, because he was on the money with which the people were buying. Let us say that it is like now in Nicaragua, with Somoza, because Somoza is on the money, and we are all used to seeing him as the owner of Nicaragua; that is the way it was at the time. I believe he wants to tell them that all things belong to God, but that the emperor wants to make himself owner of everything when he makes himself owner of people's money.[6]

---

6. Cardenal, *Gospel in Solentiname*, 3:283–84.

The Woman's Place Guaranteed

As it has developed, liberation theology has challenged the macho attitudes which are so endemic in much of contemporary culture. Women have been central to the practice of liberation theology at the grassroots whether as catechists, leaders, or through the accompaniment of women religious. That perspective may be glimpsed in the approach to the anointing at Bethany. A woman anoints Jesus and incurs the rebuke of others for the waste involved. What they could not recognize here was the significance of what was going on. Jesus the messiah was recognized as such by the woman, not in words, but in deed. In the Hebrew Bible it is the priest who anoints the King messiah (e.g., 1 Kgs 1:39). A woman claims that right and is acknowledged by Jesus to have seen in the one destined to death the true pattern of messiahship (Mark 14:8), something that was to be recognized by the soldier at the foot of the cross (15:39).

Jesus gives to this woman a central place in the proclamation of the gospel. It is quite extraordinary to note that the words "what she has done will be told in memory of her" (14:9 RSV) are similar to the words used by Jesus according to 1 Corinthians 11:23 when he speaks of the repeated act of sharing bread and wine ("Do this in remembrance of me"). In other words, the woman's place in Christian memory and story is guaranteed. Not only did she act in a priestly way by anointing the messiah who was about to suffer and die but also her action was placed on a par with the memorial of the death for which she was preparing. The most priestly moment in the Gospel story, the anointing of the messiah, is performed by a woman. Later women are depicted as Jesus' true followers and ministers (Mark 15:41) in his hour of need. The women who go to the tomb find not the body of Jesus but an empty tomb. The story ends in utter bewilderment with them meeting a young man in white who tells them of the resurrection, instructs them to announce the fact to Peter and the disciples, and promises a meeting with Jesus in Galilee. We are left with the women departing in fear without telling anyone, themselves the central figures in this climax to the story as recipients of the good news of the resurrection.

It is the open-mindedness and surprising nature of that story which are most striking. It consistently includes the marginal and embraces those involved in similar contemporary struggles. It is they who now beckon us to share in a life which includes them. They gently remind us that we ignore them and their wisdom at our peril. The poor, women, vulnerable, and people of color find themselves nearer the kingdom than those who presume to be its heirs and guardians of its truth, who risk finding themselves cast out.

Bibliography

Cardenal, Ernesto. *The Gospel in Solentiname.* Vol. 3. 4 vols. Translated by Donald D. Walsh. Maryknoll, NY: Orbis, 1979.

Mesters, Carlos. *Defenseless Flower: A New Reading of the Bible.* Translated by Francis McDonagh. Maryknoll, NY: Orbis, 1989.

Myers, Ched. *Binding the Strong Man: A Political Reading of Mark's Story of Jesus.* Maryknoll, NY: Orbis, 1988.

Pitt, James. *Good News to All.* London: CIIR, 1980.

Pixley, George. *God's Kingdom: A Guide for Biblical Study.* Maryknoll, NY: Orbis, 1981.

Rowland, Christopher, and Mark Corner. *Liberating Exegesis: The Challenge of Liberation Theology to Biblical Studies.* Louisville: Westminster John Knox, 1990.

Vallely, Paul. *Promised Lands: Stories of Power and Poverty in the Third World.* Photographs by Mike Goldwater. London: Fount, 1992.

7

That We Should Remember the Poor

I WANT TO START with a personal reminiscence. Just over two years ago, along with a colleague from Christian Aid, I visited the Northeast of Brazil, a vast area of semidesert bordering on the immense tropical rain forest of Amazonia. We were there to meet parties from Christian Aid engaged in a variety of different development programs. During that visit we travelled inland from the large city of Fortaleza, a six-hour bus journey into the interior of Ceará to a town called Sobral. There we met members of a group who called themselves *The Day of the Lord Movement*. This movement had been supported for several years by Christian Aid, but because of the remoteness from centers of population had only been rarely visited by staff.

The movement consisted of a network of communities in the countryside surrounding Sobral. They had been formed as the result of a popular education program in the 1970s organized by the local diocese. Since then, they had taken over responsibility for their own organization and had encouraged contacts between themselves. Although initially they had been organized by a local priest, they had become entirely lay-led and manifested many of the characteristics of one of the *comunidades eclesiais de base* (CEBs: Basic Ecclesial Communities) so typical of the Brazilian Roman Catholic Church. The individual communities were the church in each of those scattered villages, visited only occasionally by a priest or religious, and largely left to fend for themselves. Over the years they had built up a remarkable network of communication based on reciprocal visitations and the exchange of letters. The letters covered a variety of subjects including issues of land rights, victimization of tenant farmers, and the meaning of

Scripture and doctrine. What was so striking about the letters was the thoroughly Christian tone of each one even when mundane issues such as the rights of sugar cane workers were being discussed.

As I read the letters and listened to the story of the movement, I was struck by the resemblances between these scattered communities and the Pauline churches of the first century CE. Like the Pauline churches, they too had known their splits and the suspicions of various leaders and their styles. Also, like the Pauline churches they shared their letters. Here, it seemed, in the late twentieth century, without the benefits of technology, communication had to be carried out by more laborious means. The epistolary world of the Pauline Corpus was alive and well, enabling contact, unity of principle and purpose, and throughout creating the space for a very different perspective on life.

At the time of my visit, Brazil was in the grip of election fever, which had engulfed even this remote corner of the country. In the face of this, members of the group commented on the process in which people were being caught up: goodies and promises abounded as did adulation of the candidates by rich and poor alike. How similar, remarked one old man, was this to the graphic picture of the adulation of the Beast in Revelation, with the praises of power and influence and the threats to those who would stand aloof! Being part of this alternative network meant in some sense standing aloof, because it had become possible to see things from another perspective, different from that, say, fed them by the national TV network or the strongmen whose job it was to persuade the local peasantry to cast their votes aright.

In some way their story is unremarkable. There is little political heroism to recount or dramatic confrontations with authorities, whether political or ecclesiastical. Yet it is typical of thousands of small communities in Latin America which are the bedrock of liberation theology. In the midst of it all, there is something distinctive and authentically evangelical about it. As far as I was concerned, the evocations of the Pauline churches were most striking. They too were little more than a blip on the screen of history, scattered groups amounting at most, one suspects, to only a hundred or so persons. The connection between Pauline churches and CEBs is one that is not often made. Indeed, liberation theologians have tended to avoid the Pauline Corpus. But the activities of those Brazilian peasants should make us look afresh at Paul.

Instead of starting with themes of Romans and Galatians—the Law, righteousness, grace, and redemption—perhaps we should start with the activity of the man and the churches he founded. If we do, we shall find a story of enormous dedication and energy consisting of two parts. Firstly, there is the commitment to Christ's call which led to the formation of communities of Jews and Gentiles nurtured on the basis of reading the Bible in the light of Jesus Christ. Secondly, there is the task which occupied the last years of Paul's career: the collection for the poor in Jerusalem. It is that to which he is alluding in Galatians 2 (probably for the first time in his extant letters) in the words which offer the title for today's lecture: "all they asked was that we should keep in mind the poor, the very thing I have made it my business to do" (Gal 2:10 my translation).

These apparently innocent words rarely get the attention they deserve when commentators are preoccupied with more contentious issues of Paul's apologia in the surrounding verses. Yet here in the midst of both an extensive justification of his own authority and an attempt to distinguish himself from the sphere of influence of the Jerusalem Church, Paul surprisingly offers a concession. While asserting his distinctiveness of approach and refusal to give in, he admits that in one respect he acceded to the request of the Jerusalem apostles. Clearly, this did not have to be wrung out of him, for this pattern of behavior was one to which he was already committed. So here is a basis for a common practice in the church. When the right hand of fellowship could be exchanged at the Jerusalem conference only after hard bargaining and conflict, in the matter of relief of poverty there was immediate agreement. But that agreement receives only the barest mention. It is a salutary reminder that it is not agreement but conflict which generates greater interest.

But behind these words there lies the project which was to occupy so much of Paul's time and energy. The innovatory character of the project and the effort involved in organizing a collection which then had to be taken hundreds of miles should not be overlooked. The collection for the poor in Jerusalem has few obvious parallels in the ancient world. Attempts to relate it to the regular Temple tax for the upkeep of Temple worship have not been found compelling. The origins of the sentiments which led Paul to accede to the request of the Jerusalem apostles and to engage in such extensive activities in pursuit of it could be in the Bible itself, where provision for the poor is central. Whatever the extent to which Paul was prepared to relax laws which prevented the proper fellowship within the Body of Christ, the provision for the poor was something which had continuing validity. In this could be seen the fulfilment of the Law of obligation to the neighbor, to which he alludes later in Galatians.

The problem with the collection is not so much that it is only occasionally alluded to (in fact it is mentioned in several letters); rather it is the very humdrum tone in which it seems to be presented that gives it a less important place in discussions of Pauline theology. The lengthy discussion in 2 Corinthians has the air of a piece of administration which only serves to mask the importance of the whole enterprise. Yet closer examination reveals the centrality of this activity for Paul's theology. Not only does he justify it Christologically—"though Christ was rich, yet for our sake he became poor" (2 Cor 8:9 my translation)—but also he speaks of it as an act of grace (2 Cor 8:7). The collection was to be a channel of divine aid which was both a means of alleviating misery and also a demonstration of God's character. He speaks of it in terms which are reserved elsewhere in the Pauline Corpus for the proclamation of the gospel itself (2 Cor 9:12; cf. Col 1:24).

I have dwelt briefly on the connection between the Pauline Corpus and the network of Christian groups in Northeast Brazil for two reasons. First, it is a reminder that the mutual responsibility to offer help to the poor with whom one might have no physical contact is rooted in the gospel from the very earliest days. Second, the contemporary situation has sent us back to the New Testament with a demand that familiar passages are viewed from a fresh perspective. The pieces of tradition which are peripheral to most treatments of Paul turn out, in fact, to be central to the practice of the apostle. It is this reordering of priorities in interpretation which liberation theology has done so much to foster. And it is consideration of this change of perspective and its impact on the theology of the New Testament that I want to explore in the lecture this afternoon.

How far, for example, is a major theme of liberation theology like the option for the poor reflected in the New Testament, particularly the Gospels? My concern in part arises from my involvement with a project sponsored by Christian Aid. The object of the project is to look at the way in which members of the British churches react to poverty and relate it to their faith. That is clearly an issue to which the biblical exegete can make a contribution. Exegesis of the Bible in liberation theology has concentrated primarily on the Old Testament with its theme of liberation from oppression in Egypt and the promised land, as well as the denunciations of injustice in Amos. In the New Testament, apart from favorite proof texts they have often looked to the Gospel of Mark as a "classic" narrative in which the struggle with evil powers, the challenge to convention and taboos, and the articulation of a countercultural pattern of life is a challenge to the status quo. Mark's Gospel is a good news which contrasts with the imperial propaganda and challenges the behavior of the rulers of the earth.

Mark's Gospel is seen as a sophisticated version of the Christus Victor doctrine in which Christ's apparent defeat is really the triumph over political power based in the Temple and its priests. The challenge to the Temple and the religio-political establishment which Jesus' journey to Jerusalem provoked led to the oppressive behavior of the power of priestly authorities towards Jesus. The execution of the one who challenged the Temple polity was not the end of the matter. The rending of the veil symbolizes the end of the power of Temple and the ruling class of Judea, and the confession of the centurion was the recognition by the representative of Rome that the crucified Jewish messiah is King of Kings and Lord of Lords. Mark's Gospel has been an important resource for liberation exegesis, the results of which are widely available. However, in my lecture this evening I want to explore the potential contribution of the other Gospels, some of which have not been so widely used.

Considerations of the Gospel of Matthew and the poor almost inevitably focus on the dramatic picture of the Last Judgement which concludes Jesus' last great discourse and precedes the story of the Passion. Both the papal encyclical *Sollicitudo rei socialis* and Gustavo Gutiérrez's *A Theology of Liberation* turn to this text as a foundation for their outline of God's preferential option for the poor and afflicted. Its dramatic revelation that the assembled multitudes have already met the glorious Judge *incognito* in the persons of the hungry, naked, thirsty, and imprisoned make this a classic text for those who wish to argue for an obligation to the poor as fundamental to service of God.

The passage is a familiar one. The heavenly son of man sits on the throne of glory, a scene parallel to a contemporary Jewish text, *The Similitudes of Enoch*, where the heavenly son of man sits on God's throne of glory, exercising judgement. But in contrast to the Jewish text, Matthew's scene does not describe an expectation confined to some eschatological event. In the parable of the sheep and the goats (Matt 25:31–46) we find that the meeting with the glorious son of man is attainable in the mundane circumstances of human need. Judgement is determined at the moment of reaction to those who appear to be nonentities and who are making claims upon us from a position of weakness.

Such a universal concern is reflected in contemporary Jewish sources. Respect for the human person created in God's image, irrespective of nation or religious affiliation, is to be found. Most akin to Matthew's sheep and goats is 2 Enoch 42:8–14 where clothing the naked, feeding the hungry, looking after widows and orphans, and coming to the aid of those who have suffered injustice are criteria for blessedness.

Exegetes, both ancient and modern, have sounded a cautionary note on the use of this passage to promote service of the needy. Debate has raged over the identity of Jesus' brothers and sisters in the parable of the sheep and goats. Is it right to see in the verse, "As you did it to one of the least of these you did it to me" (Matt 25:40 my translation) a reference to all the poor, naked, hungry, sick, and imprisoned, or is it not the case that, in Matthew's mind at least, they are references to followers of Christ, particularly to those Christian missionaries who might need shelter and care? Whatever the meaning of the words on the lips of Jesus, or the meaning which a contemporary reading of Matthew might offer, powerful arguments have been marshalled for the view that Jesus' brethren refers exclusively to poor Christians and not to the poor in general. Needless to say, such an interpretation renders this passage of little immediate service in commanding service of the poor irrespective of ethnic or religious affiliation. This is not the place to explore all the detail which would be necessary to challenge a view which is now widely held among commentators on Matthew. Some of the other passages which are taken to indicate that disciples are identified with the least of Jesus' brethren are not as unambiguous as some have made out, particularly the obscure commendation of those who give a cup of cold water to the little ones in Matthew 10:42. But even if we have an identification earlier in the Gospel, there is some evidence to suggest that a close link between disciples and the little ones does not remain constant throughout the narrative. By the time we get to Matthew 25 we have no cozy reassurance of the elect, of their vindication and the punishment of those who neglect them; but, in line with so much in Matthew, a disturbing challenge to the complacency of insider and outsider alike.

A case can be made for seeing the second half of Matthew as being one in which the ideal of discipleship ceases to be embodied in the group of disciples. It is not that they are failures but that other paradigms are needed. This is seen most clearly in chapter 18 where a child is set over against the twelve as the type of true greatness. In chapter 18 the disciples ask Jesus who is the greatest in the kingdom of heaven. He answers by taking a child and declaring to the disciples that those who "humble themselves as this little child are the greatest in the kingdom of heaven" (Matt 18:4 my translation). The child is their measure of true greatness. Jesus is portrayed as speaking of the children as "these little ones," another key term in Matthew's Gospel. Response to the child or the little one is the same as response to Jesus. Just as fulfilling the needs of the hungry and thirsty means fulfilling the desire of the heavenly son of man for a response to those in need, so receiving a child means receiving Jesus himself (18:6).

There is something special about the little ones. Echoing the language of the apocalyptic traditions, we are told their angels have the privilege of beholding God's face, the highest of all privileges. The climax of the heavenly ascent is the vision of God enthroned in glory, something normally denied not only to mortals but also to angels. The angels of Matthew's little ones can be no ordinary angels, therefore (Matt 18:10). They stand in close proximity to the throne of glory and share in that destiny which is vouchsafed to the elect in the New Jerusalem, described in Revelation 22:4, of seeing God face to face. Matthew's little ones are linked with those who in worldly terms are insignificant but who from the divine perspective carry a particular privilege. The characteristic of these little ones is that their heavenly representatives are peculiarly able to gaze on the divine face.

Although Peter has his moments of insight, it is the crowd that hails Jesus as he enters Jerusalem (Matt 21:9), the blind and the lame who come to him in the Temple (Matt 21:14), and the children who cry out, "Hosanna to the son of David!" (Matt 21:15 RSV). These are the *nepioi*, babes, of whom the Psalmist speaks and Matthew quotes: "Out of the mouths of babes and sucklings thou hast perfected praise" (Matt 21:16 KJV), from Psalm 8. They are the *nepioi* referred to in Matthew 11:25, where Jesus gives thanks to his heavenly father for hiding these things from the wise and intelligent and revealing them to babes. This includes the disciples, but as the Gospel proceeds the adult disciples are those who are seen to slip over on the side of Satan, betraying, denying, and abandoning the son of man.

In contrast to them, a child briefly moves to center stage. To place a child in the midst of the disciples is to challenge the assumption that the child has nothing of worth and can only be heeded when it has received another's wisdom. The ordering of things which characterizes the adult world is not the embodiment of wisdom and may in fact be a perversion of it. Here is a perspective which challenges the traditions of older generations. To be as a little child is a mark of greatness, in terms of the values of the kingdom, for it is the children and those able to identify with them who have solidarity with the humble—and therefore with Jesus.

What is significant about the child and the little one is not their innocence. Like many other parents I would find it difficult to see innocence as the dominant characteristic of the child. Yet, equally as a parent, I do recognize the extent of the power of the parent and the possibilities of exploitation and oppression which may be inflicted on the child. We need to remember that. The position of children in the ancient world was much inferior to the more child-centered world of today. They were often, as a matter of course, treated brutally. On the other hand, in the ancient world children were believed to be in close contact with the divine world by virtue of their marginality. Thus they have an insight which disciples must emulate, not despise.

Theirs is an intuition into the nature of God which seems to be confined to those who are in some sense at a disadvantage in relation to the wise and prudent of this world. It is too simple to say that those who have such insight are the "poor." It might be more appropriate to call them the "marginal." They are, in any case, the "humble," both in terms of status and endowment. There is a privilege for this group, though Matthew's Gospel only speaks of it in regard to the understanding of divine mysteries. It is a privilege which is to be seen as a grace rather than a right. Perhaps this is the privilege which is being enunciated when Jesus proclaims the poor in spirit blessed in the first of the Beatitudes?

It is assumed that Matthew's Gospel is preoccupied with the gathered community symbolized by the disciples rather than a much wider group of marginal people. Yet the evangelist's repeated summaries of Jesus' ministry (e.g., Matt 4:24; 8:16; 9:10; 9:35) suggest a particular care for the marginal and dispossessed. The concern with the least of the little ones is particularly evident in Matthew's Gospel and finds its consummation in the declaration by Jesus immediately following the awesome woes on the towns that have rejected his message. In it he thanks God for concealing the secrets of the kingdom from the wise and revealing them to the babes (the very ones who, as we have seen, recognize the Messiah when he comes to the Temple).

The babes who understand include the disciples but also include a wider group of "little people" who are contrasted with the opponents who interpret Jesus' activity as the result of demon possession. Compared with Luke, the thanksgiving to God is followed in Matthew by a summons to those who are oppressed. In these words, the one who would demonstrate himself to be a meek and lowly king calls those who are oppressed to himself on the basis of the fact that he shares their lot of humiliation. While elements of the wisdom tradition have been found in these verses, echoes of passages like Isaiah 58 and Isaiah 61 which speak of freedom from the yoke of oppression may also be found. The spiritualizing tendency encouraged by many of our translations and liturgical use ignores the reality of oppression, exclusion, and impoverishment of many of the crowds addressed by Jesus which the one who is in solidarity with them seeks to relieve. Jesus calls people out of oppressed and oppressive circumstances to a new community in which the conditions of oppression no longer apply.

At the heart of Matthew's christology is the deliberate identification of Emmanuel—"God with us"—with the powerless and weak rather than with the strong. From the start of the Gospel, Emmanuel is the child faced with brutal repression by the rulers in Jerusalem, and this identification with the powerless is maintained consistently throughout the Gospel. It is not surprising that the vision of the one throned in glory is located also among the outcast and not merely in heaven on the last day. The privilege of seeing God's glory is no longer confined to the seer or mystic, nor to life after death, but is granted in the midst of present circumstances. In the most unlikely persons and situations the glory of God is found here and now, in this age, hidden, mysterious, but demanding a response from those who are confronted by it.

I have tried to suggest that in the Gospel which is not usually regarded as a major resource for a liberationist perspective there is in the outline of Jesus' life an identification with the humiliated. We might even speak of "an option for the poor." The pattern of Jesus' life is demanded of disciples too, and a more inclusive concern may be found in Matthew than some commentators allow. When we turn to Luke's Gospel, we find a story that has always been attractive for its humanity and inclusiveness. Its message seems to echo many of the concerns of those working for justice and peace. Without denying the appropriateness of regarding Luke in this way I want to suggest that we need to recognize that Luke's story is a little more complicated than may appear at first sight.

One of the ways whereby Christians sought to ensure the survival of their religion was through seeking to persuade and placate those in power. Part of the task of Christian intellectual production in its earliest phase was to position itself over against the dominant ideology, whether it be a dominant form of Judaism or the ideologies of the wider Greco-Roman world. Thus, Luke wrote (among other reasons) in order to present an acceptable religion which conformed to the Bible and would not completely exclude the penitent rich and mighty. Despite the concern to give it a conventional setting, the story he tells is remarkable in its subordination of the rulers of the contemporary world to the background of rural Galilee whose populace is confronted with good news which differed markedly from the propaganda of the imperial world. For all its conventional opening and setting in the context of contemporary history Luke's Gospel hardly exhibits a supportive attitude towards established institutions and beliefs.

It is, after all, Luke's Gospel which portrays Jesus as predicting the destruction of city and Temple in the light of their inability to understand what led to its peace. The attitude to Davidic messianism is not the unquestioning assumption of the expectation of the Davidic king. The manifesto of Jesus in Luke 4 questions and looks forward to the detaching of messiahship from David later in the Gospel. In Luke the message to the rich is not a very palatable one. Luke seems to be uncompromisingly hostile to Mammon, and the reader of the Gospel is left in little doubt about the appropriate response to those like Lazarus. The chapters after the infancy narratives have been seen as a contrast to more militant messianic sentiments earlier in the Gospel. Of course, this may have suited the apologetic aim of a writer who wished to portray a pacific religion. But elsewhere there is little evidence of any obsequious attitude towards Rome. Certainly it is less obvious than in Josephus. Yet even the more obviously sycophantic Josephus enables us to catch a glimpse in his pro-Roman narrative of another dimension to the story of Second Temple Judaism than the one preferred by him.

However, it seems to me important to face the contradictory signals which have been picked up by interpreters of Luke–Acts. On the one hand, there is the clarion call to liberation in Luke 4:16 and in the uncompromising attitude towards wealth and poverty. On the other hand, there are the apparent nods in the direction of accommodation, particularly in Acts. The account of Cornelius's conversion leaves open the question of the character of life of the newly-converted Gentile soldier; Ananias and Sapphira's sin is deceiving the Holy Spirit rather than refusal to share their property, perhaps a tacit acceptance of the abandonment of the principle of the community of goods in the early Jerusalem church. In addition, Luke's Gospel, traditionally regarded as being particularly favorable to women, has recently been seen as portraying women as models of subordinate service excluded from the power center of the Christian movement and from significant responsibilities. We should resist seeking to resolve these tensions. They may well have been necessitated by the competing pulls of commitment to Christ and the need to go on living in the midst of the old political and economic order. All this speaks not of growing conformism so much as the recognition of the constraints imposed upon the practice of a radical religion in inauspicious political circumstances. It is a situation familiar to many who espouse liberation theology. In refusing the revolutionary option, Christians have found that the room for maneuver and change has been small. They understand all too well how much discipleship will be hemmed in and how even the smallest space for change will need to be exploited to the full.

We need to recognize that Christian theology from Luke onwards manifests a greater concern to convince, and perhaps even placate, the influential and important rather than be a mouthpiece for the oppressed. If our major interest is the story of the poor, we shall not find rich pickings in Luke or for that matter elsewhere in the Bible. But then history is rarely the memory of the poor and insignificant; that witness is frequently lost forever from our view. Of course, the shape of a story would be different if we sought to write it consistently from the perspective of the poor and voiceless. But the retrieval of that other story is often the task of the sympathetic voices of another culture or class. Part of the task of liberation theology has been to engage in that project. As a result, as the history of liberation theology itself indicates, the presentation of the "voice of the voiceless" is almost inevitably in an idiom at a significant remove from the story that the poor might tell.

Luke in one sense fits into this category. He is certainly not primarily interested in the lot of the poor nor does he set out to be a voice of the voiceless. The interest of the evangelist enables us to glimpse the other story because of its subject matter. The Gospels have christology, albeit in narrative form, at the center of their presentation and this towers over all other concerns. The poor and outcast are incidental to that dominant concern. But that christological perspective exemplifies the orientation of Christ towards the outcast and rejects.

Luke's mediation of the story of Jesus does not set out primarily to capture the precise character of the Galilean messianic movement, the voices of those who responded to it, why it was so important for the crowds who followed Jesus (in religious and socio-economic terms), and the character of the liberation that was experienced. But in the process of convincing Theophilus of his version of the rise of Christianity, Luke at least ensured that this strange, apparently insignificant story was written. It ensured the continuing interest in the memories and culture of rural Galilee because of the interest in Jesus the Galilean. The writing of the tradition about Jesus was a formative moment for the way in which the story was appropriated. It was a decisive step to set the story in the midst of genres which largely were the prerogative of those who served the interests of the politically powerful.

Luke's is a story which might hardly merit a record in most annals of the ancient world. His primary focus is Jesus, but in writing his history, unconventional by the canons of antiquity, Luke includes a glimpse of those poor and insignificant people who were the participants in the Gospel. It is hardly surprising that frequently basic ecclesial communities in the contemporary world have found in reading Luke a voice which in some way expresses their own aspirations and hopes, a recognition that the telling of Jesus' story brings the margins to the center.

In Matthew's Gospel we have noted a picture of Jesus which demonstrates his solidarity with the afflicted. We have then suggested that it is only through such solidarity that discipleship and insight into the identity of Jesus and his way is attainable. The need for a change of perspective is a theme in other New Testament books not often quoted in the discussion of liberative themes, but their presentations are consistent with that demand for a perspective which refuses conformity and is rooted in service. In the Epistle to the Hebrews the option of discipleship is presented as being socially costly. In the concluding chapter of the Epistle, the author urges recipients of the letter to join Jesus outside the camp and share his reproach. Although there is some debate about this, the place outside the camp seems to be an allusion to Golgotha. It is there outside the security of the camp, the place where the Sabbath-breaker and the blasphemer are stoned, that the readers are urged to move. But it is there that the High Priest of the new covenant begins his movement to the presence of God; outside, away from the security of convention and status quo, it is the place of reproach that turns out to be the sacred space, not the established pattern of cultic worship.

Sharing Christ's reproach is something the recipients of the letter had themselves experienced when first converted (Heb 10:32), when they had been exposed to vilification. They had understood what it meant to be in solidarity with those who suffered imprisonment and had put up with confiscation of their property. In that they shared the experience of one who took the option for the poor, Moses. He refused the security of Pharaoh's court and preferred to share the hardship of the people of God. In this he shared the reproach of Christ. Small wonder, therefore, that in writing a christology from the perspective of Latin America, Jon Sobrino should see in this passage a *locus classicus* for the preferential option for the poor. The summons is to share the reproach of the Messiah and thereby be in a position outside the gate to see life and God from a perspective free of the distortions of the dominant way of looking at things.

There is something similar to all this in the Gospel of John. The "spiritual Gospel" has of late had a new political lease of life, not in any conventional sense, but of importance to it nonetheless. It is not necessary to accept all the hypothetical reconstruction about church/synagogue conflict at the end of the first century CE to see that John's Gospel is, in part, about the meaning and cost of identification with Jesus. We are treated throughout the Gospel to a variety of reactions and strategies by those who are confronted by one who claimed to be sent by God, ranging from overt hostility to worship. The most famous encounter of all is that between Jesus and Nicodemus. In an important article written twenty years ago, the North American biblical scholar Wayne Meeks argued that this debate focused on the need for a change in perspective to understand God and the world aright.[1]

Nicodemus, clearly a sympathetic Jewish leader, is told by Jesus that proper understanding depends on "being born again." This is no hole and corner affair, but, as David Rensberger has recently pointed out, depends on baptism: a public identification which means a move from one social position to another, especially for the member of the ruling class who might prefer to be a covert sympathizer. Secret discipleship, hinted at in Nicodemus's case in his coming to Jesus by night, is not an option. Parallel to that in John 6, discipleship involves participation in the eucharist—eating the flesh and drinking the blood of the Son of Man. This hard saying is one which some disciples could not accept and so ceased to follow Jesus. Understanding depends on public affirmation and identification which is socially and politically costly, for it could elicit the kind of abuse that was experienced by the

---

1. Discussed in Rensberger, *Overcoming*.

recipients of the letter to the Hebrews (evident in the treatment meted out to the blind man in John 9). Nicodemus briefly experiences some of the cost of discipleship when his tentative questioning of the unjust approach to Jesus' case is met with a curt response from the authorities.

A more overtly political theme is evident in the trial of Jesus before Pilate, much more extended in John's Gospel than in any of the other canonical Gospels. Part of that dialogue involves the nature of kingship and Pilate's refusal to act rightly on the basis of the truth he had discovered. In the interchange in John 18:36, Pilate asks Jesus whether he is king of the Jews. Eventually Jesus responds with the oft quoted "My kingdom is not of this world." The distinguishing mark of the different sort of kingdom offered by Jesus is that his followers do not fight. The redefinition of kingship has its parallel in Mark 10:42 where right to a position of privilege is based on service: "you know that among the Gentiles the rulers lord it over their subjects, and the great men make their authority felt; it shall not be so with you. Among you whoever wants to be great must be a servant, and whoever wants to be first must be the slave of all." In line with this, in John 13 the supper story includes the acted demonstration of that service in the form of foot washing. The king who comes proclaiming a different kind of kingdom, therefore, offers a model of it to his disciples in this humble act.

A change of sides, even of status, is required of leaders like Nicodemus, and a pattern of behavior which demonstrates the solidarity with minorities and the outcast. A different understanding necessitates a change of sides in which solidarity with the Stranger from Heaven and his way becomes all important. It is true that nothing is said in John's Gospel about Jesus' siding with the poor, and in chapter 13 it is service of the insiders only which appears to be commended. Indeed, even those acts of healing serve to demonstrate God's glory (John 9:3; 11:4; cf. 2:11). But the specifically divine dimension of these acts does not detract from the kind of solidarity and interaction which are exemplified. The emphasis is on service of the divine majesty as the supreme goal of all human endeavor. Nevertheless, the contours of that exemplary manifestation of the divine glory are found in acts of healing and restoration of the excluded, service, political confrontation, and finally the degradation of the cross.

In the Fourth Gospel, identification with the One sent from God is a political act which challenges the status quo and calls for a price to be paid in social terms. That witness to the truth cannot be the solitary pursuit carried out by the creative mind shut off from the complexities of life and the understanding of it. It is exemplified in concrete acts which must manifest faithfulness in the public arena. Fear might drive disciples to take refuge in an upper room, but that is only a temporary respite before the witness to truth pioneered by Jesus is set in motion again by the Spirit-Paraclete in tandem with those who are Jesus' faithful witnesses. This is no private affair, therefore, because the advocacy of the Spirit, of the way of Jesus, involves a conviction of the world about issues of justice, judgement, and sin. The disciple is not greater than the teacher. Exaltation and glory are located in the victim of injustice whose innocence was ignored for fear of a political backlash. But, as in Mark, the death of the victim marks the judgement on the ruler of the world when the political power of the present system is destroyed.

By starting with the brief description of the *Movement of the Day of the Lord*, I have already implied that the process of exegesis is one that has its origin in the contemporary world of the interpreter. That applies to the most sophisticated exegete just as much as it does the Brazilian peasant. The community of interpretation of the modern guild of professional exegetes, while doubtless more pluralistic than before, has its rules of membership and parameters of interpretation. Its primarily academic setting and historical orientation have not always led members of the guild to view liberation theology entirely sympathetically. Yet the perspective of liberation theology on these biblical texts is one that seeks to be faithful to the texts as a foundation document of a community of faith, and to the sense that has been given to the texts within the Christian church, in particular the too often neglected tradition of a preferential option for the poor.

As a professional exegete I am acutely aware of the suspicion that attaches to liberation exegesis from colleagues. Liberation theology seems to many to ride roughshod over the particularities of individual texts in its search for the hermeneutical thread of liberation and to sit loose to that rigorous contextualization in the ancient world which has become a *sine qua non* of exegesis. Critics may have a point in their demand that the Bible does not easily support an overarching theme. It is naive to suppose that the Bible is transparently a handbook of liberation theology—at least in any straightforward sense. My friend and colleague Itumeleng Mosala has likewise warned of the dangers in a naive appropriation of the Bible for the liberation struggle, when the texts themselves may have been formed, in part at least, by those who won the struggle for religious and political supremacy in Israel.

So, I do not want to ignore the problems liberation exegesis poses. In some situations it has seemed to identify too closely with certain political projects. Occasionally in Nicaragua between 1979 and 1990, some came close to identifying the revolution with the coming of the kingdom. This is not typical. On the whole its practitioners have never lost the sense of provisionality which is at the heart of Christian eschatology. Yet its overt commitment and practical involvement can make it more problematic for conventional theology. Its interpretative solutions can bypass the careful questioning and necessary provisionality of much of our interpretation.

Part of the problem has been that there has been insufficient dialogue between Third World and First World theology. Too often they have passed like ships in the night. Yet Third World theology, like liberation theology, poses questions to our interpretative enterprise. Though ours may not be the obvious struggle of South Africa or El Salvador, we need to ask ourselves how far our exegesis breathes a spirit of detachment and objectivity. We are asked to see that the apparent absence of partiality in our reading should not lead us to suppose that there may be no interest at stake in our exegetical activities. We need to be as candid as we can be. In liberation theology exegesis walks hand-in-hand with discipleship and action on behalf of the poor. Such commitments seem to vitiate the much-prized detachment of the exegete. But our presumed Olympian detachment may seem to offer a privileged perspective. It must be questioned whether that necessarily enables a better way to the truth of God in Christ.

We have seen how, in biblical interpretation influenced by liberation theology, there is a serious concern with the political dimension of the narrative. In the Gospels and Epistles we have found hints that there is a demand for solidarity with the poor, the humble, and the marginal in line with the option of Jesus and a sense that this may be a position where fresh understanding of the gospel may be gleaned. Perhaps Itumeleng Mosala is right to suggest that the New Testament is directed more often at the Dives to persuade them to take account of the Lazaruses either in their midst or at the gate. That may reflect the particular social composition of the churches at the time the Gospels reached their written form. If so, they are texts particularly applicable to our First World situation. But liberation theologians have argued that there is more to the Gospels than that.

In telling the biblical story from a different perspective they have enabled us to glimpse how, in the Gospels, the poor and marginalized are viewed as responsible moral agents with serious options which are valued in the sight of God. The poor do not remain merely the objects of the concern of the rich and influential, therefore. We see them emerging from the wings of the drama, albeit in tentative and fragmentary ways. This is one of the contributions of liberation theology to our generation. The other has been to remind theologians that in the midst of their fascinating preoccupations with complex and weighty matters of divinity "we should remember the poor."

Bibliography

Esler, Philip Francis. *Community and Gospel in Luke–Acts*. Society of New Testament Studies Monograph Series 57. Cambridge: Cambridge University Press, 1987.

Mosala, Itumeleng J. *Biblical Hermeneutics and Black Theology in South Africa*. Grand Rapids: Eerdmans, 1989.

Myers, Ched. *Binding the Strong Man: A Political Reading of Mark's Story of Jesus*. Maryknoll, NY: Orbis, 1988.

Rensberger, David. *Overcoming the World: Politics and Community in the Gospel of John*. London: SPCK, 1988.

Rowland, Christopher. "'Open Thy Mouth for the Dumb': A Task for the Exegete of Holy Scripture." *Biblical Interpretation* 1 (1993) 228–45.

Rowland, Christopher, and Mark Corner. *Liberating Exegesis: The Challenge of Liberation Theology to Biblical Studies*. Louisville: Westminster John Knox, 1990.

Sobrino, Jon. *The True Church and the Poor*. Translated by Matthew J. O'Connell. Maryknoll, NY: Orbis, 1984.

Wengst, Klaus. *Humility: Solidarity of the Humiliated: The Transformation of an Attitude and its Social Relevance in Graeco-Roman, Old Testament-Jewish, and Early Christian Tradition*. Translated by John Bowden. Philadelphia: Fortress, 1988.

———. *Pax Romana: And the Peace of Jesus Christ*. Translated by John Bowden. Philadelphia: Fortress, 1987.

8

"The Gospel, the Poor, and the Churches"

Attitudes to Poverty in the British Churches and Biblical Exegesis

1

For a period of two years between 1992 and 1994 I was involved with members of Christian Aid in the planning, gestation, and birth of a project entitled *The Gospel, the Poor, and the Churches*.[1] It started life as a contribution of Christian Aid to discussions about the Decade of Evangelism, as well as a means whereby the organization could signal to the churches the central importance it attached to its work within the churches and the need to persuade them of solidarity with the poor as a central feature of mission, a theme at the heart of this conference. It was decided to commission a reputable sociological research institute (*Social and Community Planning Research*) to carry out an investigation of the attitudes of British Christians to poverty. After much discussion it was decided that the institute should embark on a piece of qualitative research; that is (to quote the report's outline of its method), "an attempt to present the social world, and perspectives on that world, in terms of the concepts, behaviours, perceptions and accounts of the people it is about."[2] The report tells us nothing about the prevalence of attitudes within

---

1. Spencer and Snape, *Gospel, the Poor, and the Churches*.
2. Spencer and Snape, *Gospel, the Poor, and the Churches*, 122.

the churches but does enable us to see the spectrum of opinion that exists. Although there has been a systematic presentation of the material, we are allowed to hear the attitudes and reactions of Christians on every page as they seek to respond to the researchers' questions. It is a rich treasury of opinion which illuminates the present state of the church and enables one to catch a glimpse of how we all view the relief of poverty.

The researchers did not determine the responses or the choice of responses and organized their findings on the basis of the information they assembled. So, although they went to a range of different churches, they found that the material they assembled compelled them to present a typology of the variety of Christian responses. The types are as follows:

1. *Personal-literal*: this person's faith focuses on the need for individual conversion. The Bible is read in a literalistic way and is the main source of authority. Key indications of appropriate behavior include prayer, Bible reading, and treating others with patience and love.

2. *Personal-questioning*: similarly, personal commitment is important, but room is left for personal experience which is allowed to foster questioning. Here, greater priority is given to addressing issues of social and individual morality.

3. *Institutional-literal*: for this group the teaching of the church is central and is usually accepted without question. Living out faith can include broader social issues but is mainly concerned with personal morality.

4. *Institutional-questioning*: for this group, as for the previous, membership of worshipping community is central, and the demands of that community and the wider church are given a high priority. Nevertheless, experience and individual conscience are important. Greater emphasis is placed on addressing broader social and political issues than on personal morality.

5. *Individual-unreflective*: the defining characteristic of this particular type is an individual's morality and how it is that she or he lives life every day. Beliefs and dogma are considered to be of secondary importance as compared with individual morality. Attending church has a pragmatic purpose as it is necessary to keep the individual on the right track. There is little sense of common belief and practice and communal obligation.

6. *Corporate analytical*: interpreting the Christian message must take place in relation to contemporary existence. But that task is one that is complex, and the approach to faith and life needs a corporate

context for understanding and engaging a shared practice. Members of this group interpret the Christian message in relation to everyday life; the investigation of the social and corporate dimensions of faith is essential.

General definitions of poverty included the following: basic needs unmet (e.g., food, shelter, livelihood, health, and education), limitations on choices, and lack of power and control. There emerged differences in the understanding of poverty in the UK as compared with the Third World and in the way in which poverty should be defined either relative to context or in absolute terms:

Reference points	**UK**	**Third World**
Poverty in relation to local context	Poverty in relation to "normal" living standards in UK	Poverty in relation to "normal" living standards in Third World
Poverty compared across contexts	Poverty may be acknowledged but is considered "minor" in relation to poverty in the Third World	"Real" poverty is found in the Third World and is the standard of measurement
Poverty in absolute terms (starvation)	Poverty is not acknowledged in the UK as "genuine" or "real" poverty	Poverty is measured in relation to the most extreme cases in the Third World (i.e., people who are starving)

Although the broad definitions of poverty applied equally to the UK and the Third World, the specific qualifying circumstances necessary to be poor in each area differed. As one might anticipate, the suggestions offered about the causes of poverty varied and included decline in individual morality, fate, the growth of materialism, and lack of Christian values in society, as well as the more politically aware assessments which pointed to underlying structural and political causes. What was apparent was the different causes offered for poverty in the Third World and UK. In the latter it was seen more as the result of the individual's fault. The researchers give an impression of the different stances on poverty which are based on a variety of factors: definitions of poverty; perceptions of the origins of poverty; whether poverty is attributed to personal, environmental, or economic, and political causes; whether poverty is seen in terms of unmet needs or unequal access to choices and rights; and the extent to which parallels are acknowledged between the First and Third Worlds. In the survey, people who are concerned about malaise in political life tend to adopt structural stances (i.e., attentiveness to underlying trends which play a part in social conditions); concern about declining standards in personal morality is linked to blaming views of poverty. Whereas the laity are represented in all positions, there are no clergy in the most unsympathetic groups.

There was a variety of understandings of the purpose of the church. Some favored a more ecclesiastical and inward-looking view focused on fellowship and maintenance or the promotion of ecumenism, while others favored a more outward-looking, "secular" understanding of the church's task in playing its role in social concerns. Poverty was not a major concern for all, and frequently was in competition with other, more pressing, "Christian" concerns. There was a range of positions on the centrality of dealing with poverty in the church's life: from "the church is here primarily to preach the gospel" to one which advocated the abolition of poverty as being the central concern of Christian life (often found as part of a range of issues concerned with the relief of human need and injustice):

The Church's Priorities

Evangelism and internal welfare	Concern is with falling numbers, spiritual development of members, pastoral needs of local community, and direct evangelism
Evangelism and state of nation	Concern is with perceived moral decline in society, fellowship, pastoral needs of local community, and indirect evangelism
Evangelism and social concern in a material world	Concern is with relevance of church and of religion itself in a secular, material age; indirect evangelism; and addressing broader social issues
Practical social concern	Concern is with broader social issues and addressing them through provision of practical help
Prophetic social concern	Concern is with broader social issues and addressing them by speaking out against inequality and injustice

In the following table six basic positions on poverty are identified: (i) a comprehensive view of world poverty; (ii) similar to (i) but with a less overarching outlook; (iii) a harsher attitude towards the poor in the UK who as individuals are seen to be responsible; (iv) little sense of an overview with reluctance to recognize poverty in the UK; and (v) and (vi) poverty the fault of the poor either in the Third World or the UK:

Positions on Poverty

	(i)	(ii)	(iii)	(iv)	(v)	(vi)
	Underlying economic & political structures (UK & 3W)	Underlying economic & political factors (UK & 3W)	Individual choice/ fault (UK) & underlying structures (3W)	Unforeseen circumstances	Individual choice/fault (UK & 3W)	Entirely individual choice/ fault (3W); no poverty in UK
Explanation of origins	Political & economic structures in 3W & UK with joint responsibility between West and 3W govts.	Political & economic factors in 3W & UK with joint responsibility between West and 3W poverty never considered to be fault of individuals	Political & economic factors in 3W with joint responsibility between West and 3W. In UK origins relate to individual choice & fault	3W people are thought to be 'victims of circumstances' while in UK origins may also be related to 'personal failings'	individual choice or fault in UK & 3W (govts. play a part)	fault of 3W govts. & people
Definition of poverty	structural or summary definitions with similarities noted between UK & 3W poverty	symptomatic or summary definitions with less clearly defined view	symptomatic or summary definition with poverty seen as distinctly different in UK & 3W	symptomatic definition of poverty	symptomatic definition with only reluctant acknowledgment of UK poverty	symptomatic absolute definitions of poverty (starvation). Poverty not recognised in UK
Secular concerns	political malaise	political malaise & discrete problems	discrete problems	moral malaise & discrete problems	moral malaise & discrete problems	moral malaise & discrete problems
Experience of poverty	linked to extensive 3W experience/ some local exposure	commonly linked to extensive local exposure	linked to negative experiences of poverty in UK & more positive impressions of 3W	little or no first-hand exposure to poverty	little or no personal exposure to poverty	little or no personal exposure to poverty

When asked for the Christian teaching on attitudes to poverty, most responded with favorite ideas, like love one's neighbor, you will be judged by your actions for the poor (dependent on Matthew's account of the Last Judgement in Matt 25:31–46), or your preference should be for the poor. There was little evidence of much more than a selective series of quotations from the Christian tradition and hardly any evidence of a more sophisticated theological explanation of the causes and responses. Some thought that there was no specifically Christian message, and an oft-quoted text was Mark 14:7: "the poor you always have with you"; a text whose meaning was seen to be rather obscure.

It was apparent that the sources of knowledge about poverty were mainly the media rather than Christian teaching. Not one person spontaneously said that the church was the source of their knowledge about poverty. Striking television images were at the top of the list: "the news comes on when one's having one's meal and adds to the difficulty." Churchgoers would appear to be no different from the general public in the character and source of their knowledge. Those who were best informed and most committed often had personal exposure via an overseas visit or working in a Third World country.

One of the most interesting parts of the research was the findings of the investigation of the differing ways in which people in the churches coped with the issue of poverty. Most churchgoers are *not* hard-hearted. The levels of feelings are intense across the spectrum, but how people deal with the feelings differs. On the one hand, there was an *active coping stance*. People in this group expressed the following feelings: anger at unfairness; a desire to help; shame at the differences between rich and poor; admiration of the poor. They responded in the following ways: by seeking more information; acknowledging personal responsibility; focusing on the human aspect of particular situations of poverty; taking inspiration from the poor for their own lives; believing that however small their contribution it could help to alleviate poverty; emphasizing things that were succeeding; and, through all of this, converting negative energy into positive action.

On the other hand, there was the *passive coping stance*. People in this group expressed similar feelings: anger; a desire to help (though qualified by a sense of helplessness); a sense of being greedy; despair or panic; horror and distress. The enormity of the situation with which they were confronted led them to react as follows: avoidance of the plight of the poor; refusal to believe the reports; placing of responsibility elsewhere so that they were relieved of it; a belief that the poor had given up trying to help themselves and so were less deserving of assistance; leaving it in God's hands; making poverty an abstract problem rather than an immediate human need; avoiding issues of local poverty; focusing on others who do even less themselves; emphasizing failed initiatives ("Does it really make any difference when money is wasted or aid projects come to naught?"). If anything, the "passive copers" had stronger feelings of anguish. The act of "switching off" is one of despair.

In conclusion, the researchers drew the threads of the research together by outlining the correlation between different positions and the various types of Christian allegiance:

Overall Stances

1. *Low tolerance*: corrupt Third World governments and the poor were to blame for poverty; solutions lie in greater aid and the encouragement of greater self-reliance; by and large, poverty is a subject usually avoided.

2. *Reluctant acknowledgement*: responsibility for support lies mainly with governments and charities rather than churches; poverty is just one of many concerns facing churches; there is a tendency to avoid poverty.

These first two groups tend to be literal or unreflective in their religious allegiances and concerned about evangelism and internal welfare.

3. *Neutral sympathy*: the poor are victims and deserve our charity; poverty is one among many concerns for the church.

Passive copers tend to be found in this group, and personal-literal, individual-literal, and individual-unreflective modes of allegiance predominate.

4. *Analytical sympathy*: structural analysis of the social world is a necessary preliminary response leading to advocacy of solutions for economic and political change; there should be a general Christian responsibility for the poor.

Passive copers, personal-literal, personal-questioning, and institutional-literal are all found in this group.

5. *Compassionate criticism*: structural origins for the origin of poverty are recognized; there is a particular responsibility of the poor in this country for their own poverty; there is a clear mandate for church involvement and a "bias to the poor" is needed and should be a key priority for individuals and churches.

This perspective is found particularly among clergy[3] and among the institutional-questioning group and those with firsthand knowledge of poverty.

6. Comprehensive Concern: structural origins of poverty are recognized, and comprehensive solutions advocated; the church has a major role in such activity, so there is need for a "bias to the poor"; poverty is no fault of the poor.

This group tends to be made up of active rather than passive copers. Characteristic of this group is their questioning attitude to beliefs, with

3. The clergy were more likely to give a high priority to poverty issues and to be found in the more sympathetic positions and to be absent from the most negative positions (it was striking that in the non-conformist churches which were part of the survey the ministers were often corporate-analytic while their congregations were personal-literal, personal-questioning, or individual-unreflective types). Nevertheless, the clergy frequently answered questions on behalf of their congregations or in other ways *in role*. They spoke of their concerns for the poor but were unwilling to "burden" their congregations with too frequent reference to the issue.

personal-questioning, institutional-questioning, and corporate-analytical groups all represented.

Neither social position nor denominational membership were thought to be significant factors in determining the different attitudes. Key influences include a person's world view, perception of the church's mission, and the nature of their experience of poverty. In general, an individualist outlook combined with a literal approach to belief tends to characterize people who adopt unsympathetic or neutral stances in relation to poverty and for whom relief of poverty has a relatively low personal priority. By contrast, a corporate outlook combined with the questioning or analytical approach to doctrine tends to be found among people who see the need to explore the structural origins and socioeconomic solutions to poverty and for whom poverty is a central issue of concern. Views on the mission of the church tend to vary depending on the extent to which poverty is perceived as central for the church.

We have in the report some flesh put on the bare bones of our hunches and our anecdotal evidence. We are shown the range of views on poverty and reminded of the range of types of beliefs which are found, not just in different churches but in the same church. We cannot go on teaching without being sensitive to the very different needs which are to be found in our midst, as well as in society as a whole. Not only is there diversity of view but also an absence of any widespread evidence of ability, either among clergy or laypeople, to offer an explanation of why, as a Christian, one should want to behave in particular ways towards others. Linked with this is the almost complete dominance of non-ecclesiastical sources for knowledge and understanding of poverty. What is true in respect to attitudes to the poor is probably the case in other areas of life also.

Some reservations about the results should be noted. It is a pity that none of the views recorded is further contextualized. The impression one has is of individuals wrestling with these issues alone rather than as part of communities, however fragmented. It would have been good to have had further indication of why the researchers thought that class made little difference to attitudes. This is of particular interest to those seeking to assess the extent to which social context determines the particular use of the Bible that is adopted. Also, there is a lack of attention to the process involved in producing the reactions of passive and active coping. Perhaps the way in which poverty is presented disposes receivers to be angry and passive because there is little help offered to enable a recipient of the information to respond with anything other than anger or despair. Little attention is paid in the report itself to the effects on the process of assembling the information because the attitudes of the people interviewed might have been influenced by the interviewers' presence. There is no attempt made to reflect on how people might have reacted and answered *to them*. Finally, much of the report concentrates on what people *say* and not what they actually *do*: how did the interviewees' behavior differ from their attitudes?

The findings of this report demand a careful and circumspect assessment. What follow are some initial reactions. The first demand is for a sense of realism about the task. If this report is at all accurate, then it is necessary to enable use of the Bible in ethics to seek to recognize how little the discourse of Christian tradition informs current practice (at least in this particular area, but there is evidence to suggest that this would extend to matters of personal morality also). That will probably cause little surprise. Anecdotal evidence suggests that even religious "professionals" tend to ignore what they learned about the content and use of the tradition in training in preaching and pastoral work. This seems to be borne out by the study. It is important for the biblical theologian to be realistic about the sort of contribution she or he can make.

2

Although there was little evidence of a systematic presentation of an argument in favor of the preferential option for the poor, respondents often made reference to passages of Scripture. One of the favorites was "the poor you always have with you" (Mark 14:7). The report states that people "commonly referred to this verse but neither the clergy nor the laity were clear as to its precise meaning and varying interpretations were made." Here are a couple of examples:

> I think . . . Jesus did also say, The poor you will always have with you. . . . I found it very depressing, but I also found it encouraging that you really just keep going, you know. . . . I found it quite depressing actually. . . . I thought, why do these people have to go on the dole? But actually, perhaps they don't; perhaps we could work . . . to a better world. Perhaps there will be a better world if we keep on working towards . . . the poor who are always with us . . . sharing together. And why shouldn't we be poor together; yeah, and any way, then he said something about "blessed are the poor in spirit"—so maybe . . . it's a growing thing somehow. Hmmmmm! (Laity)

> Well you see, the first thing that comes to mind with the Bible [is] Christ said that, the poor will always be with you, and I've wrestled with that one. . . . I believe that Christ realized that he

could not get everyone to share so there are always going to be those people who have less than others; I don't know whether that's true. On the other hand I feel that Christ would never have accepted anything other than the ultimate of everyone sharing in everything, so I don't know to be honest . . . (Laity)

The poor are always with us, that is the old Victorian maxim. And I think that is true, because communities are like that. But I'm beginning to feel over some months that there is more that we could and should be doing. I don't quite know what it is. (Laity)

Christ does tell us that the poor will always be with us. He does tell us that we should help the poor, but I would probably put limiting factors on that. (Laity)

The first quotation epitomizes that tortuous attempt to articulate a Christian response to the challenge of poverty which the research suggests was typical of many respondents. There is no doubt about the extent of the concern about poverty among churchgoers, though why this should be, from a theological point of view, and what should be done about it, is much less clear. In *one* sense, the quotations above are all examples of contextual theology, where the Bible has merged into experience. It is a form of theologizing to which I am committed. If (as I happen to believe) all interpretation, in one form or another, manifests the agenda of the modern world, what is the problem with interpretations which adapt a fatalistic attitude in the light of Mark 14:7? Do we just have to admit that where you are and work determines the way you read the Bible and leave it at that?

One contribution of the professional interpreter is to assist with the use of Scripture. In all these cases one can note the way in which the text has been taken out of context, but such a criticism, of course, itself depends upon a hermeneutical method which rejects atomistic exegesis. Attention to the wider context has not been part of the hermeneutical method adopted by Jews and Christians down the centuries. Those who use Mark 14:7 in this way have a long list of patristic and other writers on their side. And yet such use has, within mainstream Christianity, been subordinated to other principles (for example, the rule of faith). The use of Scripture in the liturgy places a question-mark against the wrenching of isolated verses out of their immediate context. Even if hearers of Mark 14:7 might not be expected to know the whole of the Markan context (of which more in a moment), there is a legitimate expectation that they should attend to the story of the anointing, read, as a whole, liturgically.

Then there is the contribution of the professional interpreter of providing allusions to other parts of the Bible. Most readers of the verse who have access to marginal references will note that the words used by Jesus are very similar to those in Deuteronomy 15. In the light of Deuteronomy, Jesus is alerting his hearers to an ongoing obligation. Because of human hardness of heart there will not be a removal of poverty, and so there is a demand for continuous and vigilant action on behalf of the poor and needy. Thus the saying is not an admission of defeat, but a reminder that day in and day out there is to be no grudging attitude, nor "villainous thought," in order to avoid one's obligation. As long as the poor are there, the demand continues.

There are hints in Mark that this obligation is not being met. Indeed, the particular concern with the widow advocated by the Torah (e.g., Deut 14:29 and 16:11) is ignored by those scribes who devour widows' houses (12:40). Immediately following that condemnation is the isolated story of the poor widow who gives her whole livelihood to the Temple, an institution which in the following verses Jesus predicts is destined for destruction (13:2) and judgement (15:38). Is this a condemnation of a religio-political system (and its values) which prompts her action and leaves her a debtor rather than a beneficiary, as the Torah demanded?[4]

Many readers of Mark 14 consider that the disciples have a point: was not giving to the poor precisely what Jesus had enjoined the rich man to do in 10:21? If we have to make choices, shouldn't the poor be given first priority over this costly "wastefulness" (Mark 14:4)? Here the passage stresses the appropriateness of the action, not necessarily because it was a gesture shown to Jesus but because it was the fulfilment of an obligation to a human person, who, according to the beginning and end of this particular story, was being plotted against by a close companion as well as the political authorities. When he died, he was not honored in death—something the memories of Jesus' death indicate was omitted at the time of his burial. It is not a choice between waste and the poor, for Jesus is presenting himself as one who is about to die, "one of the poor—the guest of a leper, headed for death,"[5] to whom respect should be shown. That respect is given in advance by the woman, the ultimate act of consideration for a human person in death.

> To give money to benefit the poor but to refuse to comfort and assist the one right beside you is as wrong as ignoring the agony of the poor of the world in order to concentrate on personal concerns. *Both* public acts of almsgiving *and* private acts of sympathy and compassion are part of the religious

---

4. Myers, *Binding the Strong Man*.
5. Myers, *Binding the Strong Man*, 359.

life—neither one substitutes for the other—and one should not be harassed for doing either.⁶

Also, the carelessness with regard to money here is not out of line with the attitude to money elsewhere in the Gospel. Throughout the Gospel there is an implicit question about the financial and conventional norms which so dominate the horizon of hearers of Mark's narrative and of hearers of the Gospel today (4:18-19; 6:8; 10:17; 12:14-15; 12:41; 14:11). The life of discipleship involves battling with the snares of wealth. It is all part of an alternative perspective on life which Mark's Gospel portrays and is best summarized in 10:42-43 where the disciples want to sit and rule but are only offered baptism and a cup. They have to understand that there is to be a contrast between their nascent, alternative culture and that of the rulers of the earth: "it shall not be so among you" (10:42). Understanding may come about only by leaving everything and following Jesus (1:20; 4:10; cf. 14:10)—something that one rich man finds very difficult to do (10:22)—and may come only when one takes up the cross (8:34 cf. 10:40-45).

3

Another text which was alluded to in the report is Matthew 25:31-46 (a fundamental text for liberation theologians and papal encyclicals, too, of course). The following quotation from *The Gospel, the Poor, and the Churches* is not untypical of use of this text:

> ... We as Christians know that God is a God of judgement, not a God of love (or) not only a God of love. He's a God of judgement and every one of us in this room one day will stand in front of his throne of judgement and answer to what we have done with our life and what we have done to [*sic*] the life of the poor around us. (Laity)

It is quite clear that this passage is being interpreted here in a way which has wide currency in the contemporary church but which differs markedly from the exegetical consensus. Let me say immediately that while I am disposed towards the former view for a variety of reasons— which I am prepared to admit are conditioned in part by an agenda which is external to the text—I want to stay with my prejudices because prejudice in interpretation *may* be able to throw light on the text and enable me to read it from a different perspective.

---

6. Tolbert, "Mark," 271.

In a stimulating article Francis Watson[7] has explored the interface between this aspect of theology and conventional exegesis, ancient and modern, in which he doubts whether this famous text can be appropriately used to justify an option for the poor and outcast. In the essay he wrestles with the concerns that have been around at least since Johannes Weiss: that there is an unbridgeable gulf fixed between theological ethics and exegesis. It is a rich resource and one which would take too long to do justice to it. One paragraph deserves quoting in full as I want to explore in depth the issues it represents:

> In the conventional exegetical procedure the apparent literal sense of this text has to be subordinated to other texts scattered throughout the gospel, a procedure justified by appeal to authorial intention understood as a means of imposing relative unity on apparently heterogeneous material. What appears to be the literal sense of the parable is sacrificed for the sake of the unity of the whole as it is imagined to have existed in its author's mind. "Matthew" may indeed have understood the parable in the restricted sense, but his intention remains a hypothetical entity insufficiently externalized in the actual wording of the text as it stands. In other words, we may appeal to the letter of the text against the author who, absented from his text in the very act of writing, can only be speculatively reunited with his text by an allegorical or spiritualizing reading which seeks to penetrate the letter of the text in pursuit of the more fundamental entity that it is said to conceal: here, an imperfectly expressed authorial intention to which the entire text of the Gospel of Matthew is to be subordinated. But what if the author refuses to play this game? What if, as we tell him what he should have said to make his meaning clearer, he simply refers us back to the text with the words, What I have written, I have written? The hermeneutical principle of the absence of the author from the text is a useful way of countering the reductionist tendency to confine textual meaning to the reconstructed circumstances of origin.[8]

Watson's thesis of setting the text against the author provokes a variety of reflections. There is an implicit criticism of the subservience to the absent author which may at times lead to neglect of the details of the text itself. Watson's major concern is to explore the validity of the liberationists' use of Matthew 25:31–46 as an inclusive challenge to all to minister to the heavenly Son of Man in the needy in the present age. He points to features in the text

---

7. Watson, "Liberating the Reader."
8. Watson, "Liberating the Reader," 65–66.

which deconstruct the neat characterization of the Matthean community on the basis of a simple relationship between text and life and the water-tight notion of purpose which is bound up with a clearly enunciated authorial intention. His hermeneutical strategy is to read Matthew 25:31–46 as prolegomenon to the Passion narrative in which the earthly son of man shows himself in solidarity with the weak and vulnerable.

The force of the exclusive interpretation[9] of "brethren" depends on the data of the text: brethren are frequently disciples; the elect seem to have already been separated from the nations in 24:31; and the end of the mission discourse in 10:42 seems to indicate that the little ones—so similar, in many ways, to the least of the brethren of 25:40 and 25:45—who are to receive the cup of water are the disciples. In 10:42 there seems to be an interpretative guide to the identity of the brethren.

One can see why Matthew 10:42 has been seen as the hermeneutical key that unlocks the interpretation of 25:31–46. Giving a cup of cold water to the little ones echoes quenching the thirsty. What is more, the little ones and the least of these my brethren, have been linked at least from the time the Western manuscript tradition replaced μικρῶν τούτων by ἐλαχίστων. Several factors need to be considered. First of all, we note the change of person in 10:41 as compared with the previous verse. If the disciples are still being addressed, why the change? Secondly, the parallel with Mark 9:41 is instructive. Mark's version identifies those who are to receive the drink of water with the disciples: "Whoever gives you a drink of water because you belong to the messiah, I tell you, will not lose their reward." Even if we suppose that Matthew is not directly dependent on Mark here and has used an independent tradition that he has preferred to Mark, it is still true that the Matthaean version makes no explicit link between the little ones and the disciples. I recognize that such a comparison, standard fare in Gospel study, is a form of canonical criticism which may not be entirely appropriate for a narrative approach, and that another interpretative maneuver is being embarked on here. At the very least we can see in Mark a stage in the identification of children with disciples. Luke 17:1 has not yet reached it, and I am not convinced that Matthew has either.

So one might question whether it is obvious that the little ones here are disciples. Matthew 18 has often seemed to point in the direction of an identification of disciples with the little ones, but even there one may have pause for thought. In Chapter 18, children are offered as the models to those who are called to be disciples because they are the ones whose particular perspective allows them to recognize Jesus when others who should have

---

9. Well set out, for example, in Stanton, *Gospel.*

known better fail to recognize him (21:16; cf. 11:25–26). So the reference to little ones in 18:5 cannot readily be equated with the twelve disciples[10] (though it is intimately linked with the understanding of the character of true discipleship, for which the child is held up as the type).

If we follow Watson's principle of setting the letter of the text against an allegorizing interpretation[11] that allows the "hidden" story of community and author to place constraints upon the literal sense of the chapter, the identification of the μικροί with Christian disciples in Chapter 18 becomes less clear. While that other dimension of interpretation may make us sensitive to the imagined needs of Matthew and his world, the letter of the text does not *demand* the "ecclesial" interpretation as the only possible reading, and it presses us to recognize that whatever "internal" concerns may be inherent in the narrative and in its hypothetical original setting, the literal sense challenges the reader to identify with the child as an example of messianic humility. Meg Davies has put the point well with regard to Matthew 18: "making children exemplary for disciples does not imply that [disciples] should become childish, but that they should assume the social powerlessness of children. Children had no economic independence and were dependent on their parents for their survival. The disciples' leadership was not to mimic the powerful but the powerless."[12]

I am not saying that I can demonstrate that Matthew's Gospel is more inclusive in its attitude to the weak and outcasts than much mainstream exegesis has allowed. The points made by opponents of the inclusive interpretation are weighty and reflect strands in Matthew's narrative. My point is rather different and echoes the point made by Francis Watson: the text of Matthew, through all the vicissitudes of its narrative, does not allow the reader to rest confident that she or he can be assured of ultimate vindication. Possibly, Matthew the evangelist wanted to say this (though I am not convinced that this was the case). In contrast with the eschatological passages from contemporary texts, which seem to manifest a self-assured belief in the ultimate salvation for

---

10. Despite the Christian flavor of the words in 18:6, the phrase τῶν πιστευόντων εἰς ἐμέ is unique here in Matthew, where belief and confession are not confined to disciples (who are portrayed as betraying and forsaking Jesus). Πιστεύω is only used in this type of phrase in a variant at Matt 27:42. Elsewhere (8:13; 9:28; 21:22, 25, 32; 24:23, 26) it seems to have the force of trust rather than membership of a community of faith based on a christological confession.

11. Some forms of historical criticism that rely on the reconstruction of another story "behind" the literal sense of the text (authorial intention, community struggles, historical Jesus, etc.) have an uncanny resemblance to ancient allegorical exegesis. The major difference, of course, is the referent of the hidden story. See the suggestive comments of Barr, "Biblical Scholarship"; cf. Childs, "Critical Reflections."

12. Davies, *Matthew*, 127.

their readers, Matthew's Gospel is much more ambiguous in refusing to allow its readers to be complacent in the face of judgement.[13]

If Matthew 25:31–46 was the high point of the New Testament's teaching on attitudes to the poor, it might appear to endorse the view that alleviation of the symptoms of poverty was all that was required, and a challenge to the causes of poverty was not to be contemplated. To put it another way, Helder Camara's oft quoted dictum ("If I give food to the poor, they call me a saint; if I ask why the poor have no food, they call me a communist") might seem to apply to the New Testament teaching—but only its first part. There is charity in plenty, but the critique of an unjust society seems to be absent from its pages. Or, to put it in the words of Meg Davies from elsewhere in this collection,[14] the New Testament is replete with "a charity of consumption" but lacks any recipe for "a charity of production."[15] Such charity would not begin to be addressed until the emergence of a cenobitic monasticism within Christianity.

We should not neglect the apocalyptic tradition in Revelation and elsewhere. What we have in the apocalyptic texts is what I have described elsewhere as an unmasking of reality in which the true character of institutions is revealed.[16] It is something that is not confined to Revelation alone and is to be found also in the virulent critique of wealth in the later chapters of 1 Enoch.[17] The critique of Babylon in Revelation 18 is an *economic* critique,[18] and that of the Temple in Mark's Gospel is arguably one that does not fail to stress its part in ignoring the needs of the needy like

---

13. Stanton, *Gospel*, 228–29: "Jewish and Christian writers turned to apocalyptic in periods of historical crisis and trauma. Apocalyptic regularly functions as consolation for groups which perceive themselves to be under duress. Apocalyptic language is also often used to reinforce attitudes of group solidarity among minority groups at odds with society at large; clear lines are drawn between 'insiders' and 'outsiders.' This is the social setting of the passages from 4 Ezra, 2 Baruch, and 1 Enoch. . . . It is also the social setting of the book of Revelation which announces judgement and doom for the powerful and complacent and in so doing provides hope of ultimate vindication for the powerless and oppressed people of God. Matt 25:31–46 comes from a similar social setting and was intended to function similarly for the first recipients of the gospel."

14. "This collection" is a reference to the set of essays edited by John Rogerson et al., *The Bible and Ethics*, in which both this essay and Davies, "Work and Slavery" appear.—Ed.

15. Davies, "Work and Slavery," 316. Cf. Rowland, *Christian Origins*, 368 n. 6; and de Ste. Croix, *Class Struggle*, 419.

16. E.g., in Rowland, *Liberating Exegesis*, 131–33; also Wengst, *Pax Romana*.

17. Discussed in the context of Luke's Gospel in Esler, *Community and Gospel*. See also Moxnes, *Economy of the Kingdom*; and Johnson, *Sharing Possessions*.

18. Bauckham, "Economic Critique."

widows.[19] Similarly, the political dimension of the language about the powers and the change which is wrought via Christ's redemption has been stressed in recent study.[20] Nevertheless, we are still at the level of protest with little of the detailed prescription for a charity of production that would enable a different pattern of production and exchange.

The Gospel, the Poor, and the Churches is a survey of attitudes, and we need to recognize that there is evidence to suggest that there is a gap between attitudes and behavior. So, whatever their attitudes, people dig into their pockets in a very generous way when confronted by human need. The position of manifest concern is one that the aid agencies and the high profile given to the tragedies in Eritrea, Somalia, and Rwanda have done much to form. While there is clearly enormous concern about the poor (more particularly abroad than at home) people often find themselves at a loss to know how to respond theologically. Now in using the term "theological," I am not meaning at a level of sophistication appropriate to monographs and journals. Rather, I am thinking of the incapacity of people to respond as they would like, as ordinary followers of Christ. It is the frustration that is the lot of anyone who longs to be more literate and articulate, to be able to understand in a way in which instincts nurtured in the heart of the church would suggest. The dearth of theological resources known to be available or able to be retrieved is striking and represents a serious challenge to all of us in theological education. Familiar passages from Scripture may be quoted, but the allusions are peripheral to the basic instinct to be concerned and to want to do something. The backing of the tradition is often elicited from memory by inquirers who possess an inkling of the extent of the biblical or theological basis for the position adopted. Paul had to write and offer a rationale to the Corinthians and Romans for the collection for the poor in Jerusalem. Many contemporary Christians are searching for a language to explain, justify, and understand a much more ready response. That something must be done is not in doubt. But why (and how)? Ours may not seem to be the situation of those first Gentile Christians, for whom the whole concept of an international collection for the poor (rather than the rich) would have been quite foreign, and, as a result, needed a Paul to explain to them why it should be done. But perhaps like them we need to be persuaded that such international concern is theologically and morally grounded?

As attempts are made to offer some explanation, we know that the appeal to favorite proof-texts will not do. Something more profound is

---

19. Myers, *Binding the Strong Man*; Belo, *Materialist Readings*; Clévenot, *Materialist Approaches*.

20. E.g., Wink, *Naming the Powers*; Wink, *Unmasking the Powers*; and Wink, *Engaging the Powers*.

required. We find in the biblical texts often apparently conforming and compromised texts alongside the clarion calls to liberation and option for the poor. The temptation to read the texts in ways which suit us is one thing which exegesis has always sought to avert. Such a remedy to deal with self-indulgent reading is a necessary companion to the slow task of exploring whether and in what way Scripture can inform the judgments of people who long to act in defense of the poor, and to be in solidarity with them, or even have only the vaguest inkling that the ordering of the world is unjust but cannot quite articulate why.

Bibliography

Barr, James. "The Literal, the Allegorical, and Modern Biblical Scholarship." *Journal for the Study of the Old Testament* 14.44 (1989) 3–17.

Bauckham, Richard. "The Economic Critique of Rome." In *Images of Empire*, edited by Loveday Alexander, 47–91. Journal for the Study of the Old Testament Supplement Series 122. Sheffield: JSOT Press, 1991.

Belo, Fernando. *A Materialist Reading of the Gospel of Mark*. Translated by Matthew J. O'Connell. Maryknoll, NY: Orbis, 1981.

Childs, B. S. "Critical Reflections on James Barr's Understanding of the Literal and the Allegorical." *Journal for the Study of the Old Testament* 15.46 (1990) 3–9.

Clévenot, Michel. *Materialist Approaches to the Bible*. Translated by William J. Nottingham. Maryknoll, NY: Orbis, 1985.

Davies, Margaret. *Matthew*. Readings—A New Biblical Commentary. Sheffield: JSOT Press, 1993.

———. "Work and Slavery in the New Testament: Impoverishments of Traditions." In *The Bible in Ethics: The Second Sheffield Colloquium*, edited by John W. Rogerson et al., 315–47. Journal for the Study of the Old Testament Supplement Series 207. Sheffield: Sheffield Academic, 1995.

Esler, Philip Francis. *Community and Gospel in Luke–Acts*. Society for New Testament Studies Monograph Series 57. Cambridge: Cambridge University Press, 1987.

Johnson, Luke Timothy. *Sharing Possessions: What Faith Demands*. 2nd ed. Grand Rapids: Eerdmans, 2011.

Moxnes, Halvor. *The Economy of the Kingdom: Social Conflict and Economic Relations in Luke's Gospel*. Overtures to Biblical Theology 23. Philadelphia: Fortress, 1988. Reprint, Eugene, OR: Wipf & Stock, 2004.

Myers, Ched. *Binding the Strong Man: A Political Reading of Mark's Story of Jesus*. Maryknoll, NY: Orbis, 1988.

Rogerson, John, et al., eds. *The Bible in Ethics: The Second Sheffield Colloquium*. Journal for the Study of the Old Testament Supplement Series 207. Sheffield: Sheffield Academic, 1995.

Rowland, Christopher. *Christian Origins: From Messianic Movement to Christian Religion*. Minneapolis: Augsburg, 1985.

Rowland, Christopher, and Mark Corner. *Liberating Exegesis: The Challenge of Liberation Theology to Biblical Studies*. Louisville: Westminster John Knox, 1989.

Spencer, Liz, and Dawn Snape. *The Gospel, the Poor, and the Churches: A Research Study Carried Out for Christian Aid*. London: Christian Aid, 1994.

Stanton, Graham N. *A Gospel for a New People: Studies in Matthew*. Louisville: Westminster John Knox, 1993.

De Ste. Croix, G. E. M. *The Class Struggle in the Ancient Greek World*. Ithaca: Cornell University Press, 1981.

Tolbert, Mary Ann. "Mark." In *The Women's Bible Commentary*, edited by Carol A. Newsom and Sharon H. Ringe, 263–74. Louisville: Westminster John Knox, 1992.

Watson, Francis. "Liberating the Reader: A Theological-Exegetical Study of the Parable of the Sheep and the Goats (Matt 25:31–46)." In *The Open Text: New Directions for Biblical Studies?*, edited by Francis Watson, 57–84. London: SCM, 1993.

———, ed. *The Open Text: New Directions for Biblical Studies?* London: SCM, 1993.

Wengst, Klaus. *Pax Romana: And the Peace of Jesus Christ*. Translated by John Bowden. Philadelphia: Fortress, 1987.

Wink, Walter. *Engaging the Powers: Discernment and Resistance in a World of Domination*. The Powers 3. Minneapolis: Fortress, 1992.

———. *Naming the Powers: The Language of Power in the New Testament*. The Powers 1. Philadelphia: Fortress, 1984.

———. *Unmasking the Powers: The Invisible Forces that Determine Human Existence*. The Powers 2. Philadelphia: Fortress, 1986.

9

Reflections on the Politics of the Gospels

IN THIS ESSAY I want to consider three related issues which have had important implications for the discussion of Christianity and politics: the character of the kingdom of God, the relationship between history and eschatology, and the appropriateness of speaking of the political involvement of Jesus in the accounts as we have them of Jesus' activity in the New Testament.

1

Eschatology achieved prominence in modern theology because exegetes of the New Testament became convinced that the best way to understand one of its key concepts was in the light of future hopes of Judaism. So, from being something of an afterthought in Christian theology, nineteenth-century New Testament scholarship began to demand that eschatology be placed at the center. At the heart of this view of eschatology is the notion of the imminent irruption of God into the old order and the establishment of a new creation. On the basis of his exegesis of the New Testament, Johannes Weiss concluded that Jesus expected the coming of the kingdom in the near future, a cataclysmic event in which humanity had little or no part to play. He recognized that such a view, rooted in first-century eschatological beliefs, was unpalatable to the theological humanism of his day. Weiss (and Albert Schweitzer after him) placed eschatology at the center of the New Testament message. In the work of both, Jesus was portrayed as a proclaimer of the imminence of God's transcendent kingdom. Their picture of Jesus was of the single-minded apocalyptic zealot whose whole outlook was dominated by the coming of this future new age. They argued that this fervent belief dominated the outlook of the first Christians too. To a significant degree the story of the emergence of early Christianity involved coming to terms with frustrated and disappointed hopes. New Testament theology in the twentieth century has involved attempts to come to terms with these theories.

It is a mark of the greatness of Albert Schweitzer's creative genius that I like many others find myself interacting with his portrait of Jesus. Schweitzer argued that Jesus expected the imminent inbreaking of God's kingdom. When he sent out the Twelve on their missionary enterprise, he did not expect them back in the present age for he expected the kingdom of God to come before their return.[1] When they did return, however, Jesus came to see that it was necessary for him to share the suffering which would have to precede the coming of the kingdom. That meant a journey to Jerusalem to die, the necessary prelude to the glorious reign of God, according to the eschatological hopes of ancient Judaism.

For all its shortcomings this portrait has the merit of taking seriously those twin themes of the Gospels: the cross and the kingdom. It portrays Jesus as one who wrestles with the circumstances confronting him so that eschatological beliefs he inherited and was convinced were realized in his activity were refracted through the lens of the social realities which confronted him. Jesus is presented as one committed to the kingdom but recognizing the cost to himself that this realization involved, faced as he was with opposition and rejection of his message. There is an acceptance of the reality of the struggle and turmoil which must be gone through. In it there is little disillusionment (until the very end) and certainly no easy optimism. Jesus may, in Schweitzer's words, be crushed by the wheel of the world which he seeks to move in order to bring this age to its close.[2] Yet the costly commitment to a different vision, and the hope that the brutality of the reality of opposition need not always be so, is an inspiration for faith. Schweitzer asserts that the continued relevance of Jesus lies in the espousal of hope which enables a critical distance from the institutions of the present and at the same time a universal applicability of the "one great man." Paradoxically, in Schweitzer's view, the hope for the future guarantees that this message will go on challenging every generation:

> Men [and women] feared that to admit the claims of eschatology would abolish the significance of His words for our times; and

1. Schweitzer, *Quest*, 357.
2. Schweitzer, *Quest*, 368.

hence there was a feverish eagerness to discover in them any elements that might be considered not eschatologically conditioned. When any sayings were found of which the wording did not absolutely imply an eschatological connection, there was great jubilation—these at least had been saved from the coming debacle. But in reality that which is eternal in the words of Jesus is due to the very fact that they are based on an eschatological world-view and contain the expression of a mind for which the contemporary world with its historical and social circumstances no longer had any existence. They are appropriate, therefore, to any world for in every world they raise the man [and woman] who dares to meet their challenge, and does not turn and twist them into meaninglessness, above [their] world and time, making [them] inwardly free, so that [they are] fitted to be, in [their] own world and time, a simple channel of the power of Jesus.[3]

Schweitzer's portrayal of Jesus is provocative and perhaps even alarming. It prompts the question: if Jesus was so misguided about his expectations, how can Christians go on having faith in such a figure or even make much sense of a life which was so determined by such an unswerving, perhaps fanatical, expectation? There are obviously passages (though few in number) which indicate a hope that the coming kingdom of God would not be long delayed. Mark 9:1 (cf. 13:30) is a good example of this kind of passage. It seems to indicate that at some point in his career Jesus seriously anticipated a manifestation of the hoped-for age of perfection either in his lifetime or that of his followers. While it seems to me important to recognize this probability, this should not necessarily lead us to the dramatic conclusion that Jesus was utterly mistaken. The presentation of that hope in the New Testament demands of us a more nuanced approach.

The way in which New Testament eschatology is formulated in the Pauline Letters may help the way in which we approach the material in the Gospels. The difference in the intensity of eschatological expectation and the extent of its coverage in the Letters have long been a matter for comment. The diminution of the raw expectation of the Thessalonian letters led to the view that there was an evolution in Paul's eschatological beliefs from the Jewish apocalypticism of his early career to a less sectarian and warmer universalism later in life. In occasional pieces the specific circumstances determined the extent and shape of the eschatological language used. The (probably early) Galatians has little reference to the future hope mainly because the concern is to stress what believers already possess. In the later Philippians a conventional expectation is to be found alongside a more

---

3. Schweitzer, *Quest*, 400.

individual offer of communion with the Messiah continuing after death. The variety of eschatological formulations is the result of the influence of circumstances on eschatological terms.[4]

The important insight that circumstances determine ideas is a salutary reminder when we turn to the eschatological expectation of the Gospels. Here, of course, we are faced with a problem. The presentation of the life of Jesus may itself in each particular case reflect the circumstances of each evangelist. Thus, it is something of a commonplace in New Testament studies that the Fourth Evangelist has a diminished sense of the cosmic eschatological cataclysm and replaces it by the present crisis confronting the world in the Word become flesh.[5] In a different way Luke diminishes preoccupation with the end of the age by the insertion of the study of the church into the saga he wishes to tell, thus enabling concentration on the present task. Also, despite its increased incidence of eschatological material the Gospel of Matthew combats complacency and demands recognition of the apocalyptic Son of man in the mundane and insignificant person of the poor (Matt 25:31–46). Mark too refuses to allow the satisfaction of a consolatory eschatology in which imminent expectation removes the need for the difficulties and complexities of the response in present circumstances.

The need for sensitivity to the context in which we find eschatological material in the Gospels is an essential prerequisite for interpreting the eschatological discourses in the Synoptic Gospels. They must not be separated from the narrative of Jesus' proclamation and inauguration of the reign of God. It is that context which is necessary to prevent the discourse about the future from becoming the goal of the narrative. Discipleship involves sharing the way of the cross of the Son of man as he goes up to Jerusalem. What is offered the disciple is the sharing of the cup of suffering of the Son of man rather than the promise of sitting at his right hand and his left when he reigns on earth. It is not that this request is repudiated but, as the eschatological discourse makes plain, there can be no escape from the painful reality of the present witness with its need to endure the tribulations which precede the vindication. That is the challenge which faces those who wish to live out the messianic narrative in their own lives; no shortcuts to the messianic reign are to be found here. It is easy to see how the discourse materials in the Gospels can be extracted from their narrative context and function as instructions which abstract the reader from the challenge of facing the cost of the shadow of suffering and martyrdom.

4. Bammel and Moule, eds., *New Testament Interpretation*.

5. See Ashton, *Understanding the Fourth Gospel*; and Ashton, *Understanding the Fourth Gospel* (2nd ed.).

The narrative framework of the Gospels is a necessary medium for understanding the eschatology. In taking sayings of Jesus out of context we risk being left with no setting other than that offered by the reconstruction of the exegete. The task of getting back to the original historical setting of a saying may be an appropriate one, but can it really be allowed to override the guidance for a Christian interpretation given by the narrative contexts of the Gospels? In saying this I realize that I am in some respects turning my back on the hermeneutics of suspicion of nearly two hundred years of exegesis which refuses to remain content with the ideological distortions which the original process of production brought about. I do not want to return to a simplistic acceptance of the text as sole determinant. Nevertheless, suspicion about the fragmentary character of our information about the original settings of Jesus' sayings places inevitable limits on the amount of reliance we can place on our critical reconstructions.

We would all like to know exactly in what situation Mark 9:1 or Luke 11:20 was uttered or whether Jesus ever uttered anything like the discourse now found in Mark 13 and parallels. Amidst such uncertainty the resort to speculative alternative contexts tends to displace the narrative context of the sayings which offers crucial guidance for interpretation. The circumstances in which a particular saying is imbedded do matter. Not that this will always facilitate precise exegesis: Mark 9:1 remains as much of an enigma in its context as it does when treated in isolation. What the narrative framework does demand of us, however, is a recognition that the setting of a saying in the presentation of Jesus' short career changed dramatically. The situation in the last days in Jerusalem was very different from the heady optimism of the signs and wonders which accompanied the proclamation of the good news in Galilee. The triply attested eschatological discourse with its dark prognostications is to be read in light of the failure to win over Jerusalem and its hierarchy and the enigmatic but emphatic denunciation of the Temple. Mark 13 does not offer general predictions about the end of the world nor is it full of glib promises (Jesus had already refused to grant these in Mark 10:38–52; cf. Luke 22:24–71). In the wake of the "failure" in Jerusalem to win over the city the mood changes, and so does the character of the eschatology. That is not to deny the hints of a less happy outcome before this. It has been a realistic possibility as far back as Mark 3:6.

In the Synoptic discourses there is in fact very little attempt made to sketch the ideal society, a mark of either a lack of any political realism or of a merely utopian outlook. One of the problems of Utopianism is that it can lead the reader into construction of ideal worlds which distract him or her from the demands of the present. Utopianism can lead to an escape from reality however much its attempts betoken that yearning for something better. Writers who resort to utopianism do so as a compensation for the inability to do anything about the world as it is. Early Christian writers prefer to hint at their conviction that one is coming without being too precise about what it will involve. It is the language of myth and metaphor which is to the fore rather than the offering of any detailed political manifesto. It is about the beyond in the sense that it is both future and different from the patterns of society currently on offer. To speak of it, therefore, demands a language which is both less precise and yet more potent and suggestive, a language which after all is what is appropriate when one sets out to speak of that which is still to come.

The book of Revelation offers us a timely reminder in its own form about supposing that its preoccupation with eschatological matters offers an opportunity to avoid the more challenging preoccupations of the present. Thus, the vision of hope inaugurated by the exaltation of the Lamb is set within the framework of the Letters to the Seven Churches. Even if we can discern a preponderance of "religious" issues in these letters (warnings against false teaching, suspicion of false prophecy, loss of an initial religious enthusiasm), we should probably regard the issues being touched on here as typical of a complacent second-generation religious movement. Christianity appears to be making too many accommodations with the surrounding culture, and it needs to be brought back once again to its countercultural affirmation in the light of its witness to the new age. Thus the promise of a part in the New Jerusalem is linked with present behavior. The readers of the Apocalypse are not allowed to dream about millennial bliss without being brought face-to-face with the obstacles which stand in the way of its fulfilment and the costly part to be played by them in that process.

What the narrative of the Gospels demands of us is the recognition that the circumstances changed rapidly. The message of the kingdom of God in deed and word met by a popular response contrast with the very different reality confronting Jesus in the hostility, attempts on his life, and perceived disaffection among members of his circle. That change conditions the character of the eschatological pronouncement. Judgement, doom, pain, and the need to endure take the place of practical demonstrations of divine sovereignty in the present. Of course, the two are not mutually exclusive. It is not the case of realism displacing a naive belief in human perfectibility. The extent of the need and the resources of divine healing of the God who reigns do not disappear merely because they are confronted by the recalcitrance of the politically powerful. The agent of God's reign meets the apparently immovable force of the status quo. Something has to give: it appears to be the former rather than the latter, though the final verses of Mark's Gospel suggest another ending (15:38). In the changed circumstances of reduced opportunities and lack of faith other priorities take their place. The commitments and opportunities of Galilee remain; the program of God's reign is one to be entered into by all who will. Yet consistent refusal to do so does not mean the extinction of its influence. As Amos put it centuries before to those who refused to accept the Lord who came, the Day of the Lord was gloom and judgement not joy and bliss.

2

The importance of Schweitzer's presentation is that he exploits to the full that contrast between the early and late parts of the narrative of Jesus' life in the Gospels. He looks for an explanation of the journey to Jerusalem and the suffering in a changed eschatological perspective. In Schweitzer's presentation Jesus' outlook is still dominated by an eschatological program, so that one still has to reckon with the problem of Jesus being mistaken in his expectation. While I think that there are enough indications to suggest that Jesus' expectation about the coming of the kingdom of God may have at certain stages of his career been over-optimistic, it seems to me that it is too simple to describe Jesus' outlook as false or mistaken merely on the basis of two or three sayings. In suggesting this I do not want to be seen as trying to protect Jesus from error. I am quite prepared to believe that Jesus entertained expectations which may have been mistaken. Rather I think that we should follow the directions given to us by Schweitzer and engage with the complexities of the narrative presentation which indicate subtle shifts in the presentation of Jesus' eschatology.

What is most striking about the New Testament is that the present is seen as a time of fulfilment. The significance the present is so integral to the understanding of God's propitious time that history is the arena for eschatologically significant actions. In the New Testament the present becomes a moment of opportunity for transforming the imperfect into the perfect; history and eschatology become inextricably intertwined, and the elect stand on the brink of the new age itself. A feature of New Testament study has been the way in which the stress there on the fulfilment of the ultimate purposes of God has reduced interest in present history. Given that the age to come was nearer than it seemed, so the argument runs, there was little point in trying to change society as it was. When the kingdoms of this world would shortly become the kingdom under the lordship of Christ then human endeavor to wrest them from the grip of the ruler of the present evil age seemed either presumptuous or unnecessary. Political activity on the part of those committed to the coming of the kingdom is at best limited. Radical change is in the hands of the God who will supernaturally intervene to establish the kingdom. Humankind is merely a passive spectator of a vast divine drama with the cosmos as its stage. With their eyes so firmly fixed on what is to come, the early Christians had little concern for ordinary human history.

Such a dichotomy between history and eschatology is not entirely borne out by the ancient documents themselves. It was certainly a matter of debate between the first Christians and their Jewish contemporaries whether the promises were near to fulfilment. This was a basic issue which separated them. But it is important that we be clear that *this* was the issue. The Christians did not abandon a hope for this world. Early Christian and Jewish writings offer a this-worldly hope which did not consist only of a cataclysmic irruption from the world beyond and the destruction of the present world for the manifestation of the divine righteousness. When we recognize that the teaching in the New Testament, particularly that attributed to Jesus, is about the ideals applicable to God's reign *on earth*, the New Testament writings can certainly be seen as the struggles of those who looked forward to a new age but also recognized the obligation to live in the present *as if* they were living in the age to come.

In this, human beings thought of themselves as the agents of God's eschatological purposes. We can see this in the story of Jesus of Nazareth, and he proclaims the present as decisive in God's purposes and himself as the messianic agent for change. The carefully constructed entry into Jerusalem signifies the risk of deeming the present moment in history as ultimately significant. Similarly, Paul of Tarsus took upon himself as the result of his deep-seated convictions the role of the divine agent through whom the eschatological act of offering the gospel to the nations could be completed. The central theme of the New Testament, therefore, is of human agency as a central means of eschatological fulfilment.

As harbingers of God's propitious moment, the New Testament actors are hardly ideal role models for Christians who seek to muddle along trying to make the best of the old eon. One can understand why reserve is expressed towards a close alignment with historical projects which take sides in contemporary political struggles. After all, how can one be sure that they are of God rather than marked with the sign of the Beast? We may be less troubled if we retain a clear contrast between history and eschatology, the latter being conceived as something totally *beyond* history. Such a view is one that all too easily bolsters conservatism in church and academy. If we can only see life as consisting of different shades of grey, we may well be reluctant to take sides in struggles for justice, thereby helping to support those structures of society and patterns of relating more or less as they are.

There may be a way of dealing with this dilemma. The question is whether there is a comprehensive enough hermeneutic of suspicion which recognizes that those who profess themselves to be children of light cannot but be infected with the reign of darkness, living as they do in the midst of the old order. The reign of God has not come in all its fullness. To behave as if it had is itself a denial of the reality of evil and the extent of the struggle. Confronting the powers of the old order in the name of the new and naming the Antichrist necessarily involves the potential, indeed the reality, of the demonic within ourselves. Merely "demonizing" one's opponents can be accompanied by a self-righteous attitude which lapses into perfectionism. That itself can lead to destruction rather than the restoration which comes from God. The children of light can see themselves as the appointed agents of the divine will; matters begin to be sharply defined and the division between good and evil clearly seen. But there is no guarantee of clarity this side of the millennium. Yet the difficulty of certainty and the risk of a nostalgia for a past where greater clarity seems to be found than is actually the case should not prevent action. Jeremiah's words about the deceitfulness of the human heart (Jer 17:9) are particularly apposite for those who espouse righteous causes. Confronting the powers and the demons in others and in the institutions of church and state must be accompanied by the co-operative task of confronting them and struggling with them in ourselves. That will be a co-operative and communal task in which critical testing will help to prevent brutal shortcuts to perfection. Individual champions of sacred causes who feel the need to leave behind the critical support of the people of God are particularly vulnerable to self-deception. But to be honest about that does not diminish the importance of the task of the church to confront the powers in conformity with the ministry of Jesus.

In the old order Christianity must be a religion constantly dissatisfied with its attempts to realize the kingdom. The problem with any kind of realized eschatology (and also revolutionary activity, as Barth pointed out) is that it misses the central point that we live still in the midst of the old eon. We need to give an account of our hope but recognize that our articulation of it in word and deed is necessarily fragmentary and partial. Study of the chiliastic tradition in all its dimensions illustrates the perpetual danger that it encourages naive optimism. As Engels rightly pointed out with regard to the religious revolutionaries of the sixteenth and seventeenth centuries, they had the right ideas but wrongly believed that they could actualize them at the wrong time. The activities of those like Müntzer, who were confident in the rectitude of their ideas but ignorant of the political possibilities, were in fact profoundly reactionary. They offer a salutary message to all those who believe that activism in itself will guarantee eschatological success. To be aware of the dangers, however, is not the same as relegating such views to the mistakes of Christian discipleship, simply because of the breadth of their vision and the earnestness of their hope.

The New Testament seems to speak of a cataclysmic "irruption" from heaven, a supernatural intervention. But we need to beware of an over-literal interpretation of this in the Gospels and elsewhere. There are questions to be asked about the legacy of an interpretation of eschatology which is so pervasive in twentieth-century New Testament study. Is it really appropriate to speak of Jesus expecting some "supernatural" intervention? Indeed, how far is talk of "direct intervention" and supernatural occurrence part of the way in which we have sought to make sense of the metaphorical language of Jewish and Christian eschatological discourse? This kind of separation between present history and future eschatology is not borne out by the ancient texts themselves. Life in heaven is the ultimate destiny of the cosmos when God will be all in all. The evocation of this demands the colorful, the spectacular, and the bizarre, in order to convey the tremendous character of that which is hoped for. There is at times a woodenness about our treatment of eschatological language. Nowhere in the interpretation of the New Testament are we more guilty of a simplistic literalism. The language of myth and parable can have a historical referent but remain allusive in precisely what it specifies. That is appropriate for that which is to come, which defies our feeble attempts to encapsulate it.

There is a wider issue here which has been touched on in recent theology but has received too little attention in twentieth-century exegesis. There has been a growing criticism of the dualistic notions which undergird post-Enlightenment philosophy and theology. That critique applies to questions of biblical exegesis also. The discussion of eschatology by Weiss makes a clear distinction between God's work and human activity. We are told that there was an ancient Jewish view of the kingdom of God. We are told it is entirely transcendent; its coming is God's task alone. Here there are two histories: salvation history and secular history which only partially overlap. The reconstruction of ancient Jewish and early Christian eschatology took place in an intellectual climate where the contrast between God and the world, the sacred and the secular, was a typical way of viewing reality and God's relationship to history. The otherworldly imminent expectation has seemed to be an unchallengeable "scientific" finding of modern critical exegesis. Yet the texts themselves as well as the attention given to the philosophical context in the history of interpretation demand that we think again. The inbreaking of what appears to be "beyond" into history is at the heart of what traditional theology asserts about the resurrection of Jesus and the experience of the Spirit. The intertwining of history and eschatology is at the heart of what is distinctive about the first Christians' interpretation of the Jewish tradition and their attachment to the story of Jesus. The modern tendency to polarize eschatology and history, the transcendent and the material, God and humanity, ignores the stubborn refusal of the Bible to draw such hard-and-fast lines between them. The expression of the Christian hope in the form of the tension between the now and the not yet refuses to push eschatology and the transcendent into some other realm but demands that the present is seen as a time of eschatological significance.

Liberation theologians like Gustavo Gutiérrez have added their voices in rejecting the dualism which subtly distances God from the world and salvation from human liberation and the sacred from the secular. For them there is *one* history, and the desire to speak of God in relationship to some special sphere of existence is a product of a philosophical era where such dualism pervades our thought. That insistence on present history as the arena of the manifestation of the reign of God in the needs of the poor and the vulnerable is their distinctive contribution. That emphasis on history and the eschatological significance of the present has meant that leading liberation theologians are sometimes charged with naive optimism in their hopes for humanity. There is, however, a consistent renunciation of projects which are unrelated to political circumstances. There is little in liberation theology to suggest that their links with the reality which surrounds them are in fact so tenuous that a fantasy of a grassroots revolution, a modern-day holy war, could ever be nurtured uncritically. They have seen the human cost of so-called sacred causes and are in the business of mitigating their effects. Most are engaged in costly small-scale protests and programs at the grassroots to offer glimpses of God's eschatological kingdom amidst the injustices of the old order. The centrality of the portrait of the Synoptic Jesus in the theology of liberation places a clear constraint on the fantastic and unreal and demands of those who believe that the kingdom impinges on the life of the present the recognition that such commitment usually ends up with a cross rather than the millennium.

In recognizing the eschatological tension, however, we must not subordinate the story and practice of our hope, admittedly mind-blowing in its extent and quality, to a secular realism which is reductionist in character. The central parts of the story we tell raise questions about a version of history which maintains the status quo by closing off the possibilities which the inauguration of the kingdom of God opened up. History is always, of course, a problematic term; it presupposes a view and a particular narrative. The Christian narrative of the past does not render the arena of history unnecessary. It offers a perspective for making sense of the world, its past, present, and future in the light of a particular set of memories focused on the life, death, and resurrection of Jesus. The answer is not to look merely beyond history to some transcendental world. Rather, it demands that we remain ever open to possibilities for change, however dramatic and beyond our comprehension they may be, in accord with the spirit of the justice and mercy of God which indeed pass our understanding. Above all at the heart of the story is one who suffered at the hands of those who sought to maintain conventional political activity in their own interest. The commemoration of Jesus involves continued identification with those in whom the risen Christ meets us in his real presence in our day: the despised, the needy, and the vulnerable.

3

The politics of the New Testament has been a subject of intense debate in the last thirty years or so, as political theology has been very much in vogue. It is impossible to abstract the story of Jesus from a political framework without irredeemably reducing its significance. The use of phrases like "social activist" and "political campaigner" to describe Jesus in the Gospel narratives is misleading without a word of qualification. The character of political life in Judea and Galilee in Jesus' day was neither political in the entirely secular sense of modern political life nor was it in any sense open or democratic. The framework provided for political activity in the time of Jesus was a despotic royal court (that of Herod Antipas) and a colonial power in Judea (Rome). There was little room for formal political activity for an artisan like Jesus.

Yet Jesus' mission is thoroughly imbued with an understanding of polity which was rooted in a theocratic tradition derived from the Bible. To claim to be messiah, to promote that claim actively as he did when he entered Jerusalem and the Temple, and to conduct himself in the way in which he is described in the Gospels are political in the broadest sense of that word and constitute a campaign which may have been vague in detail but not without premeditation. Thus we are presented with narratives of one who deliberately "set his face to go to Jerusalem" (as Luke 9:51 [RSV] puts it). In the Gospel of John, Jesus is portrayed as choosing his own moment for the decisive visit to Jerusalem (John 7). His was a deliberate act, provocative and risky, something which the Jesus of the Gospels is presented as recognizing in the predictions of suffering. The activity may not be the conventional politics of Sanhedrin, hierarchy, or Roman imperium, but Jesus is portrayed as bursting in on the cozy arrangements of Jerusalem and shattering the fragile peace which existed.

The fact that Jesus does not speak in overtly political ways and address what would be for us obvious political issues does not constitute a lack of political content in Jesus' message. Jesus addressed the people of God and their way of relating and interacting. There is hardly enough detail to construct a political program, but there is enough evidence to discern the contours of a different kind of polity which differed sufficiently to lead to a challenge to current arrangements and which consisted of the controversial assertion on his part of the right to articulate that difference. We might feel that a more obviously political Jesus might have addressed himself to Roman occupation, the reasons for poverty, and the existence of slavery. Also, he might have constructed his parables with stories which were less accepting of the status quo than he did. To stand before the Sanhedrin and assert his messianic status, however, is to lay claim to a different pattern of human relationships, to be political, within the framework of late Second Temple Judaism. We can only guess at what that might have involved if Jesus would have had the chance to activate a different kind of polity. The memory of him is of one whose career was cut off with little opportunity for the measured preparation of a political legacy. We have no ground for assuming that this would have excluded the construction of a polity on the grounds that his kingdom would not have been in this world (cf. John 18:36).

So far I have concentrated on the narrative of Jesus' relationship with formal political processes. It is a measure of the way in which we have reduced the nature of the political that we should conceive of it solely in terms of a program for action in society. For most of us the political is of little direct impact in the way in which we conduct ourselves. But those interactions between individuals and in small groups, remote as they might often seem from formal political processes, deserve the description political. Not only are they shot through with the influences of the wider social setting, but in themselves they manifest the exercises of power, the subordination, and the impoverishment of human beings in the struggle for the maintenance and extension of individual interests.

The political character of the actions of Jesus in the Gospels deserves more attention than it has received. By political in this context, I mean their relationship to conventional patterns of human interaction and organization, whether formal (like a Sanhedrin or a local body of elders) or informal and traditional (like widely established practices). The political challenge posed by Jesus involved departures from norms of behavior, status, attitude, and access to social intercourse which are typical of a particular society. The narratives of Jesus' action portray a challenge to convention and imply different standards of human relating. The touching of lepers and of "unclean" women, the restoration of those excluded as "mad," the healing of paralytics and blind, whose disabilities inevitably caused impoverishment, signify sitting loose to boundaries of conviction and a preparedness to countenance in human action something different which claims to be more restorative. There is, of course, nothing that is unconventional in healing the sick but the challenge and perhaps even the breaking of "taboos" represent a shake-up of the personal relationships which constitute the fabric of human relating, the very stuff of politics. The disturbing of what counts as normal and acceptable is also evident in the reaction to Jesus. The surprise is that those who are abnormal recognize Jesus, whereas those who are supposedly normal are suspicious and hostile. The former is "blessed" with an insight which seems to be denied to "normality." But here too there is resistance to change. Jesus has come to torment. The stability or equilibrium of impoverishment and spiritual disintegration is suspicious when the possibility of temporary dislocation confronts it. How true is the maxim "better the devil you know" when it comes to being confronted with change brought about by the new and disturbing.

The wider perspective reminds us that in many of the reports concerning Jesus there is a process described which only tangentially relates to the formal political processes. But as the narratives themselves often indicate there is an exercise of power in particular and frequently controversial ways. In understanding the politics of the Gospels, we do well to note the politics of individual interaction as exemplifying patterns of relating which may offer significant steps forward in the betterment of human relations, applicable even in those situations where access to formal political power is limited. In such situations the experience of the first Christians proves invaluable. They understood the mechanics of change within situations where the levers of political power seemed to be denied to them. Perhaps that is a lesson we have to learn once more even in societies where access to political power appears to be quite open. A political theology which takes seriously the Gospel narratives will not concentrate only on gaining the levers of power. They too need to be transformed but not at the expense of the transforming politics of personal relationships, the impact of which helped send Jesus to his death.

Bibliography

Ashton, John. *Understanding the Fourth Gospel*. Oxford: Oxford University Press, 1991.
———. *Understanding the Fourth Gospel*. 2nd ed. Oxford: Oxford University Press, 2007.
Bammel, Ernst, and C. F. D. Moule, eds. *Jesus and the Politics of His Day*. Cambridge: Cambridge University Press, 1984.
Engels, Friedrich. "The Peasant War in Germany." In *On Religion*, by Karl Marx and Friedrich Engels, 97–118. Mineola, NY: Dover, 2008.
Gutiérrez, Gustavo. *A Theology of Liberation: History, Politics, and Salvation*. Translated and edited by Sister Caridad Inda and John Eagleson. Maryknoll, NY: Orbis, 1973.
Horsley, Richard A. *Jesus and the Spiral of Violence: Popular Jewish Resistance in Roman Palestine*. 1987. Reprint, Minneapolis: Fortress, 1993.
Lash, Nicholas. *Easter in Ordinary: Reflections on Human Experience and the Knowledge of God*. Richard Lectures 1986. Notre Dame, IN: University of Notre Dame Press, 1990.
Rowland, Christopher. *Radical Christianity: A Reading of Recovery*. Cambridge: Polity, 1988.
———. *Radical Christianity: A Reading of Recovery*. 1988. Reprint, Eugene, OR: Wipf & Stock, 2004.
Rowland, Christopher, and Mark Corner. *Liberating Exegesis: The Challenge of Liberation Theology to Biblical Studies*. Louisville: Westminster John Knox, 1990.
Schweitzer Albert. *The Quest of the Historical Jesus*. Tranlated by W. Montgomery. Mineola, NY: Dover, 2005.
Weiss, Johannes. *Jesus' Proclamation of the Kingdom of God*. Translated, edited, and with an introd. by Richard Hyde Hiers and David Larrimore Holland. Lives of Jesus. Philadelphia: Fortress, 1971.

10

The "Interested" Observer

I RECALL ON SEVERAL occasions in conversation with John Rogerson his recollection of an international Old Testament conference at which an exegete based in Brazil addressed the distinguished gathering about exegesis in a Third World country and the rather bemused, even hostile, reception he received. It is typical of John that this should have formed the introduction of his presidential address to the British Society for Old Testament Study in 1989.[1] Typical because John Rogerson is utterly committed to a study of the Hebrew Bible that is both rigorous and critical and because of that is sensitive to the bearing of the social and political context on its interpretation. In giving expression to these concerns in his lecture John attempted to explore the significance of the critical theory of Jürgen Habermas for theology. He concentrated on Habermas's most recent work, but I want to start from his earlier work and use it as a basis for some reflections on the practice of biblical interpretation.

In *Knowledge and Human Interests*[2] Habermas suggests a connection between the psychological condition and the nature of texts: "the . . . framework of psychoanalysis is tied to the presuppositions of the interpretation of muted and distorted texts by means of which their authors deceive themselves. . . ."[3] In other words, there is a parallel between the situation that confronts the psychotherapist and the exegete.[4] For the former

---

1. Rogerson, "Central Question."
2. Habermas, *Knowledge*, 214–19.
3. Habermas, *Knowledge*, 252.
4. There is a carefully worked out proposal for the interrelationship between

there are presenting symptoms and an increasingly obvious manifestation of those symptoms in the way in which the relationship between client and professional works itself out. A crucial part of the understanding of those symptoms is the retrieval, exploration, and testing of the diachronic account, the construction of a personal narrative, and in the course of the therapy comprehending its relationship to the symptoms manifested in the therapeutic relationship. Similarly, the way in which the critical interpreter is confronted by a particular text and its effects lead him or her to explore the antecedents of the text. There is clearly a need to take care lest concentration on the "surface" leads to an avoidance of engagement with all that contributed to its present form and imposes its way of looking at the world on the reader.[5]

The development of critical awareness in the therapeutic relationship is essential in a situation where absolute objectivity is not possible. In the transaction between therapist and client the basis of the relationship is that one partner (the therapist) has a sufficient knowledge of self and personal story to allow the possibility of a process of attentiveness and exploration to go on which is focused on the client. It is not that listening will be entirely without distortion (and indeed such distortion and its interpretation will be an important part of the process of understanding). Rather, that self-awareness that the therapist possesses contributes to an ability to distinguish his or her own agenda, so that the latter does not unnecessarily distort the conversation. There is no suggestion that the therapist ignores that material, particularly the feelings induced by the interaction with the client. Indeed, attention to the feelings engendered is an important part of the assessment that goes on and may contribute to the process of interpretation. Rather it is the case that gratuitous, spontaneous interventions deriving from the therapist's own business are to be avoided.

In a similar vein a fruitful exegesis involves acknowledgment of the importance of the two poles (text and reader). Or, following the kind of hermeneutical model adopted by Clodovis Boff (which he describes as "correspondence of relationships"),[6] there is an interaction between reader(s) and their context and the text and its context, so that the witness of the text and its context to the struggles and explorations of the past can be in a creative dialectic with the attempts at appropriate patterns of Christian response in the contemporary world. The interaction will demand in the interpreter the highest level of awareness of self and circumstances in the process of

---

exegesis and psychotherapy in Rashkow, *Phallacy of Genesis*.

5. Mosala, *Biblical Hermeneutics*.

6. Boff, *Theology and Praxis*.

reading. A critical reading will involve the ability to acknowledge prejudice and so enable the peculiarities and "otherness" of the text to become fully apparent and for the text to "speak," if not precisely on its own terms, at least with sufficient respect for its own integrity that it does not merely mirror the prejudice of the reader. Even the most rigorous process of distancing, in which a hypothetical ancient historical context is suggested, and the text firmly placed within it, is part and parcel of a complex modern set of prejudices which condition the way in which the text is understood.

Of central importance in the therapeutic relationship is the process of *transference*, whereby feelings and ways of relating reflecting experiences of the past are displaced onto the therapist by the client. Transference is the experience of impulses, feelings, fantasies, attitudes, and defenses towards a person in the present that are not appropriate for that person but are a repetition of response originating in early childhood. The process in therapy or in everyday life is a repetition of the past that distorts reality and is inappropriate to a proper, undistorted understanding of the present. Involvement in that process enables the coming to consciousness of repressed thoughts and feelings and thereby allows some disentangling of past and present. So a distance can be established from the original experiences, and hidden assumptions and fears may be examined. The therapist will refuse to be seen as the object of those emotions and will enable the client to look at them and perhaps make connections with previous occasions of hurt. Thereby a certain resistance can be established to the hegemony of the past so that the unconscious feelings no longer debilitate or paralyze the client. That kind of process of distancing is necessary in interpretation of any kind, so that facile assumptions and credence to a text or tradition may be avoided and attention may be given to the reasons behind resistance to a text or too ready acceptance of its contents on the part of the reader.

In the construction of understanding in the therapeutic relationship there will be two dimensions: diachronic and synchronic. The former will involve the discovery of a story that will enable some sense to be made of how an individual got to the present state of affairs and how it relates to present attitudes and feelings. Of equal importance, particularly where the experience of transference is concerned, is going to be the dynamics of the present interaction. Ways of relating with the therapist enable the hidden past to become apparent in the present. In biblical interpretation the diachronic approach has been refined and tested over the years and has been the foundation of critical study of the Bible. There has been much more uncertainty about the critical value of a synchronic approach, however, and the way in which prejudice conditions and even distorts reading (though the criteria for what counts as a distorted reading are almost always vague). It is here the contextual theology in all its various forms has stimulated discussion and emphasized the need for attention to *where* reading is done and the effect of text on interpreter and vice versa. So the use made of texts demands a critical assessment in terms of contemporary debate and practice as well as the perspective of their origin and history.

The critical awareness of the therapist can facilitate the refusal to collude with the demands of the client (e.g., by not being drawn into a role of fulfilling deep-seated needs) or the overcoming of resistance (whether that be to empathize with the client or the determination to keep the client's concerns at the center of the therapy). These two reactions are common enough in the reading of Scripture: Why do we allow ourselves to be carried along by a text or a particular way of reading? Has the development of resistance to a text more to say about us? Is it necessary to resist co-opting the text in order to allow space for it or the concerns of the interpreter? For example, post-Enlightenment readings have refused to be "taken in" by the text or, in the case of contextual theologies, have demanded that present experience (of oppression, doubt, etc.) set the interpretive agenda.

There are, of course, limits to the usefulness of the analogy of the therapeutic relationship. The interpersonal character of psychotherapy is different from the interpreter-text relationship. So far the focus has been on the interpreter as critic and possessor of self-awareness. Care must be taken not to treat Scripture as "a client" presenting problems which the enlightened interpreter can solve. Part of the process of reading is that critical self-awareness and attentiveness may mean a reversal of roles in which the interpreter becomes "the client." Just as in the therapeutic setting space is created to reflect, so in reading one needs to create an environment that will encourage the interpreter to explore the extent to which she or he projects onto the text or is resistant to it.

Biblical scholarship in the last two hundred years has invested an enormous amount of time and energy in the pursuit of one pole of the hermeneutical process: the diachronic elucidation of the text. The text's "pathology" and contradictions have meant that it has been the object or critical concern. That is not deny the role of the interpreter and reflection on what has gone on, but it is the text that is regarded as "pathological" and the interpreter "enlightened." Of course, this kind of pattern is endemic in the psychotherapeutic relationship also. And yet there is always the caveat that the "aware" interpreter of the client's problems is at the same time someone who recognizes problems within. If it is the case of the blind leading the blind, it is also the case that one of them at least knows where some of the ditches are.

The demand that we take seriously the diachronic perspective when it comes to the "interpreter" pole is long overdue. Some recognition of it is now becoming evident. For example, in a little noticed book John O'Neill[7] set the biblical interpretation of the giants of biblical scholarship of the last hundred years in their historical and philosophical context (something that John Rogerson himself alludes to briefly in his presidential address when he discusses his work on de Wette). Alongside this there is need for attention to the synchronic approach to the text. By that I mean not only that kind of holistic reading which has been typical of what are loosely termed narrative approaches but the kind of understanding of the interaction between text and reader that has taken place at different periods of history. The whole discipline of *Wirkungsgeschichte* ("reception history" or "history of effects") helps here. Studying the effects of a text will of necessity demand that one engages in a contextual approach as the particular moment of engagement with the text is explored.

In believing that we have much to learn from Third World liberationist exegesis I do not want to assert that everything about it is to be slavishly followed. There is much in it that I find problematic: for example, the reliance on historical reconstruction, whether it be the origins of Israel or the historical Jesus (I think John too has severe reservations about their method). Despite the impression that they make the Bible conform to twentieth-century concerns, liberation exegetes have in common with the mainstream of biblical study a concern to be critical. Indeed, Western exegesis can thank the liberationist perspective for the incessant reminder of its own partiality. We need to be reminded of the ideological character of our study, in particular imagining that we are "drawing from the text simply what it contains."[8] Ideology is not something which belongs to the overtly committed readings.[9] Indeed, it is part of the insidious character of ideology that those who are in control of the way in which the text is interpreted deny that their readings are in any way ideological and claim instead that they are the product of "scientific" methods.[10]

It is a mark of critical interpretation that it manifests an awareness of its own approach to the text but also the understandable constraints that this method imposes and the necessity of openness to other interpretative

---

7. O'Neill, *Bible's Authority*.
8. Houlden, "Schools of Thought."
9. See, e.g., Eagleton, *Criticism and Ideology*; and Jameson, *Political Unconscious*.

10. Such espousal of "science" as a description of biblical interpretation has pervaded even the in many ways the commendable summary of biblical interpretation published by the Pontifical Biblical Commission in *Briefing* 24; 4, 5 (the periodical of the Bishops' Conferences of Great Britain).

methods as both checks to and stimuli for change. Critical interpretation should, therefore, be a model of the communicative interaction that, Rogerson stresses, is at the heart of Habermas's philosophy. In so far as interpretation eschews *proper* dialogue with the contextual theologies that are such an important component of modern theology it ignores what Rogerson sees as a fundamental component of the Hebrew Bible. One may say the same for the New Testament also. The God who spoke through the Son demonstrates that kind of communicative interaction. But that communication is not merely confined to words, even if the memory of it is primarily enshrined in the words and witness of the New Testament writings. The Christian church in its common life of worship and service attests to the ongoing character of that communication, however partial and fragmentary it might be in the specific ecclesial embodiments of it. At present it may be a distorted communication, but its horizon of hope looks forward to that "ideal speech situation" when humans will see, and address God face to face.[11]

Theologians look back to a story of communication in Christ in the Gospel narratives. Those narratives have been subjected to a way of reading in the last two hundred years in which a particular Christian community's struggle for identity hidden in each Gospel narrative has been used as a determining factor for understanding the texts. That has brought great benefit as readers have had some inkling of the way in which text and (ancient) context subtly interplayed. But often that has been at the expense of themes in the text as a whole and any resonances with the contemporary readers' experience. So, if one asks students today what the Gospel of Matthew is about, one is unlikely to hear a reference to the literal meaning of the text. It is much more likely to be "the struggle between church and synagogue and the emergence of a Jewish Christian group over against emerging rabbinic Judaism at the end of the first century CE." In the interests of history and exegetical "science" it either ignores or subordinates to (at best) a secondary position both the meaning for today and the *literal* meaning of the text to the concern for the other story, that of author and community originally addressed. Liberation theology has been in the vanguard of the criticism of a narrowly *ancient* historical concern (for there is, inevitably, a contemporary historical concern whether overt or not). As Carlos Mesters puts it,

> the emphasis is placed [in liberation exegesis] not on the text itself but rather on the meaning the text has for the people reading it.... [It is a matter of] understanding life by means of

---

11. See the brief comments on Habermas's theory when applied to eschatology in my discussion of Nicholas Lash's essay, "Conversation in Gethsemane," in Rowland, "Eucharist as Liberation."

the Bible. . . . The discovery of meaning is not the product of scholarship alone, of human reasoning, but is also a gift of God through the Spirit.[12]

I think Barth is a herald of the sentiments of many liberation theologians when he says in his preface to *Epistle to the Romans*, "Why should parallels drawn from the ancient world be of more value for our understanding of the Epistle than the situation in which we ourselves actually are and to which we can therefore bear witness?"[13] The two dimensions of interpretation, the text and its context, and the readers and their context, are both necessary. As in therapy, the "here and now" of the interaction offers data for interpretation which must take priority over that tentative reconstruction of the past that led to the "here and now"—though the importance of the latter is that it facilitates the understanding of the dynamics of the interaction. To do justice to texts and to their effects necessitates that both poles should be taken seriously. In my reading of the Gospel of Matthew I recognize that it is shot through with ambiguities. It is carried out in the midst of "comfortable Britain" yet with a commitment to the intuition of liberation theology that in the act of divine grace in the incarnation there is the classic expression of "the option for the poor" that is borne out by the Gospel narrative.[14]

2

I want to stress the importance (perhaps even indispensability) of consideration of the "ancient" pole in the interpretive process (while recognizing that this is an artificially constructed ancient environment that is itself the product of the "modern pole"). This development is necessary in order to understand and not to be beholden to the vehemence of the anti-Pharisaic rhetoric as a context-related phenomenon that cannot and need not lead to anti-Semitism.

Although there have been dissenting voices, there is a widespread assumption that Matthew is dependent on Mark and was written in the wake of the devastating upheaval which struck the Jewish polity in 70 CE (see Matt 21:41, 43; 22:7; 23:7–8; 24:15).[15] Whether the Gospel was written as a reaction to *birkat ha-minim* has been keenly debated, and the consensus is

---

12. Mesters, *Defenseless Flower*, 161.

13. Barth, *Romans*, 11. See also Watson, *Text, Church, and World*.

14. There are interesting similarities and contrasts with Meg Davies's reading of Matthew's Gospel in Davies, *Matthew*.

15. Outline in Stanton, *Gospel*.

moving away from the view that there had been a uniform and widespread exclusion of Christians from the synagogues.[16]

The situation in Matthew's church seems to be a close but tense relationship between church and synagogue (8:12; 17:26; 27:25), though the frequent use of "*their* synagogues" (4:23; 9:35; 10:17; 12:9; 13:54; 23:34) suggests an already existing distance. There is a strident opposition to the Pharisees, though, unlike John, there is little sign of anti-Jewish sentiment (28:15 is the only possible polemical use of "the Jews," and that is an editorial gloss). The conflict is still an internal Jewish dispute. Like Stephen's speech in Acts 7 it reflects the tone of the persecuted minority or remnant who believe that they have the key to the truth.

The curious addition to Mark's narrative in Matthew 17:24 might give us a clue to the situation. It is possible that it could have been read in the late first-century situation as a recommendation to pay the payment of Temple Tax/*fiscus Judaicus* (we know that it was a problem at the end of Domitian's reign when Jews and supposed Jews were put under pressure to pay the tax).[17] It is worth reflecting that the advice offered by the Matthean Jesus would have the effect of making it very difficult to distinguish between Jews and Christians in the eyes of the Roman authorities as both paid the tax (though for different reasons). There is acceptance of the Gentile mission (but with reservations—5:19; 22:11?), polemic against antinomians (5:19; 7:15; 24:11–12); the close relationship with the *Didache* and Ignatius's letters suggests that relations with Judaism and true and false prophecy were issues at the period (the latter inveighs against "judaizing"; see *Phil.* 6.1; 8.2 and *Magn.* 9.1); and connections with themes in the Pauline corpus may suggest some kind of relationship with that tradition (Matt 5:19; 22:37–38; cf. Gal 5:14; Rom 13:9; Matt 1:1; 3:9; cf. Gal 3:6–29 and Rom 4).

The heightened eschatology in Matthew may have served several purposes. Firstly, it affirms the necessity of an appropriate decision in the face of the final consummation. Secondly, it serves as a setting for the story as a whole which is "earth-shaking" in its effects. It is the "end of the world" (in the sense of the imminent demise of the political order based on the Temple) even if its climax is still awaited. It is arguable as to whether the delay of the Parousia was a problem faced by Matthew's community (24:43–51 is often taken to indicate evidence that this was a "problem").[18]

---

16. Text in Schürer, *History*, 2:454; and see further Kimelman, "Birkat Ha-Minim"; and Horbury, "Benediction."

17. See Goodman, "Jewish Identity," 44.

18. See Rowland, *Christian Origins*, 287–96.

So much by way of a summary along conventional diachronic lines, an approach, I have suggested, which is necessary to guard against absolutizing sets of attitudes determined solely by the contemporary context. But what of the context? What shape will a synchronic exposition take in which the dialectic between text and contemporary reader is moved to the fore? First, Schüssler Fiorenza would have us recognize that our scholarship is to be situated within the rhetoric of political discourse in the contemporary world.[19] I have with much uncertainty engaged in an exercise in exegetical exploration since my return from my first trip to Brazil eleven years ago, when I was aware that my interpretive work could never be the same again. Being of a rather conservative bent, I could not leave behind the theological formation of twenty years, yet neither could I regard what I had learned in Brazil as something merely faddish and ephemeral. Most of us are engaged in one form or another in the experience of oscillating between different sorts of interpretive worlds, trying to make sense of them, trying to inhabit both and be heard by the inhabitants of both and trying to interpret one to the other. The chances are that one will never feel entirely at home in either. One never stays long enough in one place to achieve that sense of place which familiarity and routine bring about. My commitments demanded attention to the traditional theology course at Oxford, and my part-time concerns with a major British development agency (Christian Aid) brought a continuing challenge of liberation theology to my biblical study.

What follows is an exercise in interpretation in which the option for the poor is supported by reference to a scriptural text. To that extent the hermeneutical circle starts "outside" the text with an interpretive principle which the rule of faith leads us to suppose is an adequate summary of the text. Matthew's Gospel, it is suggested, is the story of the Son of God whose activity and message end up being a challenge to the strong who are suspicious of the means whereby the weak and marginal are restored. Jesus' work starts on the margins of his society and favors the insignificant and disadvantaged. It extends also to those who manage the political systems (tax collectors, soldiers). The Son of God ends up as a victim of systems which do not practice justice. Nevertheless, his career shakes the foundation of the world and its values: from start to finish Jerusalem turns out to be a city that is disturbed by the change brought by the messiah (2:3; cf. 21:10).

In the very first chapter, where we have a genealogy, legitimation is offered of the true child of Abraham and David (3:9; 22:41–46); in the course of that genealogy reference is made to four women—Tamar, Ruth, Bathsheba, and Rahab—who are part of this particular story though they

---

19. Schüssler Fiorenza, "Ethics of Biblical Interpretation."

hardly seem to be conventional links in the messianic genealogy possibly paralleling Mary's extraordinary pregnancy. In the face of this Joseph could have rid himself of Mary (cf. Deut 22:20), but he shows himself be a true son of David (Matt 1:20), a worthy "father" of the messiah, in contrast with Herod. Herod forms no part of the genealogy and is therefore concerned about the report of the birth of one who is the true king of the Jews (2:2; cf. 21:11; 27:37). A starkly unfavorable comparison is offered between the true king's attitude to children (18:2; 19:14; 20:31) and that of Herod (2:16–23). Herod is linked with priests and scribes (2:4) who later in the Gospel will be opponents of Jesus the true king. Although there are hints of a more positive attitude towards scribes and their activity in 8:19, 13:52, and 23:34, they do oppose Jesus, accusing him of blasphemy (9:3; cf. 26:65). The scribes together with the Pharisees are the subject of Jesus' denunciation in Chapter 23 and in 21:45, though their authority is recognized (23:2; cf. 9:11–12). The Magi manifest a different kind of wisdom, however. In addition to scriptural proof the way of God comes through dreams: 1:20; 2:13; 2:19 (cf. 27:19). Peter's confession (16:13–28) is a reminder that perception comes through divine revelation (16:17) and that insight given to the insignificant is stressed in the important Matthew 11:25–26.

The themes of the first two chapters, the surprising character of Jesus' birth in obscurity and his persecution by the powerful, are continued as the narrative begins its account of Jesus' mission (Matt 3:1–17). It starts with the message (Isa 40:3) of an eccentric prophet (cf. 11:9) in the desert. The metropolitan population goes out to him (3:5), only for their leading representatives to be upbraided by John (3:7). Jesus identifies himself with John (3:14–15) and in the desert is proclaimed as Son of God (3:16–17). Here he is tested by the devil as Son of God, rejecting self-satisfaction (4:4), self-preservation (4:6), and self-aggrandizement (4:10). It is not in Jerusalem that he settles but on the margins of Israel's life (4:16; cf. Isa 8:23—9:2). It is here that the proclamation of the imminence of God's reign begins (4:17) with the healing of every kind of disease (4:23–24).

Jesus is presented in Matthew as engaged in acts of compassion (8:10; 9:30, 35; 14:14) and healings (4:23–24; 9:35; 12:13, 15; 15:30; 19:2) which affect crowds (9:36; 14:14; 15:32) rather than leaders. It is the disabled (9:27; 11:5; 20:29–30; 21:14), women (9:20; 15:27), tax collectors (9:9–11; 11:19; 21:31–32), and children (18:1; 19:14; 21:15) who are the recipients of his attention. Jesus is depicted as a humble king[20] (20:24–25; 21:5; cf. 2:2; 5:5; 11:27; 27:11, 37, 42) yet one who brings division (21:14–15; cf. 10:34; 12:23–24). That humility characterizes those who receive divine

---

20. Verseput, *Rejection*; and Wengst, *Humility*.

approval in the Beatitudes (5:3-11). These blessings indicate the kinds of people who enjoy privileges in the kingdom, and the themes are picked up later in the Gospel when the character of Jesus is portrayed (for 5:3; cf. 11:5; for 5:5; cf. 11:29; for 5:6; cf. 3:15; for 5:20; 5:7; cf. 9:13; for 12:7; 5:8; cf. 5:28; 6:21; 15:18-20; 22:37; for 5:10; cf. 10:21).

The reaction of the crowds is to follow (4:25; 12:15; 19:1; 20:29) in amazement (7:28-29; 9:33; 13:54), regarding him as a prophet (21:11, 46) or as a Son of David (12:23; 21:9). Being one of the crowd means remaining without full understanding (13:14) and prey to influences that distort perception (27:20). Those who become disciples understand the words and works of Jesus and see them for what they are: the fulfilment longed for by prophets and righteous (13:16-17; cf. 23:34-35). That privilege should mean a greater degree of understanding (16:17-18). Often disciples fail to see (16:8-9), and the men end up forsaking Jesus (26:56; cf. 27:55, 61). Jesus has compassion on the crowds, and their needs are responded to (e.g., 14:14). Nevertheless, members of these amorphous bodies must be moved by sympathy for Jesus as prophet (21:11, 46) or as Son of David (12:23; 21:9), or by amazement at his teachings (22:33). Mere admiration is insufficient. There is a price to pay for being a disciple (8:19-20; 19:27-28), something pointed out uncompromisingly by Jesus (19:21-22; cf. 6:24).

Final judgment (25:31-46) is based on response to the hidden Son of Man in the destitute lot of his brethren (cf. 7:21-28; 10:42-43). Critique of Pharisees is that they do not practice what they preach. That must be the key to the new righteousness (5:20) with its particular concern for the little ones who may be ignored or silenced (21:15-16). These are the last who will be first (20:16). Concern for one's final destiny is a present response to those who like the earthly Son of Man have nowhere to lay their head (8:20). Meeting the eschatological Son of Man at the Last Judgment is anticipated (25:31-46; cf. 10:40-42). Speaking a word out of place has eternal consequences (12:32, 36; 10:32-33; cf. 5:22-48). The healing of the demon-possessed is an anticipation of the final struggle (8:29; cf. the torment caused by eschatological agents in the Apocalypse, especially Rev 11:10). A confession of faith is the foundation for resisting superhuman forces (16:18-19). The death of a failed Messiah has extraordinary consequences (27:51-52). The little ones are in a sense closest to God and vouchsafed an apocalyptic vision (18:10; 17:2-8). At the heart of Matthew's Gospel is the ordinary carpenter's son (13:55) who is also Son of God (3:17) and who is seen as he really is on the mount of transfiguration (17:1-13).

Despite the air of conventionality at its opening Matthew presents a story of God's messiah whose coming, from the very start, is greeted with suspicion, dismay, and persecution by those in power. Born in an apparently insignificant place, identifying with those regarded as sinners, taking children as examples of the attitude of humility appropriate for the kingdom, Jesus has an unconventional message. It is exemplified in the character of those who are blessed at the beginning of the Sermon on the Mount. Jesus' link with John the Baptist and his privileged place in salvation history confirm the impression of a story where the reversal of values and priorities and the undermining of conventional hierarchy are central. It is the rulers who misunderstand and mislead the crowd. The demon-possessed and outsiders rather than the "normal" are the ones who glimpse Jesus' true character. In this respect Matthew closely resembles Mark's theme of the subversion of the established order. In the new age the persecuted Son of Man will reign as the humble king. That rule will be according to criteria very different from those of the kings of the nations (20:23). That forms the heart of what the nations need to be taught (28:20; 7:21–22; 10:42–43; 25:40). The story of Jesus demands a rearrangement of that constellation of ideas that constituted the received wisdom as to the meaning of God's dealings with Israel. That rearrangement takes place according to different principles and concerns. It is no novelty but neither does it replicate the received view of the tradition. It reflects the unexpectedness of God's acts, the way they challenge conventional assumptions and social stratification, so that the negative reaction of the politically powerful comes as no surprise. The Gospel involves a definition of divine kingship amplified by Jesus' activity, the persons to whom he ministered, and the commentary on that activity in the discourses. This kingship does not involve force of arms (26:52–53; cf. John 18:36). It is exemplified particularly by humility and compassion.

But in one important respect this reading of Matthew's Gospel may seem to be naively oblivious of a problematic strain where one group is vilified in the text: the Jews. A particular difficulty centers on the climactic moment in the Passion narrative when the Jewish crowd seemingly constituted for the purpose as the people of God take upon themselves and subsequent generations responsibility for the death of Jesus. It is a verse which has played its part in the most virulent bouts of anti-Semitism throughout history. As we have seen, the diachronic perspective may help us to understand its role in the Gospel narrative even if it is difficult to ameliorate its effects. The problematic verse, however, comes in the context of the climax of this story when the separation between Jesus and priestly elite is complete. They are portrayed as being implicated in opposition to Jesus from the very start (2:3). Their plan to kill Jesus is facilitated by the defection of Judas (26:3, 14–15) in handing over Jesus for money (26:15). So Judas serves mammon and not God (6:24). Every means is used to get Jesus put to death including deceit (26:59). At last the crowds are persuaded by priests and elders to ask for Barabbas. On this the latter show themselves to be false shepherds (cf. Ezek 34; Matt 26:31) who lead astray. They are frequently described as being "of the people" (2:4; 21:23; 26:3, 47; 27:1), and it is they who are misled. So the crowds are now presented not just as a mob but as the people (*laos*) and accept responsibility: "his blood be upon us and our children" (27:25 my translation). Here is a verse whose effects have been catastrophic in serving the interests of virulent and inhuman anti-Semitic attitude and behavior.

Is the way in which this verse is used as a peg on which to hang such anti-Semitism justified? Does attention to the literal sense of the text suggest this? It would *appear* that full responsibility is taken by the people, a term being used here that is widely used in the Septuagint for the people of Israel. That might seem to conclude the matter. But surely such a statement, however apparently uncompromising in its assertion, still needs to be set in the context of the narrative as a whole and in particular the overall theme and its christological portrayal? In the Gospel the central character is not portrayed as laying the blame upon the *Jewish* people (unlike the Gospel of John, the phrase "Jews" is hardly ever used of the opponents of Jesus) and to use this verse as a basis for the followers of Christ simply accepting that responsibility flies in the face of the drift of the message of Jesus as it is presented in the Gospel. Why is it that a later Christian readership has acquiesced in giving authority to that *laos* to speak for the whole people of God, whether at that point in history or on behalf of children yet unborn? Can that crowd take to themselves the right to speak for their children when it is "this generation" that is held accountable by Jesus (23:26)? Or, to put it another way, does that assertion of the crowds take precedence over the point made by Jesus, the central character and "normative teacher of the narrative," that responsibility is not something which attaches to Jews and Judaism as a whole but to "this generation." Rather, within Matthew's narrative the people's statement should be seen as part of the pattern of shifting of responsibility which goes on all through the passion story. The priests persuade the crowd and so put pressure on Pilate; Pilate gives responsibility to the crowd (27:24). The people now include their children in their claim to responsibility—children are here again victims as they have been in 2:16–17, and the concern for the children manifested by the messiah which is a dominant theme in the Gospel is temporarily rejected, but that cannot be the last word since it is the way and words of the messiah that have the last word (28:19).

3

It is incumbent upon the interested interpreter to reflect on the approach taken to the text. Not only is there a question of whether the interpretation "fits" the text, or, to put it in other terms, whether exegesis rather than eisegesis has been undertaken—but also there must be as frank an assessment as possible to locate the interpretation within the quests for meaning and significance that exist within contemporary society. My location in an academic environment demands certain canons of critical application partly in order to gain a hearing and partly to gain credibility for the enterprise. Theologians have an interest in maintaining not only the existence of their subject but also their own livelihoods. There is also an assumption that this kind of theoretical activity is worthwhile and that mere practice is insufficient. For me, therefore, there is oscillation between different sorts of worlds, trying to make sense of them, trying to inhabit both and be heard by the inhabitants of both and trying to interpret one to the other.

But the canons of Christian theology cannot in the last resort be shaped by the academy. The strange encounter between Jesus and Nicodemus remains a salutary lesson. The Johannine Jesus confronts a leader of the Jews with the uncompromising statement that he needs to be born over again or from above. For Nicodemus to see the kingdom of God there is need for a complete transformation to be made which can only be likened to a birth. The transformation of which Jesus speaks here is directed to one who is part of "the opposition." Jesus bids him move from that position as a "leader" of the Jews to one where he can share that transformation of perspective that is essential in order to be able to "see the kingdom of God." His social, political, and religious position has to be put on the line. Nicodemus appears not to have been able to take the plunge of baptism. That would have been a public act that would have required him to change sides. He would have had to leave behind the political power of the national leadership and to identify himself with one whose baptism meant initiation into a community with a very different, marginal, perspective on the world. As long as he remains part of the leadership, however hard he tries to distance himself from it, he is looking at the world from the point of view of the ruling class. Just as the Synoptic Jesus had talked of solidarity with the child as the necessary condition for understanding the kingdom and being truly great, so Nicodemus has to see that however old one may be there is a necessity to go through that process of gestation and growth that will enable a new perception. For the Fourth Gospel the true perspective is not that of the political leadership or even their Roman allies but the minority group who followed the Son who has come down from heaven.

When the Ecumenical Association of Third World Theologians (EATWOT) Conference of 1976[21] spoke of the need for an "epistemological rupture" that makes commitment the first act, followed by critical reflection on praxis amidst the reality of a suffering and unjust world, it was a similar kind of challenge posed to First World theology to that made by the Johannine Jesus to Nicodemus. There is a legitimate question whether that kind of rupture is possible in Britain. Armchair radicals do well to explore their own interpretive interests as honestly as they can. What I have admired most about John Rogerson (and it is evident in his recent work) is the recognition both of this and of the need to act as well as write, so turning theological institutions towards the service of the vulnerable and marginal. Without this, theology can easily end up serving its own needs or those of its expositors rather than the service of almighty God who hears the cries of the poor and who in Christ is identified with them.

Bibliography

Barth, Karl. *The Epistle to the Romans*. Translated from the 6th edition by Edwyn C. Hoskyns. London: Oxford University Press, 1933.

Boff, Clodovis. *Theology and Praxis*. Translated by Robert R. Barr. Maryknoll, NY: Orbis, 1987. Reprint, Eugene, OR: Wipf & Stock, 2009.

Davies, Margaret. *Matthew*. Readings—A New Biblical Commentary. Sheffield: JSOT Press, 1993.

Eagleton, Terry. *Criticism and Ideology: A Study in Marxist Literary Theory*. London: Verso, 1978.

Goodman, Martin. "Nerva, the Fiscus Judaicus, and Jewish Identity." *Journal of Roman Studies* 79 (1989) 40–44.

Habermas, Jürgen. *Knowledge and Human Interests*. Translated by Jeremy J. Shapiro. Social Theory. Cambridge: Polity, 1987.

Horbury, William. "The Benediction of the Minim and Early Jewish-Christian Controversy." *Journal of Theological Studies* 33 (1982) 19–61.

Houlden, Leslie. "Schools of Thought." *Theology (Norwich)* 93.754 (1990) 259–60.

Jameson, Fredric. *The Political Unconscious: Narrative as a Socially Symbolic Act*. Ithaca: Cornell University Press, 1981.

Kimelman, Reuven. "Birkat Ha-Minim and the Lack of Evidence for an Anti-Christian Jewish Prayer in Late Antiquity." In *Jewish and Christian Self-Definition*. Vol. 2, *Aspects of Judaism, in the Greco-Roman Period*, edited by E. P. Sanders, with A. I. Baumgarten and Alan Mendelson, 226–44. 3 vols. Philadelphia: Fortress, 1980.

Mesters, Carlos. *Defenseless Flower: A New Reading of the Bible*. Translated by Francis McDonagh. Maryknoll, NY: Orbis, 1989.

Mosala, Itumeleng J. *Biblical Hermeneutics and Black Theology in South Africa*. Grand Rapids: Eerdmans, 1989.

---

21. See Torres and Fabella, *Emergent Gospel*, 269.

O'Neill, J. C. *The Bible's Authority: A Portrait Gallery of Thinkers from Lessing to Bultmann*. Edinburgh: T. & T. Clark, 1991.

Pontifical Biblical Commission. "The Interpretation of the Bible in the Church." Vatican City: Libreria Editrice Vaticana, April 23, 1993. https://catholic-resources.org/ChurchDocs/PBC_Interp-FullText.htm/.

Rashkow, Ilona N. *The Phallacy of Genesis: A Feminist-Psychoanalytic Approach*. Literary Currents in Biblical Interpretation. Louisville: Westminster John Knox, 1993.

Rogerson, John. "'What Does It Mean to Be Human?' The Central Question of Old Testament Theology?" In *The Bible in Three Dimensions: Essays in Celebration of Forty Years of Biblical Studies in the University of Sheffield*, edited by David J. A. Clines et al., 285–98. Journal for the Study of the Old Testament. Supplement Series 87. Sheffield: JSOT Press, 1990.

Rowland, Christopher. *Christian Origins: From Messianic Movement to Christian Religion*. 2nd ed. London: SPCK, 1985.

———. "Eucharist as Liberation from the Present." In *The Sense of the Sacramental: Movement and Measure in Art and Music, Place and Time*, edited by David Brown and Ann Loades, 200–215. London: SPCK, 1995.

Schürer, Emil. *The History of the Jewish People in the Age of Jesus Christ (175 B.C.– A.D. 135)*. Translated by T. A. Burkill and others. Revised and translated by Géza Vermes and Fergus Millar. 3 vols. in 4 parts. Edinburgh: T. & T. Clark, 1973–1987.

Schüssler Fiorenza, Elisabeth. "The Ethics of Biblical Interpretation: Decentering Biblical Scholarship." *Journal of Biblical Literature* 107 (1988) 3–17.

Stanton, Graham N. *A Gospel for a New People: Studies in Matthew*. Edinburgh: T. & T. Clark, 1992.

Torres, Sergio, and Virginia Fabella, eds. *The Emergent Gospel: Theology from the Underside of History; Papers from the Ecumenical Dialogue of Third World Theologians, Dar Es Salaam, August 5–12, 1976*. Maryknoll, NY: Orbis, 1978.

Verseput, Donald. *The Rejection of the Humble Messianic King: A Study of the Composition of Matthew 11–12*. Europäische Hochschulschriften XXIII, Theologie 291. Frankfurt: Lang, 1986.

Watson, Francis. *Text, Church, and World: Biblical Interpretation in Theological Perspective*. Grand Rapids: Eerdmans, 1994.

Wengst, Klaus. *Humility: Solidarity of the Humiliated: The Transformation of an Attitude and Its Social Relevance in Graeco-Roman, Old Testament-Jewish, and Early Christian Tradition*. Translated by John Bowden. Philadelphia: Fortress, 1988.

11

The Second Temple

Focus of Ideological Struggle?[1]

THIS ESSAY SETS OUT to collect and survey some texts, mainly from the apocalypses but also some other pseudepigrapha of the Second Temple period or just after, relating to the theme of the Temple and Jerusalem in the present age and the age to come. The apocalypses form a major segment of the Jewish pseudepigrapha and are a significant witness to Jewish eschatological beliefs of the period. While brief allusion will be made to the Dead Sea Scrolls, the problems posed by these texts, particularly with regard to the attitude to the Temple, demand a more detailed study than is possible here.[2]

In the table below there are various passages in which there is a differentiation between those dealing with the Temple and those which refer primarily to Zion/Jerusalem. While there may in most instances have been a presumption that Zion would have included a Temple, the fact that the book of Revelation contemplates a new Jerusalem without a Temple makes

---

1. For a discussion of this theme see Nickelsburg, "Enoch, Levi, and Peter"; Ford, "Heavenly Jerusalem"; Strack and Billerbeck, *Kommentar*, 3:796; Gaston, *No Stone on Another*.

2. This is particularly true since the discovery and publication of the Temple Scroll. There might even be a case for regarding the latter as an example of an apocalypse, set as it is in the context of a divine revelation to Moses on Sinai (there are some formal similarities with the book of Jubilees) but the complexities of interpretation of this document mean that it demands a study in its own right and will not be treated here. Some passages where a negative attitude to the Temple is expressed may be noted: 1QpHab 8:8–13; 9:3–7; 12:7–9; 4QTest 28–30; CD 4:17; 5:6–9; 6:11–14; 12:1–2; 20:22–23.

it imperative to note that distinction. Indeed, it is worth noting that in the eschatological program sketched, for example, in Sibylline Oracles 5:422 (cf. 3:286; 3:652; 5:108) there is specific reference to the Temple in the restored Zion (as also in the Shemoneh Esreh), though such specific reference is often absent elsewhere. It needs to be borne in mind, therefore, that a restored city might conceivably be without a Temple as in Revelation, for there would be no need of a special holy place reserved for God.

In looking at the apocalyptic material we should resist the temptation to find an apocalyptic or even late Jewish understanding of the Temple, as if the chance survival of documents which may well come from very different provenances and social milieux might witness to a uniform view of the Temple. An examination of the apocalypses hardly encourages us to suppose that there is enough cohesion in the contents of these works to offer anything approaching an "apocalyptic" concept of *anything*. Even though we shall continue to hear talk of apocalyptic eschatology as if there were a discrete body of ideas in Second Temple Judaism linked with particular works, the view should be resisted that we can easily reduce the apocalypses, still less the pseudepigrapha, to a neat body of leading motifs.[3] Apocalypses may have a common literary form but cannot for that reason necessarily be supposed to have much else in common. It is all too often assumed that what we call apocalyptic must have been associated with particular circles in Judaism, possibly on the fringes of mainstream Jewish religion.[4] We do not know enough about the apocalypses to be able to say with any assurance that they are products of a particular group. Indeed, close analysis suggests that within this body of literature there are significant differences of concern (e.g., between 1 Enoch and 4 Ezra) which point to differences of function of the apocalyptic outlook in differing circumstances. Most of the apocalypses which we shall be examining come from a wide range of dates and circumstances. We should not be surprised, therefore, to find differences in the form of the visions and subject-matter. Apocalyptic offered a mode of discourse which would have been available to a wide range of groups with very different religious and political options. It is important to remember that it could be made to serve the needs of conservatives just as much as radicals.[5] The works which have formed the basis of this study are the Jewish apocalypses which date from the period of the Second Temple or shortly after: 1 Enoch, Daniel, 2 Enoch (Slavonic Enoch), Jubilees, Testament of Levi,

   3. See Rowland, *Open Heaven*, particularly 23-48.
   4. See Davies, "Social World."
   5. This point is well illustrated by a study of the way in which apocalyptic ideas functioned in different periods of history. See, e.g., Hill, *Antichrist*; and Cohn, *Pursuit of the Millennium*.

4 Ezra, 2 Baruch (Syriac Baruch), 3 Baruch (Greek Baruch), the Apocalypse of Abraham, and Revelation, together with one or two apocalyptic pieces contained in works of different literary genre (e.g. Life of Adam and Eve 29). The Sibylline Oracles exhibit sufficient coherence of religious outlook for them to be included. Even if in their present guise they purport to be pagan oracles, their concerns and content are thoroughly Jewish and exhibit several similarities with the apocalyptic tradition.

The approach taken in this essay is to look at the material thematically. There are dangers in so doing precisely because it can link together works which are not related either in time or space and give a false sense of homogeneity. The alternative would be to attempt to treat the material chronologically. That has its disadvantages too, however. Not only are several of these works of a composite nature, but also it is not easy to determine with any degree of precision the time and place of writing in the majority of cases. Accordingly, at the risk of offering a false sense of coherence, and, with due regard for the framework imposed on disparate material by such a systematic presentation, I have set out to treat the material thematically in order to enable some general picture of attitudes to emerge from the literary remains of the period. That kind of approach is of some value when the questions being asked of the material concern the strands of thought and trends within material. If we are to understand the character of the ideological struggles which were going on in the Second Temple period, then some attempt at tracing common themes and patterns is a necessary contribution to the fulfilment of that task. In so doing we can only remind ourselves that the accident of history has left us with the literary remains at our disposal, and that may distort our understanding of the centrality of the Temple and the perception of it by Jews in our period. The survey of material included here needs to be set in the context of the evidence of the importance given to the Temple in the writings of Philo, Josephus, and the tannaitic literature. Philo indicates how important the Temple was for the Alexandrian Jewish aristocracy even when there was a much nearer focus of Jewish cultic activity at Leontopolis (which Philo never mentions). The inclusion of a tractate dealing with the measurements of the Temple in the Mishnah (Middoth) as well as records of disputes about the Temple service are reminders of what a central place the Temple (and the restoration of its worship) had. We have to rely on the hints that are available to us and run the risk that in magnifying them we are in danger of distorting the reality of the past by our hypotheses. Of course, there is no other way forward for the historian of this period. To these fragmentary comments we are indebted for some understanding of how an apocalyptic outlook colored the views of this central organ of Jewish life.

Table of References

Solomon's Temple
1 Enoch 89:50; 89:67; 93:7–11; Life of Adam and Eve 29:5; 2 Baruch 44:5–7; 59:4; 61:2; 67:6.

The Second Temple
1 Enoch 26*; 89:73; Daniel 8:11–12; 8:14; 9:17; 9:25–27; 11:31; Life of Adam and Eve 29:6; Jubilees 1:27; 2 Baruch 68:5; Testament of Levi 8:17.

Indestructibility of Temple and Eschatological Assault
Sibylline Oracles 3:665; 5:401; Jubilees 1:27; 23:22–32; 25:21; 1 Enoch 56:5–8; 90:13; 4 Ezra 13:34.

Sacrifice and Temple Questioned
1 Enoch 89:73; 2 Enoch 45:3; Testament of Levi 9:9; 14:5; 16:1; Psalms of Solomon 2:3; Jubilees 23:21; Assumption of Moses 4:8; 6:1.

Temple's Destruction
Apocalypse of Abraham 27; Sibylline Oracles 4:115–245; 5:150; 5:398; 4 Ezra 10:21; 12:48; 2 Baruch 6:7; 8:2, 5; 10:10; 11*; 20:2*; 85:3*.

New Temple and Jerusalem
1 Enoch 90:28–29*; 91:13; 2 Baruch 6:8; 32:4*; Apocalypse of Abraham 29; Life of Adam and Eve 29:7; Jubilees 1:26–29; 4:26*; Sibylline Oracles 3:702; 3:718; 5:424–34; Testament of Benjamin 9:2; Tobit 14:5; Targum to Zechariah 6:12–15; Psalms of Solomon 17:32–34

Heavenly Jerusalem
2 Enoch 55:2; 2 Baruch 4:2–7; 4 Ezra 7:26; 8:52; 9:26–47; 13:36; Revelation 21.

Heavenly Temple
Testament of Levi 3:6; 5:1; 18:6; 4QShirot (4Q510); 1 Enoch 14:8–25; Revelation 3:12; 7:15; 11:19; 14:15, 17; 15:5–8; 16:1, 17; cf. Hebrews 9:24.

Altar in Heaven
b. Hagigah 12b; 3 Baruch 11:8; Revelation. 6:9; 8:3; 9:13; 14:18; 16:7.

*References to Zion/Jerusalem which *might* imply reference to the Temple.

Solomon's Temple

In 1 Enoch 89–90 we have a retelling of salvation history from creation to the coming of the kingdom. This was probably written during the Maccabean period (the end of the historical review in 90:6–17 focuses on the Seleucid period). In 1 Enoch 89:50 there is a clear distinction made between the house built for the sheep and the lofty tower built for the lord of the sheep. This is a distinction between Jerusalem and the Temple, a fact which is confirmed by the reference to this passage in Testament of Levi 10:5: The reference to the full table offered to the Lord indicates the proper nature of the sacrificial system at this stage in Jewish history. A house is mentioned earlier in 1 Enoch 89:36 and 40, where both of these passages refer to the tabernacle. Subsequently the house which Moses built for the Lord of the sheep becomes a house in which the sheep also dwelt (a reference to Zion). The tabernacle thus became the focal point of the worship of Israel in Jerusalem. In 1 Enoch 89:67 the destruction of the house and tower are referred to (cf. Mic 3:12).

In a section in which the history of the world is divided into ten weeks of years (93:1–10; 91:12–17) a house and a kingdom are built (93:7; clearly a reference to the Davidic dynasty). In the Life of Adam and Eve 29:5 (a short apocalyptic section in a pseudepigraphon which does not seem to presuppose the fall of the Second Temple) the divine plan is to establish a kingdom and habitation for the divine majesty. In 2 Baruch 59:4 (a part of the vision of the black and bright waters, another historical review similar to the two examined from 1 Enoch) Moses on the mountain is shown the likeness of Zion. This indicates a link between the settlement in Jerusalem and the foundational revelation of God's covenant establishing the Davidic decision as part and parcel of the divine plan. The measurements are to be made "after the likeness of the present sanctuary" (cf. Exod 25:10; 26:30).[6] In 2 Baruch 61:2, the dedication of the sanctuary is linked with a period of rest and peace for God's people.

Second Temple

It is already clear from the Bible that the origins of the Second Temple are surrounded in controversy. The inclusion of Haggai and Zechariah in the canon represents the triumph of the point of view which looked to the re-establishment of the cult as the fulfilment of the prophetic promises.[7] There are enough hints from elsewhere that there was considerable skepticism, even opposition, if the enigmatic oracle in Isaiah 66:3–24 is anything to go by.

As part of Enoch's journey, he visits Jerusalem (1 En 26; cf. Jub 8:19). In 1 Enoch 89:73 reference is made to the building of a house and the raising of a tower. Here the table placed before the tower has food on it which is polluted and impure. We may note that nothing is said about the Lord of the sheep standing on the tower here (cf. 89:50), which suggests that this temple

---

6. 2 Bar 59:4 in Charlesworth, ed., *Old Testament Pseudepigrapha*, 1:642.

7. See, e.g., Plöger, *Theocracy and Eschatology*.

was without the divine presence. The profanation of the Second Temple is alluded to on several occasions in Daniel (8:11; 9:17; 11:31) and its restoration predicted (8:14; 9:25). In the Life of Adam and Eve 29:6 the return from exile and the building of the Temple is mentioned without further comment. Zion's rebuilding features in 2 Baruch 66:5 when the offerings are restored, and Zion is honored by the nations. Nevertheless, the inferior quality of this restoration is noted when the text points out that the whole process was carried out "not as fully as before" (though this might conceivably refer to the absence of a restored monarchy).[8]

Sacrifice Questioned

In 1 Enoch 89:73 the sacrificial offering of the Second Temple is considered inadequate (cf. 1QpHab 9:1–7; 12:7–9; 4QTest 28–30). It is worth noting that we find this reference in a work which exhibits views which may have been opposed to mainstream opinion with regard to the calendar (1 En 82:4; Jub 6:32–38). The problem with the Second Temple according to this apocalypse dates back to its very foundation, possibly reflecting the tensions which existed at the time.[9] In the Assumption of Moses we have several passages in which the validity of the sacrifices offered in the Second Temple is questioned. In 4:5 the post-exilic restoration is questioned: "And two tribes shall continue in their prescribed faith, sad and lamenting, because they will not be able to offer sacrifices to the Lord." In 6:1 there is polemic against the Hasmoneans who "assuredly work iniquity in the Holy of Holies."[10] There is a general allusion to the essence of religion not being sacrificial offering in 2 Enoch 45:3, though it seems difficult to regard this as anything other than the rather general statement in the spirit of the prophets.

The Indestructibility of the Temple

There is some evidence to suggest that the sort of mythology connected with the Temple and Zion in some of the psalms (e.g., Ps 46) and in the early part of Isaiah continued well into the Second Temple period.[11] These ideas centered on the Temple as a place where God dwelt which would be

---

8. 2 Bar 68:6 in Charlesworth, ed., *Old Testament Pseudepigrapha*, 1:644.

9. See, e.g., Hanson, *Dawn of Apocalyptic*.

10. This translation is adapted from Charles et al., eds., *Apocrypha and Pseudepigrapha of the Old Testament*, 2:407–24.

11. See Clements, *God and Temple*.

inviolate. It seems to be hinted at in two passages from Jubilees where the Temple is regarded as an eternal building (1:27; 25:21). In Jubilees 1:27 the building of the sanctuary is seen as something which would be eternal, as is also the case in 25:21. The most explicit reference to this myth comes in the fifth book of the Sibylline Oracles in a context dealing with the destruction of the Second Temple by the Romans (5:400). This work is not easy to date but may be as early as the second century CE, though the presence of the Nero Redivivus myth may place it somewhat earlier (5:138–710). The myth of indestructibility seems to have been behind some of the fantastic stories preserved in Josephus's *Jewish War* (e.g., *War* 6:300), which recalls the departure of the divine *kabod* from the Temple in Ezekiel 10. Earlier Josephus tells of rash beliefs of those who expected supernatural deliverance in the moment of greatest trial, probably a reference to the Sennacherib incident (*War* 6:285, 295; cf. Isa 38–39). In Sibylline Oracles 3:657–1030 an assault on the Temple is repulsed by supernatural means. In 1 Enoch 90:13 (cf. 56:4) we have a passage which is surprisingly not more attested in the apocalypses, the eschatological assault on the Jews, which finds some general parallel in the intensified last assault mentioned in Jubilees 23:22–32.

The Temple's Destruction

As we might expect, the most extensive of the references to the Temple's destruction are to be found in the apocalypses which are to be dated in the immediate aftermath of 70 CE, particularly the Syriac Apocalypse of Baruch (2 Baruch). Elsewhere, in the Apocalypse of Abraham 27, the destruction of the Temple is justified because of idolatrous practices. In Sibylline Oracles 4:115–24 the destruction of the Temple by Rome is explained as "whenever they put their trust in folly and cast off piety and commit repulsive murders in front of the Temple," probably an allusion to some of the strife which Josephus describes during the siege.[12] This book is to be dated to the end of the first century CE; there is a reference to the eruption of Vesuvius in 5:135–710, which is seen as a punishment for the desecration of the Temple. Elsewhere in the Sibylline Oracles there are brief allusions in 5:398 (the destruction of the Temple by fire) and in 5:150. In 4 Ezra 10:21 Ezra tells the lamenting woman about the destruction of Zion and the sanctuary and pleads with her to recognize an even greater reason for grief (cf. 12:48).

Of the passages listed above those from 2 Baruch call for special attention. While it is only Zion which is mentioned explicitly in 20:2, there is a link between the destruction of the city and the fulfilment of God's

---

12. Charlesworth, ed., *Old Testament Pseudepigrapha*, 1:387.

eschatological promises. In two passages in 6:7 and 80:1 mention is made of the Temple vessels being hidden. In the former an angel descends from heaven, goes into the Holy of Holies and takes the veil and the holy ark as well as other items, which are then committed to the earth to await the last times (6:8-10). This is a theme which emerges elsewhere in Jewish literature (e.g., 2 Maccabees 2:4-8 and Josephus, *Ant.* 18:85-108, the latter passage being connected explicitly with eschatologically orientated movements). In 2 Baruch 7:1 and 8:2 we have the notion of the release of divine protection from the Temple, which enables its destruction at the hand of Israel's enemies. This probably reflected the passage in Ezekiel 10 already alluded to (cf. Josephus, *War* 6:300). In 10:10 the destruction of the Temple has an air of finality about it. There seems to be little prospect of the restoration hinted at in Barnabas 16 despite the imminent eschatological expectation that emerges from time to time (e.g., 20:2). Instead there is the concentration on the centrality of the Law as the vehicle of God's revelation and the means of maintaining the relationship between God and the people (see e.g., 85:3).

Building of the New Temple and City

The reference to the messianic building of the Temple in Sibylline Oracles 5:424-34 is one of the few passages in the literature of this period where the messiah's task is to build the Temple (though it may be hinted at in Pss. Sol. 17:32-34).[13] The fifth Sibylline Oracle has been dated in the second century CE, but this passage which links the building of the Temple with the coming of the messiah may reflect that peculiar eschatological enthusiasm which arose when the Second Temple was destroyed and expectations of restoration and messianism intensified (e.g., Berakot 5:1). In Jubilees 4:26 there is a clear reference to the central role of the renewal of Zion as a focal constituent for the renewal of creation ("Mount Zion . . . will be sanctified in the new creation for a sanctification of the earth"[14]).

In 1 Enoch 91:13 in the Apocalypse of Weeks, in the eighth week, the week of righteousness, after the period when an apostate generation emerges, there is a time of bliss centered on Israel. In the next period righteous judgment is revealed to the whole world. At its close a house shall be

---

13. Gaston, *No Stone on Another*, also adds Targum to Zechariah (Tg. Ps.-J.) 6:12-15: "Thus said Yahweh of Hosts: This man, messiah is his name, will be revealed and grow and build the Temple of Yahweh. He will build the Temple of Yahweh, and he will exalt its splendor and he will sit and rule on his throne, and there will be the High Priest by his throne and the kingdom of peace will be between them."

14. Charlesworth, ed., *Old Testament Pseudepigrapha*, 2:63.

built for the Great King for evermore, and all humankind shall look for the path of righteousness.[15] Here the building of the Temple forms part of the establishment of the earthly kingdom of righteousness. In 2 Baruch 32:4 the building of Zion will be shaken in order that it may be built again. But that building will not remain forever but will again after a time be destroyed to make way for renewal and an eternal perfection.

In Apocalypse of Abraham 29, at the end of the period of messianic woes the righteous who are left will return to the devastated Jerusalem and the Temple (27) and offer proper sacrifices (perhaps another hint that what had hitherto been offered left much to be desired). In Life of Adam and Eve 29:7 the building of the house of God comes after the return from dispersion. The house of God built then "will be ... greater than of old"[16] and there will be a period when the enemies of the righteous will no more be able to hurt the people who believe in God. In 14:4 there is a prediction of a period of destruction and desolation for the house of God. Once again the gathering of the people of God which had been dispersed will be followed by the rebuilding of the Temple. In Tobit 13:16 (which is probably to be dated c. 250 BCE) there is a prediction of the rebuilding of Jerusalem "with sapphire, emerald and precious stone" (my translation).

The character of life around the new Temple is described in Sibylline Oracles 3:702–1030 (a passage which should be compared with the description of eschatological bliss in Jub 23:23–32). This leads to the fulfilment of Isaiah 2:3: "then all the isles and the cities shall say ... come, let us fall on the earth and supplicate the Eternal King, the mighty, everlasting God. Let us make procession to his Temple for he is sole potentate" (Syb. Or. 3:710–18 my translation; cf. Tob.13:11).

The Animal Apocalypse in 1 Enoch offers us one of the most important references to be considered in connection with any discussion of the eschatological Temple (1 En 90:28–29). After the judgment of the angels of the nations[17] there is a reference to the house.[18] After the reconstruction

---

15. The Qumran Cave 4 (4Q212) Enoch text reads: "a royal Temple of the Great One in his glorious splendor for all generations forever" (my translation).

16 Adapted from Charles et al., eds., *Apocrypha and Pseudepigrapha*, in Horne et al., eds., *Sacred Books and Early Literature*, 14:19 (https://ia904706.us.archive.org/13/items/TheBooksOfAdamAndEve/the-books-of-adam-and-eve_text.pdf/).

17. On this see Dexinger, *Henochs Zehnwochenapokalypse*; and Wink, *Naming the Powers*, who lists all the relevant material. On the heavenly temple see also Charles, *Eschatology*, 179, 199. For a contrary interpretation, see Strack and Billerbeck, *Kommentar*, 3:796; and further, McKelvey, *New Temple*.

18. This passage is alluded to in Barnabas 16:3.

of a new house and the acceptance by the Gentiles of the primacy of Israel (90:30) there is a time of eschatological bliss centered on the city.

While the animal symbolism is not always easy to interpret, the section on the house is quite explicit:

> And I stood up to look until he folded up that old house, and they removed all the pillars, and all the beams and ornaments of that house were folded up with it; and they removed it and put it in a place in the south of the land.... And I looked until the Lord of the sheep brought a new house larger and higher than the first one; and he set it up on the site of the first one which had been folded up; all its pillars were new and its ornaments were new and larger than those of the first one, the old one which had been removed. And the lord of the sheep was in the middle of it. (1 En 90:28–29 my translation)

We may note: (1) the old house is destroyed and its various parts placed in the south of the land; and (2) God brings about a new house, larger than the first one, built in its place.

The question we have to ask is whether in this passage we have a reference to the Temple at all. If we examine this passage in the light of 1 Enoch 89:50, we have reason to doubt whether it is in fact a reference to a new Temple. In that passage there is a house built for the sheep and a tower for the lord of the sheep. It would appear, therefore, that it is the *tower* which the Animal Apocalypse sees as a symbol of the Temple. The tower is also a symbol of the Temple in 89:73 where the reference to polluted sacrifices makes an identification of the tower with the Temple virtually certain. So in the description of the eschatological Zion, it is possible that we might well be faced in this passage with a restored city without a Temple, as no new tower is mentioned in the new house.

Another question which arises in connection with this passage is whether we have a reference here to a heavenly Jerusalem. The main reason for supposing this is the fact that it is God who is said to have built the house. There seems to me to be insufficient evidence to develop the theory that we have here a reference to the heavenly Jerusalem. The passage is in marked contrast to 4 Ezra 10 where there is much clearer stress on the appearance of the celestial city in a place where there was *nothing* before (cf. 4 Ezra 7:26; 2 Bar 4:2–6). It seems preferable to suppose that what the author has in mind is *either* human agents fulfilling the divine purposes *or* a miraculous building rather than the descent from heaven of a pre-existing city (cf. John 2:17). We cannot rule out the possibility that this passage may have been interpreted by later readers as a reference to the heavenly Zion, but it is more likely that the original version spoke of a new city built in the last days fulfilling the divine purposes. There are similar sentiments enunciated in the Shemoneh Esreh, for example, the prayer to God to "bring back worship into the Holy of Holies of thy house" (my translation). One assumes that this act would have been fulfilled by human agents in pursuance of the divine purposes.

Related to this issue but probably offering evidence of a pre-existing heavenly city/temple is 2 Baruch 4:2–6 (cf. 59:4 with its allusions to Exod 25:40; 26:30), though it is worth noting that this apocalypse is not exactly replete with references to a restored Temple. The reference to a heavenly mystery can hardly be simply the heavenly secret written on the divine palms similar to the secrets on the tablets revealed to Enoch (1 En 93:2). The fact that the reference is made to both Paradise and the city being removed from Adam suggests that the seer has in mind both a garden and a city existing in heaven (cf. the way in which the manna is stored on high in 29:8). Similarly in 4 Ezra 7:26 the seer is shown "the city which is now seen... and the land which now is hidden shall be disclosed"(RSV).[19] The reference to Abraham's vision of Zion "by night among the portions of the victims" (my translation) once again connects the establishment of Zion to the founding of the nation. It reflects the type of tradition which we find in the Apocalypse of Abraham where this event in Genesis 15:9–21. becomes the basis for an ascent to heaven and a vision of celestial and eschatological mysteries, including the restoration of Zion and the cult.

In 2 Esdras (4 Ezra) 9:26—10:57 there is the vision of the woman mourning the death of her son. The passage is a complex one and falls into the following sections:

Vision

1. vision of a woman in mourning: Ezra hears that she was barren and after 30 years gave birth to a son who died on entering the wedding chamber.

2. Ezra's rebuke: "For Zion, the mother of us all, is in deep grief and great humiliation. Zion ought to mourn over her children who are on their way to perdition" (4 Ezra 10:7, 10 my translation).

3. the transformation of the woman: her face shines; she utters a cry and in place of a woman a city is built.

---

19. *ecce enim tempus veniet, et erit quando venient signa quae praedixi tibi, et apparebit sponsa et apparescens civitas et ostendetur quae nunc subducitur terra* (Vulgate: hopper/text.jsp?doc=Perseus%3Atext%3A1999.02.0060%3Abook%3D2+Esdras%3Achapter%3D7%3Averse%3D26).

Interpretation

a. the woman is Zion (10:44).

b. the barrenness means the period (3000 years) before the offering was made (10:45).

c. the birth of the son means Solomon's building of a city and the establishment of sacrifice in Jerusalem (10:46).

d. the death of the son is the destruction of Jerusalem (10:48–49).

e. in the wake of the destruction of the city something new is required and a divine construction is initiated (10:53–54; cf. 9:24).[20]

f. Ezra is then instructed to go in and see the splendor and vastness of the building.

There has been much dispute over this passage. G. H. Box and many others have argued[21] that the woman stands for the heavenly city and her son who dies represents the earthly city. This, however, seems to represent an oversimplification of the complexities of the passage. The woman is transformed into the heavenly, eschatological city only at the end of the vision. Until then she had been the earthly Zion. This seems the most obvious way of construing the interpretation. Verse 44 of 4 Ezra chapter 10 states explicitly that the woman is Zion and the life of the son is the period of the cult from Solomon to the destruction by Nebuchadnezzar. Thus we are dealing in this vision with stages of Zion's history culminating in the appearance of the heavenly Zion corresponding to the transformation of the woman in the vision. It is apparent in 10:51 that the heavenly origin of what Ezra sees is emphasized. In a place where there was nothing before, the city of the Most High appears. It seems likely that at the conclusion of this passage we have material indebted to Ezekiel 40–48. This is most evident in 2 Esdras 10:55–59. where Ezra is commanded to go in and note the character of the new building (cf. Ezek 40:4; 43:10). Even though there is no explicit reference to the Temple, the vague references to the new Jerusalem may presuppose the existence of a Temple in the new Jerusalem. The most cogent reason for this is the reference to the sacrificial system in 10:46. The replacement of the old Zion together with its cult by a heavenly city might be expected to include all that was present in the old (as is apparent in the eschatological passages in Sib. Or.).

20. Cf. 2 Bar 29:3 and 39:7 where we have reference to the revelation of the messiah and the messianic kingdom. On this vocabulary see the discussion of the Aramaic terminology of revelation in Chester, *Divine Revelation*.

21. See Box, "Introduction to 4 Ezra," 2:553–54; see also Myers, *I and II Esdras*.

The Heavenly Temple

Already in the Bible there are hints that heaven may have contained at least a pattern of earthly entities like the cult (e.g., Exod 25:40).[22] In Testament of Levi 3:6 we find a description of the heavenly Temple. Although there is some textual variation, mainly relating to the number of heavens, the main textual streams witness to the existence of a heavenly Holy of Holies where God dwells. There with God are archangels who offer propitiatory sacrifices to the Lord on behalf of the sins of ignorance of the righteous. They present to the Lord a pleasing odor, a rational and bloodless offering. The similarity with Romans 12:1 raises the question of Christian influence.[23] Whatever may be the arguments for Christian influence and insertions in other parts of the Greek Testament of Levi there do not seem to be strong reasons for supposing that it can be found in this section. A major reason for suggesting this is that in b. Hagigah 12b[24] we have evidence of a very similar belief. Speaking of the fourth heaven, Zebul, it states that "it is that in which the heavenly Jerusalem and Temple, and the altar is built, and Michael the great prince stands and offers upon it an offering" (my translation). In Testament of Levi the likelihood is that we have a reference to a heavenly altar of incense (cf. Exod 30; 37:25) similar to that alluded to in Revelation 8:3. In similar vein to Testament of Levi 3, though less explicit in its formulation, is 3 Baruch 11:8. Here Michael carries a large bowl, full of the virtuous deeds of the righteous which are then brought before God (14:2). Unlike the Testament of Levi nothing is said of theophany, a curious absence in a work which otherwise follows the standard pattern of cosmography.

We turn now to consider a remarkable passage in the Jewish apocalypses, 1 Enoch 14:8–35:[25]

> And there was shown to me in my vision as follows: Behold, in my visions clouds were summoning me, and mists were calling me, and the courses of the stars and lightnings were hurrying me along and were bewildering me. The winds in my vision
> 5 carried me away, lifted me up and brought me to heaven. I entered until I drew near to a wall built of hailstones with tongues of fire around them, and they began to make me afraid. I entered into the tongues of fire, and I drew near to a great house built from hailstones. The walls of the house were like flat stones. All were

---

22. See McKelvey, *New Temple*; Maier, *Gnosis*; Bietenhard, *Die himmlische Welt*.
23. Jonge, *Twelve Patriarchs*.
24. See Rowland, *Open Heaven*, 81–82.
25. Translation of the Greek from Black and Denis, *Apocalypsis Henochi Graece*.

10   made of snow, and the foundations too were of snow. Its roofs were like the courses of the stars and like flashes of lightning, and between them were fiery cherubim, and their heaven was as water. A burning fire was around the walls, and the doors were burning with fire. I entered the house, which was as hot as fire
15   and as cold as snow, and there were no means of nourishing life there. Fear covered me and trembling overtook me. I was shaking and fearful and fell down. I continued to see in my vision, and behold, another door was opened before me. There was another house greater than the first, and the whole of it
20   consisted of tongues of fire. All of it excelled in its glory, splendor and majesty, so that I am not able to tell you of its glory and majesty. Its foundation was of fire. The upper part of its roof was of fiery flame. I looked and saw a lofty throne, and its appearance was of crystal and its wheel as the shining sun. There was
25   also a vision of cherubim. From underneath the throne there came forth rivers of flaming fire, and I was not able to look at them. The Great Glory sat on a lofty throne. His robe was as the appearance of the sun, brighter and whiter than any snow. No angel could enter the house and see his face because of his
30   magnificence and glory. No human being could look at his flaming fire which was around. A great fire stood by him and no one was near him. Ten thousand times ten thousand stood around him and before him, and his word has power. The holy angels who are near him do not depart by night nor do they leave him. Until
35   this time I had been prostrate on my face trembling.

Most are agreed that it comes from the earliest phase of the apocalyptic tradition. Milik[26] in his edition of the Qumran Enoch fragments wants to push the date of this section back to a time *before* the P reference to Enoch in Genesis 5:24. The reason for considering this heavenly ascent in the context of a discussion of references to the Temple is that the description of heaven seems to follow the geography of the cult. Thus we read in 1 Enoch 14:10 and 15 that there are two parts to heaven, a "great house" and a "second house greater than the former." Unlike the Testament of Levi, no mention is made of a heavenly cultic activity.

The immediate context of this account of a heavenly ascent is Enoch's commission to announce judgment on the watchers and Azazel (13:1) and the request by them that Enoch should intercede with God on their behalf (13:4–10). The watchers' petition is rejected (14) and Enoch recounts his experience in 14:2–25, which leads to the heavenly ascent and another

---

26. Milik, ed., *Books of Enoch*. See also Barker, *Older Testament*.

account of the divine rejection of the petition. Here we have an account of a mortal taken into the divine presence (parallel to other early Enoch traditions such as Jub 4:20–33, which may be dependent on 1 En 14). Connections with other parts of the biblical tradition abound as the following summary indicates:

> line 2 (14:80): Dan 7:13; T. Ab. 10; Ezek 8:2; 14; 2 Kgs 2:11
>
> line 6 (14:9): Exod 24:10; 38:22; Ezek 1:27
>
> line 7 "tongues": Ezek 1; Dan 7:9; Acts 2:3
>
> line 9 (14:10): two houses following the two major parts of the Holy Place?
>
> line 12 (14:11): Exod 19:16; Ezek 1:13
>
> line 13: heaven as water: Ezek 1:22; Rev 4:6; T. Levi. 2:7; b.Hag15a ("When you come to the place of the marble plates, do not cry, 'Water, water'")
>
> line 19 (14:15): no veil mentioned; cf. Exod 31:33
>
> line 23 (14:18): Isa 6:1; Ezek 1:26; Dan 7:9; Rev 4:2; 2 En 22:2; Life of Adam and Eve 25
>
> line 24 (wheel): 2 Kgs 2:11; Ezek 1:16; 10:2; Dan 7:9; 4QShirot; 1 En 71:7
>
> line 26 (14:19): fiery stream: Dan 7:10; 4QShirot; 1 En 71:2; Rev 22:1
>
> line 27 (14:22): glory: Ascen. Isa 11:32; T. Levi. 3:4; 5:1
>
> line 27: raiment: Dan 7:9; Isa 6:1; Mark 9:3 and parallels; T. Ab.12
>
> line 32 (14:23): angelic attendants: Rev 4; Dan 7:10; 1 En 1:9

This remarkable passage has received greater attention in recent years. Its concern with a heavenly journey and its obvious indebtedness, at least in general terms, to Ezekiel 1 have made it a focus of interest for those interested in exposing the character of the mystical tradition in the Second Temple period. There seems little doubt that it offers us the earliest evidence of the expansion of Ezekiel 1. Opinion will be divided over whether it indicates a vital speculative or visionary interest. A comparison with its biblical antecedents suggests that we have come a long way from the typical prophetic commission. While the connection with Ezekiel 1 is obvious, this passage differs from other throne-theophany passages in the extent of that indebtedness.

Rejection of the Temple?

It is the book of Revelation which offers the clearest evidence of the redundancy of the Temple in the eschatological age. The celestial city *as a whole* reflects the proportions of the Holy of Holies (21:15). That connection might lead us to suppose that there is nothing other than influence of the dimensions of the tabernacle and no allusion to the Temple itself, though there are affinities with 1 Kings 6:20. The city itself was one large holy place (just like the new Jerusalem in the Temple Scroll) from which anything unclean was rigorously excluded (Rev 21:27). With the design of the Holy of Holies forming the basis of the design of the city, the faithfulness of the new to the Scriptures is ensured, while at the same time an institution which had clearly been a cause of strife in Judaism could be abandoned in favor of the unmediated access of the saints to God (21:3; 22:4; cf. Jub 1:26-28). It is apparent from the references to the heavenly Temple elsewhere (e.g., Rev 11:19; 15:5; 16:1, 17) that the position taken by the book is not totally anti-cultic. In a situation where God's will is not done, the presence of the Temple in heaven is a symbol of the divine dimension to existence. The tabernacle/Temple is a reminder of obligation, and the heavenly worship represents the divine remembrance of the cost of faithful witness which will not ultimately be ignored. Indeed, the earthly Temple is the basis for the inspiration of the vision of the two witnesses in Revelation 11. Measurement of the Temple offers the seer a potent way of speaking about the extent of the divine presence in a recalcitrant world.

Another feature of Revelation which may also have contributed to the absence of the Temple is imbedded in its cosmology. There is an eschatological resolution of the cosmological contrast in Revelation. Dualistic cosmology derived from the apocalyptic tradition is used to stress the transcending of the alienation of the world from God and humanity from one another. Starting in Revelation 4 we are introduced to God's throne world where the Almighty sits receiving the praises of heaven. In heaven there is a Temple with an altar and angels ministering, similar to what we find in Testament of Levi. This world above where God is acknowledged as creator and the source of messianic redemption by the heavenly host in songs of praise contrasts with the unrepentant world below. Despite the start of the eschatological woes initiated by the Lamb opening the seals, humankind refuses to repent (Rev 9:20). We have a contrast between the world above and the world below under the dominion of a regime inspired by the devil (13:2). Revelation 6-19 tells, with several interruptions, of the overthrow of this hostile dominion, culminating in the binding of Satan and the millennium. In a new creation there is a very different cosmological pattern. In the new heavens and new earth, the dwelling of God is not in the world above seated on a fiery throne (4:5) but tabernacling with people in the new Jerusalem on a throne from which flows the river of the water of life (22:1). The contrast between heaven as a haven of righteousness and an evil earth has disappeared, as also has the Temple (21:22). It is a mark of the perfection of the new creation that there is no need of a peculiar dwelling for God either in heaven or on earth.

The development of a heavenly Temple (or in 1 En 14 a description of the heavenly world which owes something to the layout of the cult) is not easily explained. Once again we may resort to the theory that the heavenly Temple offered a radical alternative to the inadequacies of its earthly counterpart. The presence of a heavenly-throne passage from Qumran may add some weight to this belief. Other explanations seem more convincing, however. There was developing in ancient Judaism a more sophisticated cosmology in which God was believed to be enthroned in glory far above the heavens. Well before the beginning of the common era if 1 Enoch 14 is anything to go by, some Jews had taken the step of establishing the *merkabah* of Ezekiel in a heavenly palace which only the privileged seer could view. Such a cosmological development may tell us something also of their theology. God was absent in heaven; signs of the divine presence were indirect and not immediate. Such a lack of immediacy should not blind us to the importance attached to divine immanence at particular moments in history and ritual devotion. Care should be taken not to overplay such dualistic contrast, as it is clear from the apocalypses that the whole of human history is not a random series of events but follows the plan laid down in heaven.

Concluding Comments

We do not have a great amount of material on which to base judgments about the attitudes to the Temple in the apocalyptic tradition, but the absence of much detailed discussion of the Temple is striking. This could be because this institution is taken for granted as an essential component of both this age and the age to come. In the material dating from the years immediately after the destruction of the Second Temple the relative paucity of references is noteworthy. It might have been expected that the end of the Temple would have at least led to nostalgic hopes, though a hope for its restoration is included in the Shemoneh Esreh. That there was a significant increase in eschatological urgency is indicated by several passages (e.g., 2 Bar 85:10; 4 Ezra 5:50-56; 14:10, 16). It is remarkable that the detailed prescriptions such as are found in the Temple Scroll are completely absent in the extant apocalypses. We might conclude from this that the writers of the apocalypses were against the cult. That would be too precipitous a conclusion to draw. But we need to remember that fantasizing about the details of the new age in a utopian fashion is hardly typical of the apocalypses. They show an interest in history as a whole in which *detailed* concern with the Temple would have been out of place.

The explicit concern with the heavenly Zion which we found in apocalypses from the second half of the first century CE may well derive in part at least from the catastrophe of 70. It is apparent in other subject matter in 4 Ezra, 2 Baruch, and the Apocalypse of Abraham that the disaster had an effect on the content of the revelations and the concerns expressed in them. All three are virtually unique in including questions of theodicy. It should come as no surprise, therefore, that the destruction of the city led to developments in their doctrine of Zion just as it appears to have done in their emphasis on the temporary nature of the messianic kingdom and the emergence of the doctrine of the two ages.

There is some evidence of a growing concern with Zion at the expense of specific reference to the Temple. Explicit doubts about the Second Temple are occasionally expressed, for example, in 1 Enoch 89:73 and 2 Baruch 68:5. In the light of the protests raised in some of the Qumran texts about the Temple it is reasonable to suppose that some of the dissatisfaction expressed itself in the visions for the future by a concentration on Zion rather than the Temple. Still, there is nothing to compare with the hint in Stephen's speech that the whole cultic enterprise based on the Temple was flawed from the very start and was the consequence of the massive rebellion at the golden calf (Acts 7:40).[27]

The socio-economic context of the apocalyptic literature we have been considering was one in which the Temple played a central role in the lives of Jews both inside and outside Judea. The regular flow of income to the Temple from all parts of the empire led to the enrichment of this institution and those who ran it. As far as Jerusalem itself was concerned, the Temple provided a central feature of the local economy. Throughout the years leading up to the First Revolt in 66–70 CE there was a program of rebuilding which would have involved employment. More important was the regular round of sacrifices which demanded provision and was a significant component of the local economy. The removal of the Temple must have necessitated a cataclysmic shift in the pattern of life, so anyone predicting its destruction was pronouncing a threat not only on an ideological focus but also on the most significant part of the Jerusalem economy. We can

---

27. See Epistle of Barnabas 16, and further Simon, *Verus Israel*, 86, 120.

only with difficulty reconstruct the real-life struggles of which the literary remains are the ideological expression. There is obviously a complicated relationship between the two. Indeed, as we have seen, the apocalyptic literature cannot readily be identified as the repository of the ideas of the marginalized when only occasionally do we find critical or deviant ideas in them. The language of revelation can be used by the powerful just as much as the weak and marginalized as a way of cloaking their positions of power with the mantle of divine authority.

One of the interesting developments in biblical studies over the last decade has been the recognition that social and economic forces must be allowed their place in the understanding of religious movements. Of course, as Ernst Bammel has catalogued,[28] there has been a long history of attempts to place Jesus and the early Christians within social and revolutionary struggles for change in the last years of the Second Temple. Some of these are testimony to the ingenuity of the writers concerned and seem to have only tenuous links with the sources. Our doubts about particular solutions should not make us any less conscious of the issues that they raise. We may want to voice doubts about the whole fabric of the edifice of the "hermeneutics of suspicion" which has dominated our reading of biblical texts, in which the surface is rejected in favor of underlying tendencies. Nevertheless, biblical scholarship has drunk deep of the "spirit of the age" and in its various results has shown how productive it can be for theological as well as historical inquiry, in order to maintain a credible critical awareness in giving meaning to ancient religious texts. Recent scholarship with an avowedly liberationist or Marxist bent[29] which sees Jesus as part of a diffuse movement opposed to the hegemony of the Temple both ideologically and economically is an attempt to restore to our interpretative consciousness the socio-economic dimension of the struggles for power among men and women.[30] We may not want to reduce the religious to epiphenomena of class-conflict, but to deny the importance of the struggle for power is to reduce the scope of the religious to a compartment of human experience instead of allowing full weight to its social function. The literary form of our New Testament texts disguises as much as it reveals, not least in that central area of the social formation out of which and for which the texts were written. It is the task of the interpreter to restore that hidden story in a way which can ground the

---

28. Bammel, "Revolution Theory."

29. See, for example, Kautsky, *Foundations of Christianity*; Pixley, *God's Kingdom*; Belo, *Materialist Reading*; Segundo, *Historical Jesus*; Myers, *Binding the Strong Man*; Kreissig, *Die sozialen Zusammenhänge*. Most recently on the circumstances of the First Revolt, see Goodman, *Ruling Class of Judaea*.

30. See Williams, *Marxism and Literature*.

"political unconscious"[31] dimension firmly in the narrative we are offered and recognize the role of the text in the social and political struggles of the ancient world as well as in our own. That will demand attentiveness to what lies before us in the particularity and peculiarity of the form and language and not wholesale dismissal of its form and content. Equally, it must encompass the recognition that there is another story to be told which is never absent from the text but can disappear in our readings of it, particularly when we are tempted to see religion as merely a "spiritual" matter.[32] Nowhere is this more true than in the discussion of the Jewish Temple. Apparently it is the focus of religion and not of politics. Yet the Temple was a powerful economic factor in Judean life as well as an influential ideological symbol. There are occasional signs, however fragmentary, of peripheral movements devoted to a challenge to powerful vested interests at the center of Jewish life. Early Christianity wrestles with and ultimately transcends the Temple by arguing for its obsolescence. This is hardly a noncontroversial position in a society where power and wealth were linked particularly with one institution. A biblical study must be allowed to cast light on the social formation in which the text was created and has hitherto been read. Biblical exegesis must take care not to allow it to be divorced from the social world of today and yesterday. In this respect the emerging biblical interpretation from the so-called Third World has much to teach us.[33] The oppressive role of centers of power in the contemporary world and the fate which awaits those who challenge them have their echoes in the fate which awaited those who dared to go up to Jerusalem and of whom it could be said: "We heard this man say, 'I will destroy this Temple and in three days build a Temple not made with hands'" (Mark 14:58 my translation).

Bibliography

Bammel, Ernst. "The Revolution Theory from Reimarus to Brandon." In *Jesus and the Politics of His Day*, edited by Ernst Bammel and C. F. D. Moule, 11–68. Cambridge: Cambridge University Press, 1984.

Barker, Margaret. *The Older Testament: The Survival of Themes from the Ancient Royal Cult in Sectarian Judaism and Early Christianity*. London: SPCK, 1987.

Belo, Fernando. *A Materialist Reading of the Gospel of Mark*. Translated by Matthew J. O'Connell. Maryknoll, NY: Orbis, 1981.

---

31. To quote the title of Jameson, *The Political Unconscious*, where some attempt is made to deal with this aspect of literary criticism.

32. For a further discussion of this, see Lash, *Easter in Ordinary*.

33. Its implications are recognized in Bammel, "Revolution Theory."

Bietenhard, Hans. *Die himmlische Welt im Urchristentum und Spätjudentum.* Tübingen: Mohr, 1951.
Black, Matthew, and Albert-Marie Denis. *Apocalypsis Henochi Graece.* Pseudepigrapha Veteris Testamenti Graece 3. Leiden: Brill, 1970.
Box, G. H. Introduction to 4 Ezra. In *The Apocrypha and Pseudepigrapha of the Old Testament*, edited by R. H. Charles et al., 2:553–54. 2 vols. Oxford: Clarendon, 1913.
Charles, R. H. *Eschatology: The Doctrine of a Future Life in Israel, Judaism, and Christianity; A Critical History.* Schocken Paperbacks. New York: Schocken, 1963.
Charles, R. H., et al., eds. *The Apocrypha and Pseudepigrapha of the Old Testament.* 2 vols. Oxford: Clarendon, 1913.
Charlesworth, James H., ed. *The Old Testament Pseudepigrapha.* 2 vols. Garden City, NY: Doubleday, 1983–1985.
Chester, Andrew. *Divine Revelation and Divine Titles in the Pentateuchal Targumim.* Texte und Studien zum antiken Judentum 14. Tübingen: Mohr Siebeck, 1986.
Clements, R. E. *God and Temple.* Oxford: Blackwell, 1965.
Cohn, Norman R. C. *The Pursuit of the Millennium.* London: Secker & Warburg, 1957.
Davies, Philip R. "The Social World of the Apocalyptic Writings." In *The World of Ancient Israel: Sociological, Anthropological, and Political Perspectives: Essays by Members of the Society for Old Testament Study*, edited by R. E. Clements, 251–71. Cambridge: Cambridge University Press, 1989.
Dexinger, Ferdinand. *Henochs Zehnwochenapokalypse und offene Probleme der Apokalyptikforschung.* Studia post-Biblica 29. Leiden: Brill, 1977.
Ford, J. M. "The Heavenly Jerusalem and Orthodox Judaism." In *Donum Gentilicium: New Testament Studies in Honour of David Daube*, edited by Ernst Bammel et al., 215–26. Oxford: Clarendon, 1978.
Gaston, Lloyd. *No Stone on Another: Studies in the Significance of the Fall of Jerusalem in the Synoptic Gospels.* Supplements to Novum Testamentum 23. Leiden: Brill, 1970.
Goodman, Martin. *The Ruling Class of Judaea: The Origins of the Jewish Revolt against Rome, AD 66–70.* Cambridge: Cambridge University Press, 1987.
Hanson, Paul D. *The Dawn of Apocalyptic: The Historical and Sociological Roots of Jewish Apocalyptic Eschatology.* Philadelphia: Fortress, 1975.
Hill, Christopher. *Antichrist in Seventeenth-Century England.* Riddell Memorial Lectures, 41st ser. University of Newcastle Upon Tyne Publications. London: Oxford University Press, 1971.
Horne, Charles F., et al., eds. *The Sacred Books and Early Literature of the East.* 14 vols. New York: Parke, Austin, and Lipscomb, 1917.
Jameson, Fredric. *The Political Unconscious: Narrative as a Socially Symbolic Act.* Ithaca, NY: Cornell University Press, 1981.
Jonge, M. de. *The Testaments of the Twelve Patriarchs; a Study of their Text, Composition, and Origin.* Van Gorcum's theologische bibliotheek 25. Assen: Van Gorcum, 1953.
Kautsky, Karl. *Foundations of Christianity: A Study in Christian Origins.* New York: Monthly Review, 1972.
Kreissig, Heinz. *Die sozialen Zusammenhänge des judäischen Krieges. Klassen, und Klassenkampf im Palästina des 1. Jahrhunderts v. u. Z.* Schriften zur Geschichte und Kultur der Antike 1. Berlin: Akademie, 1970.
Lash, Nicholas. *Easter in Ordinary: Reflections on Human Experience and the Knowledge of God.* Richard Lectures 1986. Charlottesville: University Press of Virginia, 1988.

Maier, Johann. *Vom Kultus zur Gnosis*. Kairos: religionswissenschaftliche Studien 1. Salzburg: Müller, 1964.

McKelvey, R. J. *The New Temple: The Church in the New Testament*. Oxford Theological Monographs. London: Oxford University Press, 1969.

Milik, J. T., ed., with Matthew Black. *The Books of Enoch: Aramaic Fragments of Qumrân Cave 4*. Oxford: Clarendon, 1976.

Myers, Ched. *Binding the Strong Man: A Political Reading of Mark's Story of Jesus*. Maryknoll, NY: Orbis, 1988.

Myers, Jacob M. *I and II Esdras: Introduction, Translation, and Commentary*. 1st ed. Anchor Bible 42. Garden City, NY: Doubleday, 1974.

Nickelsburg, George W. E. "Enoch, Levi, and Peter: Recipients of Revelation in Upper Galilee." *Journal of Biblical Literature* 100 (1981) 575–600.

Pixley, Jorge V. *God's Kingdom: A Guide for Biblical Study*. Translated by Donald D. Walsh. Maryknoll, NY: Orbis, 1981.

Plöger, Otto. *Theocracy and Eschatology*. Translated by S. Rudman. Richmond, VA: John Knox, 1968.

Rowland, Christopher. *The Open Heaven: A Study of Apocalyptic in Judaism and Early Christianity*. New York: Crossroad, 1982.

———. *The Open Heaven: A Study of Apocalyptic in Judaism and Early Christianity*. 1988. Reprint, Eugene, OR: Wipf & Stock, 2002.

Segundo, Juan L. *The Historical Jesus of the Synoptics*. Translated by John Drury. Jesus of Nazareth, Yesterday and Today 2. Maryknoll, NY: Orbis, 1985.

Simon, Marcel. *Verus Israel: A Study of the Relations between Christians and Jews in the Roman Empire (135–425)*. Translated by H. McKeating. The Littman Library of Jewish Civilization. New York: Published for the Littman Library by Oxford University Press, 1986.

Strack, Hermann. L., and P. Billerbeck. *Kommentar zum Neuen Testament aus Talmud und Midrasch*. 6 vols. in 7 bks. Munich: Beck, 1922.

Williams, Raymond. *Marxism and Literature*. Marxist Introductions. Oxford: Oxford University Press, 1977.

Wink, Walter. *Naming the Powers: The Language of Power in the New Testament*. The Powers 1. Philadelphia: Fortress, 1984.

12

Friends of Albion?

The Danger of Cathedrals

1

WILLIAM BLAKE, IN *JERUSALEM*, called the English cathedral cities "the friends of Albion" (Albion being the embodiment of Britain in Blake's idiosyncratic myth).[1] What kind of friends are being talked of here? Are they merely companions who go along with every whim and desire of their friend, or are they those who have the true interests of their friend at heart and are prepared to talk about those things that make for their friend's peace and well-being? Blake's poem suggests that they behave as the former but should be acting in the latter capacity. Too many of them are infected with the same disease which eventually kills Albion, despite the prophetic call to recognize their mission. The disease is a religion of sacrifice, of rules, which lacks mutual forgiveness and the promotion of human kinship. Like the rest of the inhabitants of Albion, the friends either collude with, or promote, life committed to the senses and without the transforming power of imagination, and so they betray true art, which is the gateway to the eternal and to a set of values.

Blake had the highest regard for the Gothic artists who built the medieval cathedrals, seeing them as persons fired by imagination. But, despite exceptional prophetic spirits who emerged from some of the

---

1. Blake, *Jerusalem* 40:3; 48:27; and especially 71:13–14: their villages, towns, cities, seaports, temples, and sublime cathedrals, all were his friends.

cathedrals, he saw that the Christian religion was severely compromised by the cathedrals' cultural ethos and opposed to the way of Jesus. The cathedrals point to a God of "mercy, pity, peace, and love," and yet often seem entangled in the values of a world opposed to God, as Jerusalem and Babylon mingle together. They are touched by God's Spirit and can offer a glimpse of another dimension to existence, while at the same time they are tainted with barbarism and based on "the anonymous toil of their contemporaries," as Walter Benjamin put it.[2]

Blake's ambivalence towards cathedrals is shared by many, both inside and outside the Christian churches. We can go into these wonderful buildings and may catch in them a glimpse of eternity—but in their structures, in their particular relationship with society at large, and in their seeming cultivation of privilege in worship and life, they seem to be opposed to the values of the Lamb of God. That ambivalence is reflected in various parts of the biblical tradition which pose serious theological questions about church buildings, including cathedrals, in the life of the people of God. To paraphrase a recent Church of England report: the criticism of worldly splendor, which lay at the heart of the Cistercian ideal, leads one to ask whether the glory of the medieval cathedrals is really the most authentic representation of the religion of Galilean fishermen or Francis of Assisi.[3]

There is therefore a serious theological issue concerning the nature and operation of cathedrals which is often ignored or bypassed, perhaps because it seems to have been settled long ago. Churches which hear the Scriptures and seek to respond to them will, however, sooner or later find a discrepancy between contemporary practice and key aspects of the scriptural vision. Of course, questions are raised about all sacred places, and the attitudes of Christians to them—not just cathedrals. Cathedrals, because of their place in a nation's culture and affections, offer an acute example of the wider theological problem. Even if I were competent to do so, I can hope to do no more than scratch the surface of a subject which deserves the sort of treatment in our day given to it by Bede, our great ancestor in the faith.[4] My particular interest is biblical studies, and it is to the scriptural witness that I turn to suggest that

---

2. Benjamin, "Philosophy of History," 248 (Thesis 7): "[Cultural treasures] owe their existence not only to the efforts of the great minds and talents who created them but also to the anonymous toil of their contemporaries. There is no document of civilization which is not at the same time a document of barbarism."

3. Archbishops' Commission on Cathedrals (Church of England), *Heritage and Renewal*, 190. One of the curious features about this report is the absence of any theological rationale.

4. Bede, *Bede: On the Temple*.

we cannot easily sidestep the theological challenge to our attitudes to buildings, nor ignore the questions it poses to our practice.

In the Torah, provision for liturgy centers on the tabernacle, though the ancestors had worshipped regularly at a variety of holy places. As with human monarchy, which has an important though ambiguous position in the history of the people of God (1 Sam 8; 2 Sam 7:14), the role of the Temple and (more often) of other places of religious worship is viewed with a mixture of approbation, unease, and downright condemnation. Despite the divine sanction for the building of the Temple in Jerusalem and its conformity to the divine plan (1 Chr 28:12, 19), the description of the building of the Temple suggests that, from its very inception, its structures were infused by the spirit of Canaan. First Kings 11 records Solomon's departure from the worship of God, continued in the deeds of his descendants which, in the books of Kings, becomes a litany of catastrophic decline from the single-minded devotion to the God of Israel's ancestors. The story of the books of Kings would have been familiar to Blake: Temple worship involved compromise with local cults, with the world of the senses, and with the values of the settled society of the Canaanite cities. God who is beyond human comprehension, recognized as such in Solomon's prayer in 1 Kings 8:27, came to be too closely identified with a place, a temple made with hands (1 Kgs 8; Isa 66:1–2, quoted in Acts 7:49–50), a dynasty, a city—and perhaps inevitably with oppression and injustice. God's approval of the building did not extend to the form, content, and actions in it, as the conditions laid out in the response to Solomon's prayer make clear (1 Kgs 9:3). The Temple, decorated and influenced as it was by the culture of Canaan, rapidly became a shrine to Baal and not to Yahweh.

As the years went by, the extent of this departure from God's purposes was recognized from time to time, particularly in the reigns of Hezekiah and Josiah. There appears to have been a lack of awareness, among elites and people alike, of the extent of the discrepancy between the practice of the Temple and the demands of God. There were those who kept the Sinaitic vision alive: a vision of a people formed in the desert, who had shed the false consciousness of Egypt and its fleshpots, but who had not yet been corrupted by Canaanite life. Theirs was a vision of a God who required concern for the orphan, the widow, and the stranger, and whose presence was particularly connected with the portable tabernacle rather than the permanent and glorious edifice of the Temple. The Exodus vision had almost disappeared in the Jerusalem of the monarchic period. It makes only a rare appearance in the psalmody of Solomon's Temple and in the oracles of Jerusalem's prophets. Even the celebration of the Passover had fallen into desuetude (2 Kgs 23:22). In place of the story of the Exodus and the giving of the Law, the myths of the Davidic dynasty (together with the invincibility of Zion and its Temple) so dominated the culture that the austere story of the formation of a people with a religion of tabernacle and social justice was almost forgotten. Prophets like Isaiah called a people to seek justice, rescue the oppressed, defend the orphan, plead for the widow, rather than for "the multitude of your sacrifices" (Isa 1:11, 17 NRSV). The prophetic critique reaches its climax in Ezekiel and Jeremiah, when Solomon's Temple is regarded as a place of idolatry, nowhere more stingingly rebuked than in Jeremiah's Temple sermon (Ezek 8:5–18; Jer 7:4, 8).

We can only guess what a shock it must have been to the Temple culture which echoed the conviction, "God is in the midst of the city; it shall never be moved" (Ps 46:5 my translation), when the Temple was destroyed after the invasion of Nebuchadnezzar. After the return from exile there seems to have been a struggle between those like Haggai and Zechariah, who wanted to see the Temple rebuilt as a symbol of Israel's life, and those who held out against such a move with a grander vision, more universal in scope. Haggai prophesies that the impoverishment of Israel is the result of the neglect of "old-fashioned" Temple religion. If only the Temple were rebuilt (and scarce resources thereby diverted to the restoration of cultic activity), then all would be well in the land (Hag 1:4–15). It is likely that the oracles which make up the final chapters of Isaiah bear witness to the growing disillusionment of a prophetic group who find themselves outmaneuvered by the protagonists of Temple reconstruction, and thus marginalized in Israel's life. As Jews sought to survive in the hostile world of ancient Near Eastern power politics, figures like Ezra and Nehemiah consolidated the life of Jerusalem centered on priesthood, Temple, and Law. But, as even Nehemiah 5 indicates, there can be no escape from the priority given to social justice, with the ruling elite, in the person of Nehemiah, taking the lead. The Temple continued to play a central role in the lives of Jews, both inside and outside Judea, in the years preceding the Christian era. The regular flow of income to the Temple from all parts of the Roman empire led to the enrichment of this institution and those who ran it. It was the focus of religion and was a powerful economic factor in Judean life as well as an influential ideological symbol. But the Temple's pre-eminent place should not lead us to forget the evidence of the questioning of the Temple which continued in the intertestamental literature.

The priests who held power in Jerusalem preserved the Temple as a holy space at the heart of Jewish life in the holy city, in order to maintain the pattern of worship that they believed God had prescribed for that place. All that might defile the holy place was excluded from the Temple.

In Jesus' day the maintenance of the cult necessitated some kind of coexistence with the Roman authorities (cf. John 11:48). This priority for the preservation of the holy place was highest on the agenda. Small wonder that, with the destruction of this holy place, the *raison d'être* of priestly religion should perish with the sacrifices they were pledged to preserve. The maintenance of a holy space was not, however, confined to the Temple. During the period of the Second Temple, this search for a holy space was carried out in a variety of ways. The members of the Qumran sect lived in the desert, and in their common life created a holy environment where the holy angels assembled and shared their life. The Pharisees' view of holiness was rooted in practical living in the midst of the variety of human communities, both near to and far from the Temple. The detailed regulations of the Mishnah, the earliest code of Jewish practice outside the Bible, bear witness to the seriousness of the endeavor of their rabbinic successors to ensure the preservation of a holy space in all aspects of existence. It was that vision which enabled Judaism to survive the destruction of its holy place in 70 CE and for Pharisaism to become the driving force of what was to emerge in the second century as rabbinic Judaism.

Pharisees, like other Jews and Christians, may have been devastated by the destruction of the Temple in 70 CE, but the emerging practice of religion based on the synagogue (which could meet anywhere and was not necessarily attached to particular places which were deemed to be holy) was a factor in enabling them to survive the events of 70. Buildings did not, in the last resort, matter in the life of the people of God; what mattered was obedience to the divine Law in all circumstances. Judaism has survived without a Temple for the last two thousand years. Judaism has maintained a religion which does not depend on Temple or even holy places, so paralleling the words of the third-century Christian writer Minucius Felix: "We have no temples; we have no altars."[5] Judaism contrasts with what the Christian religion has become.

2

Initially, the early Christians shared the ambivalent relationship to the Temple evident in some Jewish circles during the Second Temple period (e.g., Acts 6:13; cf. Mark 14:58; John 4:23). On the one hand, we find them using its imagery to describe their common life, hinting that this life replaces the holy life of the Temple in Jerusalem. On the other hand, some of the earliest

---

5. Marcus Tertullian and Minucius Felix Octavius, *Minucius Felix Octavius*, 389–90 (ch. 32).

Christians continued to worship in the Temple. The Gospels leave us with a picture of Jesus who, in the last days of his life, prophesied the demise of the Temple. According to the Gospel of Mark, Jesus' death comes at the end of a narrative in which, from Chapter 11 onwards, the Temple is a dominant theme. Jesus enters the Temple. In Mark the story of the cursing of the fig tree, which sandwiches the "cleansing," is a comment on the bankruptcy of the institution. Its fate will be that of the cursed tree. Jesus condemns scribes for devouring widows' houses and, before leaving the Temple for the last time, gets his companions to note the way in which the widow, out of her poverty, puts in everything she has to live on, while the rest contributed out of their abundance (Mark 12:41–44). The incident is described without comment. But, in the light of Mark 12:40, where the scribes are condemned for devouring widows' houses, the fact that an institution allows an impoverished widow to give all that she has, sits uneasily with the demand in the Torah to care for the widow (Deut 24:17; Jer 7:6).

The death of Jesus is the moment when the heart of the old economic, political, and religious institution is destroyed, truly "the end of the world" for those who set great store by it. At his baptism a heavenly voice had proclaimed Jesus as God's son and the heavens were rent apart. So also is the veil of the Temple rent at Jesus' death (Mark 1:10; 15:38). Heaven and earth are linked at the rending of the heavens. But at the moment of Jesus' death, the tearing of the veil suggests something more destructive—the end of the Temple (cf. 1 Sam 15:27). The veil, which symbolizes the mystique of the Temple's power, is torn asunder signifying its demise. The Temple is replaced by a way of life based on service and an alternative "holy space" focused on commemoration of Christ: "in place of the Temple liturgy Jesus offers his body—that is, his messianic practice in life and death."[6] The destruction means an end to an institution and an ideology which had dominated life, politically, religiously, and economically. So the stones of the Temple, however beautiful, deserve no special attention except as monuments to an obsolescent form of religious life (Mark 13:2). In the days of Israel's exile the departure of the divine glory from the Temple was a sign of imminent destruction (Ezek 1; 10). But, in contrast to Ezekiel's prophecy, there is no promise in the New Testament that any building would ever again be set apart as a particular place of the divine presence and worship—except "the temple of Jesus' body" (John 2:21). The juxtaposition of death and rending at the climax of Mark's Gospel means that the moment of defeat of a prophet of the Temple's doom precipitates the institution's collapse. It is left to a representative of the

---

6. Myers, *Binding the Strong Man*, 364.

Roman military to recognize in this moment the reign of another sort of king than Caesar (Mark 15:37; cf. John 18:36; Phil 2:10–11).

According to Acts, the first Christians continued to worship in the Temple, but in their articulation of the worship of God, the Temple had become a metaphor for the holiness and sense of divine presence in the lives of men, women, and children. The importance of the physical Temple diminished, particularly in those texts which now form the canon of our New Testament: "The hour is coming when you will worship the Father neither on this mountain nor in Jerusalem. . . . The true worshippers will worship the Father in spirit and truth, for the Father seeks such as these to worship him" (John 4:21, 23 NRSV). Among the early Christians are radical voices like Stephen's, whose implicit criticism of the Temple provokes a hostile reaction leading to his death. In the speech attributed to him in Acts, he dwells on the rebelliousness of the majority of his ancestors, and in his review of Israel's history he points to Solomon, who built a house for God which, if the quotation from Isaiah 66:1 is anything to go by, marked a departure from the divine intention; as the prophet says: "Heaven is my throne, and the earth is my footstool. What kind of house will you build for me, says the Lord, or what is the place of my rest? Did not my hand make all these things?" (Acts 7:49–50 NRSV). Bede, in his *Commentary on the Acts of the Apostles*, regards Stephen as a spiritual pioneer who explains to his hearers that "the Lord does not place a high value on dressed stone, but rather desires the splendor of heavenly souls."[7]

Throughout the New Testament, sacred buildings, however glorious, seem to have been of little concern to its writers. Their prime concerns were the reign of God, the witness to the ways of God's justice, and the hope of heaven on earth, all anticipated in the common life of small groups of men, women, and children. Christians began to explore a variant way of being God's people: their priority was the temple of the Holy Spirit, men and women of flesh and blood. Emmanuel, God with us, is met in the persons of the hungry, thirsty, naked, and imprisoned, for the weak and marginal are the ones with whom Jesus identified (Matt 1:23; 25:31–46). In the Pauline Epistles we have glimpses of communities struggling to maintain a style of life at odds with contemporary culture. The locus of Christ's presence in the world is to be found in a variety of different places which share the holiness of God (1 Cor 1:2–31; Rom 12), and therefore where people seek to work as a community under God, distinguished by its quality of life and practical service (Rom 15:25; 2 Cor 8:4; Phlm 13). The community witnesses before the world at large and maintains a "divine presence" in

---

7. Bede, *Acts of the Apostles*, 7:44.

the face of disregard for the justice of God (Rev 10–11). Heaven and earth meet no longer in tabernacle or Temple, but outside the camp, in a place of shame and reproach where the blasphemers and sabbath-breakers are stoned. Those who share the way of Jesus can expect to go with him outside the camp, into the secular world.[8] God's love and solidarity are demonstrated in human beings in ways which the elaborate performance of cultic ritual never can show. The gate of heaven opens up to a solitary visionary on a Greek island (Rev 1:9; 4:1), just as in the dark days of a people's exile in Babylon, when a prophet saw the divine glory move from above the cherubim in Solomon's Temple and encountered it in his place of exile by the waters of Babylon (Ezek 1; 10). The unseen glory of cherubim and seraphim behind the veil in the Temple had burst beyond the veil. Despite the pessimism of the people who despaired of so doing, it was now possible to sing the Lord's song in a strange land. The Temple was superfluous as a witness to the divine presence. In the New Testament the human community is where God may now be found, acknowledged, and served, and where the alternative vision of reality is maintained and celebrated. The hope in, and commitment to, the crucified Messiah, which are folly to humanity (1 Cor 3:19), are incarnated in people where God's Spirit can dwell. But those communities of faithful people need to recognize that the divine often comes as a disturbing, apparently alien, presence, from outside the warmth of the gathered community. The risen Christ stands outside the door of a complacent Church and knocks, seeking entrance.

The sentiments of early Christian writers make disturbing reading, as Karl Barth appreciated in lectures of 1920:

> The *church* of the Bible is, significantly, the Tabernacle, the portable tent. The moment it becomes a Temple, it becomes essentially only an object of attack. One gathers that for the apostles the whole of the Old Testament is summarized in Stephen's apology. Undeniably the center of interest of both Testaments is not in the building of the church but in its destruction, which is always threatening and even beginning. In the heavenly Jerusalem of Revelation nothing is more finally significant than the church's complete absence: "And I saw no Temple therein."[9]

When Christianity became the religion of the Roman empire, things began to change. While some of the seeds of these developments antedate the Constantinian settlement, a significant shift took place after Constantine, whose reign offered fertile soil in which those seeds could grow. From

---

8. Heb 13:13; Exod 33:7; Lev 24:16; Num 15; 35. See also Isaacs, *Sacred Space*.
9. Barth, *Word of God*, 72 (italics original).

about 260 CE, but especially after 313 CE, church buildings began to gain in size and become public structures. This reflected the growth in the size of congregations, and (after 313 CE) of imperial favor. In the fourth century the Church grew, according to one estimate, from 10 percent of the populace to about 50 percent. Big buildings became necessary. Christians chose the basilica (associated with the emperor and with law courts) rather than the temple (associated with paganism) as the design template. So ecclesiastical buildings, which had hitherto been domestic (although getting larger), became public and were beautifully decorated to reflect imperial iconography. Space was divided into areas for clergy and laity. Because of the large congregations, the worship became large-scale rather than relational and communitarian.[10] As the number of worshippers grew and the places of worship likewise, ceremonial flourished and the importance of human relationship in divine service withered.[11] So there begins to emerge a pattern of Christian activity which sits uneasily with the biblical vision of the common life. Passages in the Hebrew Bible anticipate Blake's prophetic critique of the Anglicanism of his day, whose buildings, ethos, and way of life had succumbed to a contemporary religion of Canaan, a culture of abstract reasoning and moral virtue. In the New Testament the identification of Christ with the Temple, and with the divine presence in unexpected places and persons, and the priority given to human relationships in ministry, leads us to widen our quest for the gates of heaven.

Supporters of cathedrals may well suggest that the money which goes to their appeals and which pays for the upkeep and pattern of worship would not go to the poor and needy. Nevertheless, one has to ask what is the theological rationale for the huge expense involved in cathedral building and preservation. For example, a new cathedral is being built in Managua, Nicaragua, after the colonial building was destroyed in the 1972 earthquake. Why is this happening when hundreds of thousands are homeless, and half the population is without regular employment? One answer is to allude to the anointing at Bethany, or to say that it is the Judases of the world who complain about the expense while saying that the money should be given to the poor.[12] Such building projects can be replicated in other poor countries throughout the world—although, by way of contrast, in the archdiocese of São Paulo which is a pioneer of the Roman Catholic

---

10. See Cobb, "Architectural Setting," 528.

11. See Kreider, *Worship and Evangelism*.

12. On the ways in which the passage about the anointing at Bethany is used by contemporary British Christians, see Spencer and Snape, *Gospel, the Poor, and the Churches*.

Church's "preferential option for the poor," the bishop's palace and the cathedral have been given over to community use.

Much is made too of cathedrals as spaces where people of all degrees of explicit allegiance or none may feel they belong. Yet there are limits to the use of this space. What place do flags and other military insignia, which sit so uneasily with the way of Christ, have in a Christian church? Services of remembrance can and should take place, but without "religion hid in war," as Blake puts it.[13] Incarnation is a theological concept often used to support the open-minded and inclusive ministry of churches alongside all sorts and conditions of people. But incarnation does not mean baptizing the status quo or accepting its values, for the coming of the Word into the world means judgement: "The light has come into the world, but people preferred darkness to light because their deeds were evil" (John 3:19 my translation). Christian groups, with the spaces they inhabit, seek through God's grace to bear witness to the alternative culture of the gospel: "Among the Gentiles, kings lord it over their subjects; and those in authority are given the title benefactor. Not so with you: on the contrary, the greatest among you must bear themselves like the youngest, the one who rules like one who serves" (Luke 22:24–27 my translation). Christians offer love and acceptance, seeking to embody that love and acceptance in which they have shared. They are part of a living temple, ministering to persons of flesh and blood with the human and financial resources at their disposal; only then do they turn to the care and preservation of bricks and mortar, glass, and other artefacts.

3

Cathedrals have been transmitters of British culture, and as such have nurtured a much broader, open relationship between English society, culture, and history on the one hand and the church which bears witness to Christ on the other. A continuing problem for any cosmopolitan and nondualistic ethos, incorporating the best from the culture of the surrounding society, is that it runs the risk of ending up in the same predicament as the wonderful edifice erected by Solomon, which opened up the puritanical religion of Yahweh to the richer, less austere culture of Canaan. The kings of the earth may bring their gifts into the new Jerusalem in repentance, yet their acceptance must be of the ways of God's justice for all, not of the privileges of the few. So I find myself among those whose concern is reflected in the following words from the recent report of the Archbishops'

---

13. Blake, *Milton*, 42:17–22 ("religion hid in war named moral virtue"); and Blake, *Jerusalem* 75:20.

Commission on Cathedrals: "For some, both inside the Church and outside [the close affinity of cathedrals and private education] raises questions about the political or professional desirability of the Church being involved at all in independent [fee-paying] education."[14] To which may be added a question of theological propriety too.

I agree with the sentiments of Blake's *Jerusalem* that cathedrals and churches may have a continuing part to play in the religion of these islands. While it would be wrong to ignore the attempts to play such a part, some of which are described in this book, the shape of our medieval churches and their distinctive ethos can make it difficult for them to be responsive to the priorities of the Church's mission. Churches have an ambivalent position in society, and as a result, like all institutions, they have a continuous struggle to work out a *modus vivendi* with contemporary culture. The civic role of cathedrals demands even greater vigilance of their staff in the maintenance of an alternative horizon within their life, their preaching, and their practical discipleship. My impression is that the peculiar position of cathedrals has made it particularly difficult for them to be countercultural signs. We now have an opportunity to think again about mission and ways of bringing the Gospel of Jesus Christ to our generation. Those of us who use and are responsible for cathedrals, churches, and chapels should apply the Five Marks or Strands of Mission to our buildings and their use, demanding as they are of human and financial resources. These arose out of the 1988 Lambeth Conference and were commended by the General Synod of the Church of England to Anglican dioceses. They are proclaiming the good news of the kingdom; teaching, baptizing, and nurturing new believers; responding to human need by loving service; seeking to transform unjust structures of society; striving to safeguard the integrity of creation; and sustaining and renewing the life of the earth. The role of our buildings in fulfilling these tasks demands of us a theological, as well as a purely pragmatic, answer.

Perhaps there is a way for the cathedrals to go on seeking to work out a vision of service in liturgy and practical action. According to the monastic ideal, buildings for divine worship, living, and service were alongside each other. So often in the cathedrals of the "new foundation" (that is, the old monastic communities which became cathedrals at the Reformation), the buildings which enabled service as a witness lie in ruins or have been adopted for other purposes. They remain as a poignant testimony to a monastic ideal which has partly fallen into desuetude, and a challenge to us to recapture that balance between worship and action in the divine service. The devastation of

---

14. Archbishops' Commission on Cathedrals (Church of England), *Heritage and Renewal*, 45.

monastic life in this country was a tragedy for British religion. Whatever may have been wrong with the monasteries in the sixteenth century, the wholesale destruction of a way of life in which worship and welfare were, in theory, closely intertwined, warts and all, is one of the less appealing parts of British social history. The remnants of those old monastic communities, which form the closes of many of our cathedrals, testify to that monastic ideal of divine service in the worship of lips and of lives, devoted in practical service, the latter being in no way inferior to the former.

In this essay I have echoed Blake's sympathetic description of the cathedrals as the "friends of Albion," and his belief that they can be true friends in helping to point out and alleviate Albion's disease. I share Blake's hope that they will be beacons for our nation and a means of offering more than an aesthetic or vague religious experience. Jeremiah's stunning indictment of the Temple of the Lord—and the complacent attitude of its supporters long ago—is a salutary reminder of the constant vigilance demanded of us as we seek to wrestle with the legacy of buildings and their contemporary use. Many will come into cathedrals echoing the disciples' wonder at "the fine stones and ornaments" of the ancient Temple (Luke 21:5 my translation). Peter desired on the Mount of Transfiguration to build tabernacles to preserve or encapsulate the divine. Our need to create and maintain holy spaces is strong and its consequences far-reaching, but the glorious stones must never become an end in themselves. Christian institutions which seek to be true to the call of Jesus Christ must, as a first priority, respond to people who suffer hardship and dislocation, and who find themselves vulnerable or ignored. The risen Christ, the living Temple, is found (disconcertingly for most of us) in surprising and unprepossessing people, in a manner which is disturbing to a comfortable British Christian like myself. With whatever significance we, as humans, seek to endow Christian buildings, theologically they are no more deserving of attention as places where God may be found than, on the one hand, any place where two or three are gathered together, or on the other hand, than the persons of the poor, the outcast, and the vulnerable. That will affect the way in which we view buildings, however grand and however venerable:

> The ugly, concrete block worship-space . . . can be a holy place, because it is occupied by and associated with a community of Christian people who are known, publicly known, for their acts of charity and peacemaking and who have drawn their building into the struggle for a radical openness to the will of God. . . . To

root the holiness of Christian sacred space in anything else is to be involved either in idolatry or in magic.[15]

Liturgy and service go hand in hand as parts of what constitutes the divine service, just as in the Torah, the service of the tabernacle went hand in hand with the practice of justice and mercy. All Christian communities must manifest that poverty of spirit which does not count worldly success as its sole criterion for devotion to Christ, is open to criticism, and is not sustained by self-righteousness. Where God is praised and reverenced and, in Ignatius of Loyola's words, no inordinate attachment is placed between oneself and God, a balance between tabernacle and social justice can be preserved. To be so attached to the sign is to be enslaved to the world of appearances, the world of the fallen senses. Many would see cathedrals as ways of opening the "eternal worlds." But too often a narrow aesthetic experience turns out to be no real opening to the eternal world, for it lacks encounters which produce the recognition that we cannot "exist but by Brotherhood,"[16] and appropriate action to match.

I believe that Blake would have beckoned us to see the importance of the ambiguities of cathedrals as opportunities for imaginative creativity. The existence of what Blake describes as "two contrary states" is not to be transcended with the result either that one dissolves into the other, or that one is in effect subordinated to the other. Rather, adequate attention is to be given to both poles, particularly the "contrary" which we admire less and which most causes us discomfort. Cathedrals and holy places have become an established part of Christian culture; yet they do not fit easily with a theological tradition which is hardly warm in its support of sacred edifices, and which gives the central place to the nurture of "living stones" (1 Pet 2:5). While we await that "place where Contrarieties are equally true,"[17] the tantalizing and disconcerting effects of the contraries evident in cathedrals, churches, and chapels can provoke us to be more vigilant for glimpses of Jerusalem in the midst of Babylon, and less complacent in our assumption that we know where these are to be found—for we will surely, to our surprise and consternation, find them in the least expected persons and places.

---

15. White, "Theology," 42–43.
16. Blake, *Jerusalem*, 96:28.
17. Blake, *Jerusalem*, 48:14.

Bibliography

Archbishops' Commission on Cathedrals (Church of England). *Heritage and Renewal.* London: Church House, 1995.

Barth, Karl. *The Word of God and the Word of Man.* Translated with a new foreword by Douglas Horton. Harper Torchbooks. New York: Harper, 1957.

Bede. *Bede: On the Temple.* Translated with notes by Seán Connolly. With an introduction by Jennifer O'Reilly. Translated Texts for Historians 21. Liverpool, UK: Liverpool University Press, 1995.

———. *Commentary on the Acts of the Apostles.* Translated with an introduction and notes by Lawrence T. Martin. Cistercian Studies Series 117. Kalamazoo, MI: Cistercian, 1989.

Benjamin, Walter. "Theses on the Philosophy of History." In *Illuminations*, 253–64. Edited with an introduction by Hannah Arendt. Translated by Harry Zohn. London: Fontana, 1979.

Blake, William. *Jerusalem.* Edited with an introduction and notes by Morton D. Paley. Blake's Illuminated Books 1. Princeton: Princeton University Press, 1991.

———. *Milton, A Poem, and the Final Illuminated Works.* Edited with introductions and notes by Robert N. Essick and Joseph Viscomi. Paperback ed. Blake's Illuminated Books 5. Princeton: Princeton University Press, 1998.

Cobb, Peter G. "The Architectural Setting of the Liturgy." In *The Study of Liturgy*, edited by Cheslyn Jones et al., 473–87. London: SPCK, 1978.

Isaacs, Marie E. *Sacred Space: An Approach to the Theology of the Epistle to the Hebrews.* Journal for the Study of the Old Testament Supplement Series 73. Sheffield: JSOT Press, 1992.

Kreider, Alan. *Worship and Evangelism in Pre-Christendom.* Alcuin/GROW Liturgical Study 32. Cambridge: Grove Books, 1995.

Myers, Ched. *Binding the Strong Man: A Political Reading of Mark's Story of Jesus.* Maryknoll, NY: Orbis, 1988.

Spencer, Liz, and Dawn Snape. *The Gospel, the Poor, and the Churches: A Research Study Carried Out for Christian Aid.* London: Christian Aid, 1994.

Tertullian, Marcus, and Minucius Felix Octavius. *Apologetical Works and Minucius Felix Octavius.* Translated by Rudolph Arbesmann et al. 1950. First paperback reprint, Fathers of the Church. Washington, DC: Catholic University of America Press, 2008.

White, Susan. "Theology and Sacred Space." In *The Sense of the Sacramental: Movement and Measure in Art and Music, Place and Time*, edited by David Brown and Ann Loades, 31–43. London: SPCK, 1995.

13

Render to God What Belongs to God

1

THE FORM FOR MY Poll Tax registration is sitting in my kitchen as I procrastinate about how to deal with it. The whole process of registration and the tax to which it is a prelude seem so despicable that I would gladly decide at this point not to fill in the form and begin the process of non-compliance. When Ministers say that this tax is fairer than the present system, I feel anger and also a sense of powerlessness. There seems to be little doubt about the injustice of a tax which charges the richest person in a locality the same as the poorest. Yet another part of me recognizes what a fruitless gesture non-compliance would be, seeing that the mechanism exists to sequester my resources: I will have to pay it whether I like it or not. Is there room for maneuver in responding to this injustice? How best can I work constructively to remedy this injustice when there seems to be little space for any alternative action?

In situations like this there are two important tasks for me as a Christian. Firstly, I am determined to join with those who feel similar revulsion to this piece of legislation, with its regressive attitude to taxation and alarming implications for civil liberties. Secondly, while I have to renounce my desire for ready-made answers to my problem, whether in Scripture or Tradition, I must attend to what the Spirit is saying to the churches today but use the necessary discernment to enable my path of discipleship to be in continuity with our ancestors in the faith. What I want to attempt in this article is to put on paper some of the clearing of the biblical ground that enables me to continue the journey of faith and take into account this new challenge to our contemporary witness.

2

According to Mark's Gospel, Jesus of Nazareth preached the reign of God and thus the vision of salvation and heaven which eschatological hope had kept alive. The present order would not last. The imminent arrival of the messianic age heralded new priorities and broadened horizons (Matt 11:2–28; Luke 4:16). But the Gospel portraits do not present Jesus as the wide-eyed visionary whose preaching was not matched by his practice. In Mark, for example, the paradigm for the Christian gospel, the rejection of the message of the kingdom of God is accompanied by an emphatic distancing of Jesus from contemporary political arrangements. The messianic demonstration is followed by action in the Temple, which is condemned in words borrowed from the earlier denunciation of the Temple by Jeremiah and Isaiah's vision of the Exile. The juxtaposition of action in the Temple with the cursing of the barren fig tree indicates the redundancy of an order whose priorities conflict with the kingdom of God. Attempts to turn this polarization into a dichotomy between the religious and the political miss the point that *de facto* political authority in Jerusalem was wielded by the priestly aristocracy and the Judean ruling class. The fact that the challenge is against this group rather than the Romans is merely indicative of the force of the former's political power. The concluding chapters of the Synoptic Gospels leave the disciples with little idea of what the messianic reign would be like. They can be left in little doubt, however, that followers of the messiah will want to maintain a critical distance from contemporary institutions.

From a different point of view, the Gospel of John is misunderstood if the tag "the spiritual Gospel" deceives us into thinking that it is little concerned with the politics of real life. Indeed, as David Rensberger has recently reminded us, this Gospel insists that the key events in Christian life are highly political acts in which the participants demonstrate their allegiance to a different way of being the people of God.[1] For Nicodemus, who would be a secret disciple, and for the disciples who cannot cope with Jesus' eucharistic teaching in John 6:51–70, the risk involved in participation in these acts is socially costly. Likewise in its treatment of Jesus' confrontation with Pilate there is a rival interpretation of kingship in which the "non-worldly" (i.e., re-defined) understanding of kingship is articulated in the story: this king is one who washes his disciples' feet. Jesus' reply to Pilate,

---

1. Rensberger, *Johannine Faith*.

"My kingdom is not of this world" (John 18:36 RSV) is not a statement about the location of God's kingdom but concerns the origin of the inspiration for Jesus' view of the kingdom. Its norms are the result of God's spirit and righteousness. It is otherworldly in the sense that it is wrong to suppose that the definition of kingship and kingdom is to be found among this world's rulers or in their sway. This apparently inward-looking Gospel bids the followers of Jesus not to fight "but remain in the world bearing witness to the truth before the rulers of synagogue and empire."[2]

Such distance from the powers that be and such questioning of unquestioning subservience is to be found even in that passage which has formed the cornerstone of conformity and participation in the establishment: Romans 13. A reading of the passage indicates quite clearly that subservience to the powers is not a matter of blind obedience. The reason for obedience is that it serves the good of the readers. What is offered is an ideal pattern which States should implement. It is a message to the ruled rather than the rulers, possibly because some of the ruled in the Christian community in Rome were actually questioning the necessity or indeed competence of the State. The necessity of the State is reaffirmed. It is a mark of the old age which is still very much in force. But the State has to seek the good of its subjects. Such good must be defined by the character of God's goodness (the word elsewhere in Romans refers to that goodness). In so far as the State fails to do this or interprets the good as what serves the interests of the powerful, it undermines the contractual obligation so carefully enunciated in these verses. What is more, Paul's expectation of Christ's coming and reign necessarily casts its shadow over the permanence and rightness of any political regime. All, by virtue of their pursuit of sectional interest, are marked with the mark of the Beast: a reading of Romans 13 will always need the corrective of Revelation 13, so that accommodation and cooperation can at all times be seen for what they are in the "messianic light."[3]

The uncompromising rejection of State power and accommodation in the book of Revelation challenges the complacent and encourages the hard-pressed. In its stark contrast between the Lamb and the Beast, the Whore of Babylon, and the Bride of New Jerusalem, it juxtaposes the choices facing men and women and reminds the Lamb's followers of the dangers of becoming entangled in a political system based on a completely new set of values. What is particularly disturbing is the ruthless probing into the motives behind the benevolence of the powerful. The deceit involved by practitioners and gullible recipients is frightening. The remedy

---

2. Rensberger, *Johannine Faith*, 100.
3. To borrow a phrase of Theodor Adorno (*Minima Moralia*, 247).

is simple: social separation. "Here is a call for the endurance of the saints, those who keep the commandment of God and the faith of Jesus" (Rev 14:12 my translation). As Klaus Wengst has put it: this sentence can be regarded as a summary of all that John wants to say. "This endurance puts Christian life into the role of the outsider."[4]

Thus, while still living in an age which is passing away, the churches must make choices about the extent of their involvement and participation by judging just how far particular policies and political orders manifest the way of the Messiah. This brief survey of merely some New Testament approaches indicates the complexity of a task in which one can expect to encounter many different opinions. But, when the churches today wrestle with the issues in a situation where inexorable integration into the current political system is a continuing process, the chances of critical awareness are greatly diminished, and the dangers now mount that the churches will be used to baptize social, political, and economic systems which are far from reflecting the righteousness of God.

3

The pattern of conflict, so often recognized as a dominant theme within the Synoptic Gospels, is all too often relegated to the "spiritual" sphere. The persistence of the acceptance of such a separation is testimony enough to the pervasiveness of the dualism in contemporary theology.[5] No happier hunting ground for that separation between sacred and secular, spiritual and material, has been found than in the discussion about the tribute money. Here, surely, they say, is a passage which indicates that Jesus was not prepared to disturb the existing order? This view is buttressed by contemporary attempts to separate the kingdom of God from the human kingdoms, rooted in Augustine's and Luther's emphatic separation of the human and divine realms.[6] Paul's unequivocal support for the payment of taxes indicates that it was taken as an injunction to pay taxes to Caesar and recognize the demands of the State as legitimate (Rom 13:6). But then, Paul's setting, particularly the situation of the Roman Christians, left little room for maneuver. Whereas Jesus was not directly under Roman jurisdiction for much of his life, the Christians in Rome had no alternative to paying their taxes unless they wanted to court imprisonment and death.

4. Wengst, *Pax Romana*, 133–35.

5. See Lash, *Easter in Ordinary*; and Kerr, *Theology after Wittgenstein*, concisely expressed in Brown, *Spirituality and Liberation*.

6. See Skinner, *Foundations*, vol. 2, part 1.

Four ways of interpreting this passage have been canvassed which allow that Jesus was giving Caesar a valid role in the political life of his day.[7] The conventional assumption is that Jesus is allowing a limited autonomy to Caesar provided that this does not infringe the demands of God. Secondly, there is the view that what Jesus is recommending is a complete separation of spheres of influence under God between the spiritual and the temporal, between religion and politics. Thirdly, there is the view that the kings of the earth receive their sovereignty by divine permission and accordingly the saying means that by giving Caesar what is Caesar's the Jews would be giving God what is God's.[8] A fourth approach asserts that the second half of Jesus' reply "Render to God what belongs to God" is to be understood as undermining the obligation to Caesar by subordinating it to obligation to God. The land of Israel belongs to God alone (Lev 25:23), and no part of it may be handed over to a pagan ruler.

With regard to the second view, it is most unlikely that Jesus' words involved a separation between the sacred and secular spheres. That kind of separation, such a feature of our Western Christianity, was certainly not typical of the Judaism of Jesus' day. Jews regarded God as the creator of the world. The whole universe was seen as God's domain, and no earthly ruler had any absolute right of possession or authority. Thus, giving God what was God's due meant offering to the supreme ruler of the whole world all that belonged to God.

But why did Jesus not say this? A simple answer is that the context in which the question was asked demanded circumspection. Jesus was not here offering a definitive ruling on relations between his followers and the State, but a clever, if ambiguous, answer given in a situation where he had been put in a tight corner by his opponents.[9] Ambiguity was an essential part of a response in a situation where there were those who were seeking to trap him in his speech (cf. Luke 12:54). Luke, who was probably drawing on a version of the passion narrative that was independent of Mark, indicates that the answer *was* a factor in the accusation before Pilate (23:2). That it was included as part of the basis for the case against Jesus should make us pause before assuming that the meaning of the saying is entirely transparent. In any discussion of the passage, it is important to note that Jesus' prophetic role and radical preaching could conceivably have comprised a program for radical change and a short-term acceptance of the reality of Rome pending its demise in the face of the divine sovereignty.

7. There is a survey of research in Bruce, "Render to Caesar."
8. Derrett, *Law in the New Testament*, 335–36.
9. Bruce, "Render to Caesar," 259.

Such acceptance would then arise from the politico-religious strategy of one whose primary challenge was to the Jewish nation, its institutions, and life as God's means of offering a light to the nations. The focus of attention on Rome would have distracted attention from the inadequacies of the Jewish polity as a reflection of the order which God required.[10] We may compare the ministry of Jeremiah in this respect. Jeremiah had warned that Babylon was God's servant and that obedient well-being lay in submission (Jer 27:4–22; 38:17–28) and a concomitant direction of the hearer's attention to the inadequacies of their response to divine justice. So this lack of evidence of Jesus' concern with Rome should not be interpreted as a separation between the religious and the political but between the primary and secondary spheres of political concern for Jewish prophets.

The discussion takes an interesting turn when Jesus makes his opponents show him a coin. Jesus diverts the question from mere theory to the reality of the means of exchange whereby the tribute was expected to be paid. Whether we can place great weight on the fact that he himself does not appear to possess a coin is uncertain, but it may be another indication that Jesus is here dealing with a jurisdiction and set of issues both unfamiliar to a Galilean and incompatible with the style of life which he had been leading. After being presented with a coin bearing the image of the Roman emperor, he asks whose image and superscription it is. Why? Is it in order to indicate rights and duties to the one whose image is before him? Or does he wish to point out that the possession of the coin by Jews is evidence that the possessors are contaminated by an alien ideology which, in direct contradiction to Jewish law, allowed images of human beings to be engraved? Those who possess such objects of an alien system might expect, therefore, to have to abide by the rules of that system. As Bruce comments: "whatever else belongs to God, a coin which by its very form and appearance contravenes God's Law cannot be regarded as his."[11] Jesus' response, therefore, may indicate that participants in the Roman economic system were bound to pay the tax. But those who recognized the supremacy of God over the universe maintain their distance from Rome and its exploitative and idolatrous practices, a point noted by Robert Eisler:

> Jesus . . . rejects money on principle for himself and his disciples. . . . He postulates the gratuitous gift of all service to one's neighbor as an act of free love. Thus only the discourse on the tribute money becomes intelligible. The "lovers of money" who carry about with them and possess the Roman emperor's

10. See further Borg, *Conflict, Holiness & Politics*; and Caird, *Jewish Nation*.
11. Bruce, "Render to Caesar," 260.

money, and with it, the image of the "lord of this world," the enemy of God who claims worship for himself, owe his money, the poll tax, to that lord. They have fallen away from God and so have irretrievably incurred servitude and the payment of tribute to the emperor. But he, who like Jesus and his disciples disdains Caesar's money and the whole monetary system of the empire, and who enjoys with his brethren the loving communion of all possessions of the "saints," such a one has renounced the service of idols and is no longer indebted to Caesar but merely to God, to whom he owes body, soul, thoughts, words and works—in short, everything. . . .[12]

Whether or not we agree entirely with Eisler's interpretation, it is a potent reminder that Jesus' reply must be set within the context of the difficult discussion of appropriate responses to the lordship of God within the limitations imposed by Roman sovereignty. That is not a fatalistic acceptance of the powers that be, but a recognition that there is a price to pay for "supping with the devil." Maybe that is what has to be done, though, if Eisler is right, that was not the only option open to the people of God. Communities of protest which could maintain the counterculture of God's holiness could offer a way of keeping out of Caesar's grip, though a way that may have meant some political powerlessness in the abandonment of the political process. The appropriate political response might be maintained by cutting oneself off from the system in ways possible in the wilderness of Judea but inconceivable in most modern societies.

4

I have concentrated on the discussion about the tribute money. There is, of course, another passage dealing with the Temple Tax in Matthew 17:24–27. Here Jesus argues that God's parenting is the key to the whole business of taxation. God's rule is different from that of an earthly king: just as kings do not tax their own children, so neither does God. God is like a father who provides for the children's needs (cf. Luke 11:9–13). The payment of the tax is made on pragmatic grounds, and even then payment is provided by God.[13] At first sight, the Pharisees' question and Jesus' subsequent response about the payment of tribute to the emperor seems to show Jesus offering a different approach and to accept the right of kings of the earth to levy their taxes. We have seen reasons why such a reading of the story might

12. Eisler, *Messiah Jesus*, 332–34; cf. Bammel, "Revolution Theory," 32–68.
13. Bauckham, *Bible in Politics*, 75.

not be as obvious as it first appears. The story is included not to give advice over taxation (even though it may well have been used in this way if Rom 13:8–14 is anything to go by). Rather, it is an example of Jesus' wisdom and insight. He refuses to take sides in a situation where both options left much to be desired. There is nothing particularly commendable about the refusal to pay taxes if it is to result (as it did in the disastrous revolt against the Romans in 66–70 CE) in wholesale destruction of human life. The Zealot option, which refuses any kind of accommodation with Caesar, is attractive in its refusal to compromise but potentially disastrous in the course of action which can ensue. The evidence suggests that Jesus did not want to be identified with the Zealots. This was not only because he held to the deep-rooted tradition of non-violence but also because the Zealot strategy was in fact a much more reactionary one than his own. They were merely in the business of reforming the status quo so that the Temple could function properly. Jesus was much more concerned to establish a new pattern of relations with God where injustices rooted in religious practice would also be rooted out. Jesus' political option was altogether more radical.[14]

The story is placed in Mark's Gospel after Jesus has entered Jerusalem and "cleansed" the Temple. Meek acceptance of Caesar is what one would expect of an elite for whom the Temple was a central part of their power. Jesus had challenged that power and the whole ideology which undergirded it, a fact dramatically reinforced with the destruction of its mystique at the moment of Jesus' death (Mark 15:38). In a sense the issue of taxation was a diversion from the major challenge to the Jewish status quo which had been made: the discussion of the tribute avoided the issue whether the Jewish nation would accept its messiah and his way. In a situation of overarching political and economic power such as wielded by the Romans the question of tribute demanded a recognition of what was involved in complicity with the Roman system and a frank recognition of what were constructive and what were futile ways of furthering the life and prophetic witness of the people of God. Jesus did not shirk paying the ultimate price of his life when there was no other option available, but to the last in Gethsemane there was always the struggle to avoid paying that ultimate price.

Where Jesus would have agreed with the Zealots is in emphasizing that rendering to God takes precedence over all else (cf. Matt 6:24 and Acts 5:29). How that will be done will depend on the circumstances in which we find ourselves. That may be illustrated by the struggles of our sisters and brothers in the varied situations of Latin America. What seems to be a relatively harmless gesture of human compassion in the context of Brazil will be a

---

14. Clévenot, *Materialist Approaches*, 93.

life-threatening act in El Salvador. In such situations the acts of martyrdom are not confined to the moment of the termination of one's life but are brought to bear by the incessant demand to witness appropriately and wherever possible effectively to the justice and peace of God. We shall not expect those acts of martyrdom to be uniform in their direction though they will have a common focus of seeking to practice the justice of the God who stands over against all political systems and refuses to be identified totally with them. They may not be at all times as far-reaching as we would like. There may well be acute differences between those of us who seek to protest and those of us who aim to promote justice. At all times vigilant attention to the detail of the motives of the oppressor and awareness of the self-righteousness of the victims can assist in the prosecution of justice for the poor and the gentle but firm challenge to the powerful. Nothing less can be rendered to the God to whom all creation owes allegiance.[15]

Bibliography

Adorno, Theodor W. *Minima Moralia: Reflections from Damaged Life*. Translated by E. F. N. Jephcott. London: Verso, 1974.

Bammel, Ernst. "The Revolution Theory from Reimarus to Brandon." In *Jesus and the Politics of His Day*, edited by Ernst Bammel and C. F. D. Moule, 11–68. Cambridge: Cambridge University Press, 1984.

Bauckham, Richard. *The Bible in Politics: How to Read the Bible Politically*. Louisville: Westminster John Knox, 1989.

Borg, Marcus J. *Conflict, Holiness & Politics in the Teachings of Jesus*. Studies in the Bible and Early Christianity 5. New York: Mellen, 1984.

Brown, Robert McAfee. *Spirituality and Liberation: Overcoming the Great Fallacy*. Philadelphia: Westminster, 1988.

Bruce, F. F. "Render to Caesar." In *Jesus and the Politics of His Day*, edited by Ernst Bammel and C. F. D. Moule, 249–64. Cambridge: Cambridge University Press, 1984.

Caird, G. B. *Jesus and the Jewish Nation*. Ethel M. Wood Lecture 1965. London: Athlone, 1965.

Clévenot, Michel. *Materialist Approaches to the Bible*. Translated by William J. Nottingham. Maryknoll, NY: Orbis, 1985.

Derrett, J. Duncan M. *Law in the New Testament*. London: Darton, Longman, and Todd, 1970.

Eisler, Robert. *The Messiah Jesus and John the Baptist: According to Flavius Josephus' Recently Rediscovered "Capture of Jerusalem" and the Other Jewish and Christian Sources*. London: Methuen, 1931.

Kerr, Fergus. *Theology after Wittgenstein*. 2nd ed. London: SPCK, 1997.

Lash, Nicholas. *Easter in Ordinary: Reflections on Human Experience and the Knowledge of God*. Richard Lectures 1986. Charlottesville: University Press of Virginia, 1988.

---

15. For further reading, see Rowland and Corner, *Liberating Exegesis*.

Rensberger, David. *Johannine Faith and Liberating Community*. Philadelphia: Westminster, 1988.

Rowland, Christopher, and Mark Corner. *Liberating Exegesis: The Challenge of Liberation Theology to Biblical Studies*. Louisville: Westminster John Knox, 1990.

Skinner, Quentin. *The Foundations of Modern Political Thought*. 2 vols. Cambridge: Cambridge University Press, 1978.

Wengst, Klaus. *Pax Romana: And the Peace of Jesus Christ*. Translated by John Bowden. Philadelphia: Fortress, 1987.

14

Three Essays from *The Way*

14.1

Reading the Bible in the Struggle for Justice and Peace[1]

> Every theology is political, even one that does not speak or think in political terms. The influence of politics on theology and every other cultural sphere cannot be evaded any more than the influence of theology on politics and other spheres of human thinking. The worst politics of all would be to let theology perform this function unconsciously, for that brand of politics is always bound up with the status quo. Liberation theology consciously and explicitly accepts its relationship with politics ... insofar as direct politics are concerned, it is more concerned about avoiding the false impartiality of academic theology than it is about taking sides and consequently giving ammunition to those who accuse it of partisanship.[2]

RECENT MONTHS HAVE ONLY served to remind us of the accuracy of Juan Luis Segundo's words. We have seen evidence that biblical interpretation has certainly become part of the ideological struggle, as the language of religion becomes a means by which men and women once again seek to pursue particular interests. Historically, there is nothing particularly surprising about that. Indeed, it is something that Christians should welcome. What is difficult for church people and theologians to come to terms with

---

1. Themes from this article were later developed more fully in Rowland and Corner, *Liberating Exegesis*.
2. Segundo, *Liberation of Theology*, 74–75.

is that minority concerns have been suddenly thrust into the center of the stage in an increasingly divided economic and political arena. Theological and ecclesiastical concerns are not merely matters of private concern but a contested area of discourse where the dominant economic forces and powerbase seek to recruit the language of religion to their ideology. From the age of Constantine onwards that has ever been so. We have become so unaccustomed to the language of religion being a contestable area of debate that we are not as well equipped as we might be to deal with the competing claims. What that means for those who have been accustomed to have the field to themselves as they seek to use the Bible in the discussion of justice and peace issues is that they now find that they have powerful and sophisticated competition. That will demand of those who believe that the way of Jesus is a way of peace, justice, and good news for the poor the fullest possible use of the resources available in the struggle and in the problems confronting us in our present approach to Scripture. We need to be aware of the problems. There is a clear challenge from those who want to affirm a clear religious tone to the Christian tradition and would prefer to isolate the Scriptures from the political struggle and confine religion to the things of the soul.[3] More problematic, however, is the simplistic way in which the Scriptures have been used as part of debate about justice and peace issues. Some who would be sympathetic to the issues find themselves alienated by the way in which texts are taken out of context and used as proof texts for particular political projects while contrary indications found in other parts of the canon are ignored. There are important questions to wrestle with. There is also an urgency, particularly for those who do not consider that the Thatcherite project corresponds to the major themes on justice as set out in the Christian tradition and that the time has come to take issue with a complacent acceptance of variety in interpretation when that can allow injustice to abound.

The problems, however, do not by any means arise from the contemporary political scene. There are deep-seated problems in the character of contemporary exegesis. There is a homogeneity about our mode of interpretation and its setting in its preoccupation with the texts and their original meanings and settings. The hegemony of this interpretative approach is firmly rooted in theological education and the churches. Indeed, successive generations of ministers have been taught to read the Bible using the historical-critical method. Few will have been given a glimpse of the variety of exegetical practice in the Judeo-Christian tradition, except as a way

---

3. See further Forrester, *Theology and Politics*. For a detailed account of some of the history of this process see Lash, *Easter in Ordinary*.

of contrasting the scientific character of present methods with the eisegetical excesses of the past. In the process of acquiring the tools of historical scholarship we have all been enabled to catch a fascinating glimpse of the ancient world as it has been reconstructed for us by two hundred years of a biblical scholarship of increasing sophistication. But all too often our attention devoted to the quest for the original meaning of a Pauline phrase or saying of Jesus has left us floundering when we are asked to relate our journey into ancient history to the world in which we live and work. We may find ourselves resorting to obscurantist and ill-thought-out beliefs or recitation of favored proof-texts which happen to prove our point. While the journey into the past has offered us insights aplenty, our preoccupation with the past has left us with the feeling that the world we have constructed is alien to us.[4] So the biblical text, instead of being a means of life, can become a stumbling block in the way of our contemporary discipleship. The enormous investment of our energy in the quest for the original meaning has frequently led us to ignore the more important task of relating that complex of meanings and the biblical world which we have constructed to the pressing needs of the contemporary world. It would not have been so bad if we had given sufficient attention to the exploration of the whole of the hermeneutical enterprise at the same time. As we are finding to our cost, we have ignored this. Consequently, when it comes to using the Bible in wrestling with the contemporary problems of Christian discipleship, we find that our exegetical efforts frequently leave us without the necessary skills when it comes to the provision of guidance for the exploration of those questions which our generation is asking.

Many today are willing to accept, at least in principle, that a text may be the vehicle of a variety of meanings to different readers. Yet there is a deep divide among interpreters of Scripture. On the one hand, there are those who think that the original meaning of the text is not only retrievable but also clearly recognizable and should be the criterion by which all other interpretations should be judged. On the other hand, there are those who argue either that the quest for the original meaning of the text is a waste of time or that, even if it is possible to ascertain what the original author intended, this should not be determinative of the way in which we read the text. This means that whatever the *conscious* intention of the original author, levels of meaning can become apparent to later interpreters, granted that the text is free from the shackles of the author's control and has a life of its own in the world of the reader.

---

4. For some pertinent comments on these points see Lash, *Theology*, 75–92.

Understandably, the first group is worried that the freedom implied in the second approach might lead to exegetical anarchy. It wants some kind of control over interpretation, and where better to find it than in the original meaning of the text? It is a desire which lies at the very heart of the problem of authority in the church, which has always been such a pressing issue within the Judeo-Christian tradition. No doubt most biblical exegetes would chafe at the imposition of any kind of hermeneutical control on their endeavors. But the fact of the matter is that there is a "magisterium" of the historical-critical method in many parts of the church today: the critical consensus of the biblical exegetes, preoccupied as most of them are with the original meaning of the text and its controlling role in the quest for meaning of the Scriptures. That may be no bad thing; but we should recognize precisely what is going on, in particular the extraordinary influence this particular exegetical approach has had on the reading of the Bible in the churches over the last century. We have become so sophisticated in forging for ourselves tools for the retrieval of the original meaning that we have failed to see how defenseless we have become when it comes to using the Bible in the discussion of contemporary social ethics. Our practice has been divorced from our research, and we are struggling to put the pieces together again.

Liberation theologians have drunk deep at the well of European biblical scholarship and are grateful for it. Their method of work differs from what is customary in the UK. Many spend a significant part of each week working with grassroots communities in the shantytowns on the periphery of large cities or in rural communities. As part of their pastoral work, they listen and help the process of reflection on the Bible which is going on in the grassroots communities. They gain insights from listening to the poor reading and using Scripture in the whole process of development and social change. They find that this process of listening and learning has given them a stimulus to their exegesis and, more importantly, has opened up new vistas and questions in the interpretative enterprise. This grassroots biblical interpretation provides a basis for the more sophisticated theological edifices they wish to build. Yet it is clear that the different experiences and worldview of the poor offer an unusually direct connection with the biblical text, which, whatever its shortcomings in terms of exegetical refinement, has proved enormously fruitful as far as the life of the Christian church is concerned.

Also, they are much more concerned to take full account of the social formation of the biblical texts and the movements which produced them. Thus the issues which they are dealing with include the connection between the text and social formation and the way in which a particular text either challenges or affirms that social formation. Most exegetes who are influenced by liberation theology would not want to claim that they have the hermeneutical key which unlocks the meaning of the whole of the Scriptures (though there *are* some who think the perspective of the poor is the criterion for a true reading of Scripture). They are insistent that European and North American exegetes need to take fuller account of their perspective, because, they argue, the immediacy of the relationship between biblical narratives and the situation and experiences of the poor has enabled them to glimpse interpretative insights which have so often eluded the sophisticated, cerebral, and largely upper-class, orientation of First World biblical exegesis.

Carlos Mesters, who has worked with peasants and urban shantytown dwellers in Brazil for many years, points out that weariness translated itself into Brazilian biblical study with the growth of learned works on exegesis which had little appeal or relevance for the millions seeking to survive in situations of injustice and poverty.[5] In that situation, however, a new way of reading the text has arisen, not among the exegetical elite of the seminaries and universities but at the grassroots. Its emphasis, derived from the insights of Catholic Action, is on the method: *see* (starting where one is with one's experience, which for the majority in Latin America means an experience of poverty), *judge* (understanding the reasons for that kind of existence and relating them to the story of the deliverance from oppression in the Bible), and *act*. Ordinary people have taken the Bible into their own hands and begun to read the word of God in the circumstances of their existence but also in comparison with the stories of the people of God in other times and other places. Millions of men and women abandoned by government and church have discovered an ally in the story of the people of God in the Scriptures.

This new biblical theology in these Basic Christian Communities is an oral theology in which story, experience, and biblical reflection are intertwined with the community's life of sorrow and joy. That experience of celebration, worship, varied stories, and recollections, in drama and festival is, according to Mesters, exactly what lies behind the written words of Scripture itself. That is the written deposit which bears witness to the story of a people oppressed, bewildered, and longing for deliverance. While exegete, priest, and religious may have their part to play in the life of the community,

---

5. Note: the original article used Mesters's article, "Com se faz Teologia hoje no Brasil?" This chapter instead cites Mesters, *Defenseless Flower*, since Chapter 4, "Biblical Theology in Brazil Today," is an English translation of that article. See also the series of articles by Margaret Hebblethwaite in the *Tablet*. On the pastoral practice of the Brazilian church see the concise survey in Regan, *Church for Liberation*.

the reading is basically uninfluenced by excessive clericalism and individualistic piety. It is a reading which is emphatically communitarian, in which reflection on the story of a people can indeed lead to an appreciation of the *sensus ecclesiae* and a movement towards liberative action. So revelation is very much a present phenomenon: God speaks in the midst of the circumstances of today.[6] In contrast the vision of many priests is of a revelation that is entirely past, in the deposit of faith, something to be preserved, defended, transmitted to the people by its guardians.

So the Bible is not about past history only. It is also a mirror to be held up to reflect the story of today and lend it a new perspective. Mesters argues that what is happening in this new way of reading the Bible is in fact a rediscovery of the patristic method of interpretation, which stresses the priority of the spirit of the word rather than its letter. God speaks through life, but that word is one that is illuminated by the Bible: "the main purpose of reading the Bible is not to interpret the Bible, but to interpret life with the help of the Bible."[7] The major preoccupation is not the quest for the meaning of the text in itself but the direction which the Bible is suggesting to the people of God within the specific circumstances in which they find themselves. The popular reading of the Bible in Brazil is directed to contemporary practice and the transformation of a situation of injustice. That situation permits the poor to discover meaning which can so easily elude the technically better equipped exegete. So, where you are determines to a large extent what you read. This is a reading which does not pretend to be neutral and questions whether any other reading can claim that either. It is committed to the struggle of the poor for justice, and the resonances that are found with the biblical story suggest that the quest for the so-called "objective" reading may itself be unfaithful to the commitments and partiality which the Scriptures themselves demand. Of course, Mesters recognizes the difficulties of this approach. Nevertheless, he asks us to judge the effectiveness of the reading by its fruits: "One sign of the coming of the kingdom is when the blind begin to see, the lepers are cleansed, the dead rise, and the poor are evangelized."[8]

In his essay on a liberation theology for the British situation Charles Elliott succinctly sums up the challenge to contemporary interpretative procedures:

> Liberation theology is about a fundamental change in the way in which persons, personal relationships and therefore

---

6. Mesters, *Defenseless Flower*, 160.
7. Mesters, *Defenseless Flower*, 160.
8. Mesters, *Defenseless Flower*, 163.

> political relationships are conceived and structured.... Why is liberation theology so important intellectually?... Firstly it is true to elements... of the biblical tradition which were long neglected by the colonialist church.... Neither a colonialist church nor an established church can bear to think that the biblical tradition is actually about challenging power: but if you see the essence of the nature of God as being to free the oppressed from their oppression, then you are necessarily engaged in a challenge to power.... Secondly it marks a quite different theological method.... What liberation theologians are saying is... the only way you will derive theological truth is by starting where people are, because it is where poor and particularly oppressed people are that you will find God. Now that stands on its head sixteen hundred years of philosophical tradition in Christendom. From the third century, Christians have thought the way to establish theological truth has been to try to derive consistent propositions, that is to say propositions that are consistent with the facts of the tradition as revealed primarily in the Bible.... What the liberation theologians are saying... is that this will not do as a way of doing theology. If you want to do theology, you have to start where people are, particularly the people that the Bible is primarily concerned with, who are the dispossessed, the widow, the orphan, the stranger, the prostitute, the pimp and the tax collector. Find out what they are saying, thinking, and feeling, and that is the stuff out of which the glimpses of God will emerge.[9]

Few would want to turn their backs on the insights which two hundred years of historical scholarship on the Bible have offered. Yet liberation theologians rightly point out that the insights of the poor and the marginalized have breathed new life into our understanding of the concerns of the Bible. Reading the story of the people of God and the Gospel stories in particular with the eyes of the poor can cast much new light on parts of the text which the bourgeois reading of the first-century church and the academy can so easily miss. The rediscovery of God's option for the poor in the Bible is a case in point.[10] Also, the concern with the socioeconomic context of the Christian movement has helped our understanding of the way in which the radical message of Jesus was blunted in the urban environment of the Pauline churches.

---

9. Elliott, "Liberation Theology for the UK?"

10. E.g., Santa Ana, *Good News*; and from an evangelical perspective Hanks, *God So Loved*.

We cannot be content to regard the biblical texts merely as manifestations of the social processes of the past because they are part and parcel of our world and continue to contribute to the ebb and flow of ideological formation in our day. It is inadequate to concentrate in any social hermeneutic on what the text *meant* only. Of equal (if not greater) importance is the analysis of contemporary usage, whether in academy or in church, and the investigation of the particular interests that are being served by various patterns of interpretation. That point is neatly encapsulated in the diagram taken from the work of the Brazilian theologian Clodovis Boff.[11]

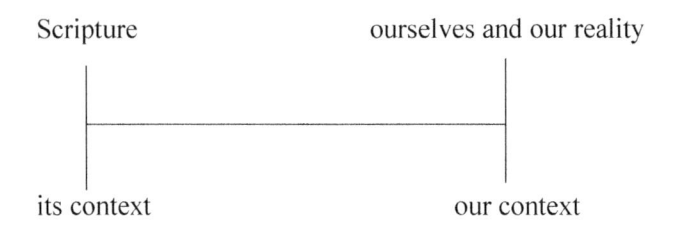

```
Scripture                    ourselves and our reality
   |                                    |
   |————————————————————————————————————|
   |                                    |
its context                        our context
```

Bearing such matters in mind will equip us for the quest for a truly critical reflection on the Scriptures and our use of them in order to be better able to lay bare the role they are playing in ideological struggles in various and different social contexts. This outline of the position of much contemporary biblical study and the contribution of the liberationist exegesis from Latin America are a prolegomenon, though a necessary one, to the task of working out a critical awareness of our interpretative task. In so doing we cannot erect another set of boundaries which will hinder a creative and imaginative use of Scripture in contemporary struggles. At the same time we cannot easily tolerate a situation where individual contexts so relativize the way in which we read that we find that we have little in common with those in positions different from our own. What kind of approach to Scriptures should we be looking for?

Provisional Guidelines for a Contemporary Interpretation[12]

1. A prime task of the exegete is to watch the way in which the biblical material is and has been *used*. In so doing it is necessary to make sure

---

11. Boff, *Theology and Praxis*, particularly Chapter 8, 132–58.

12. There are interesting parallels to what is said here, though he is approaching the issue from a rather different ecclesiastical background, in Swartley, *Slavery*, 211–28. For a useful discussion on the role of the Bible in social ethics see also Ogletree, *Use of the Bible*.

that readers are engaged with the text in its various parts and are as attentive as possible to it. For example, if we concentrate solely on Mark 12:17 ("Render to Caesar," etc.) as the clue to Jesus' attitude to the Roman occupation of Judea, we lose some of the force of the context in which that saying is uttered. What is more, when the way in which we hear this saying is governed by the interpretation of this which seems to be offered in Romans 13:8, then we may find ourselves rapidly assuming that Christian attitudes to the state are unproblematic. That may be all right when we live in a relatively benign democracy, but that does not apply to many of our brothers and sisters, say in South Africa or Guatemala or El Salvador. Are they put in a position of having to choose between following Jesus and our own inclination to resist or rebel in some circumstances? With some justification they look to parts of the Scriptures which we may prefer to ignore, for example, the book of Revelation. In Revelation 13 there is a much less optimistic assessment of the state (to put it mildly). There the state is seen as an agent of the powers of darkness, and in the picture of its power and rule in Chapter 17 the seer indicates that this power is insecure, based on self-aggrandizement and oppression.

In the light of this we may be driven back to the Gospels again and begin to ask questions about the context of Jesus' saying in Mark 12:17. The reference there to the handling of the coin and the discussion of its superscription raise a question about the rectitude of Jews dealing in coinage which bore an image in direct contravention to God's law. Also, we cannot forget the context of the saying: the journey to Jerusalem, the so-called triumphal entry, and the political dimension of the challenge to the Temple.[13] In that situation Jesus found himself in a vulnerable position, and the whole incident as described in Mark has the air of a trap being laid from which Jesus extricates himself by an ambiguous reply.

What I am suggesting is that there is more than meets the eye in the way in which we are wont to read and use the Scriptures. That may well be because our churches school us to read in particular ways because of the ways in which particular texts are juxtaposed. Thus, for the Sunday eucharistic readings in the Anglican Church when the incident with the tribute money is discussed, the readings from the Epistles are Romans 13 and Titus 2. Both of these texts urge subservience to the ruling powers and as a result condition the way in which we

---

13. See, e.g., the survey in Clévenot, *Materialist Approaches*; and Pixley, *God's Kingdom*.

hear the account of Jesus and the tribute money (which alternates in its Matthaean rather than Markan form with the account of the murder of John the Baptist). No sign of Revelation 13 here, which would temper the complacency of Christian attitudes towards the powers given by the more positive accompanying readings (Isa 45; 1 Kgs 3:4–15).

2. It is necessary to contribute alternative horizons to our contemporary use of Scripture. Firstly, we may do this by exploring to the full what might have been the original setting and circumstances of the various texts *as well as the history of interpretation within and outside the church* as a challenge to self-indulgence and the belief that our application of the texts tells the whole story of their meaning. Secondly, the language of the kingdom itself offers an alternative perspective on the arrangements of the present. A broader horizon is offered, and the reader is asked to consider the present in the light of the threat of judgement and the glory of the age to come. It has protested against those arrangements which have the appearance of order, but which in reality have brought about the prosperity and progress of some at the expense of others. It is frequently those who have to bear that suffering who can see the fragility of those structures which appear to offer peace and security. Those whose lives are fragmented and who live at the margins can discern the signs of the times in ways which are frightening to those of us who cannot see from what is apparently a more favored vantage point. Many throughout history have been attentive in ways which would not be possible for those in more comfortable surroundings, for whom life does not seem to present such stark choices or an oppressive threat.

3. We should accept the inevitable eisegesis which is part of the variety of the exegetical (i.e., the complex process of finding meaning in texts) to enable one another to be aware of the kinds of eisegesis which we are carrying out in all their subtlety and sophistication. That must concentrate just as much as the various human interests which may be at work in the maintaining of particular positions of individuals and groups. That is going to necessitate that we take seriously the patient analysis of the particularity of each situation and whose interests are being served by various interpretations.

4. This will mean that there will be a greater sensitivity to methods of finding meaning which do not necessarily attribute much weight to authorial intention or even the original setting of the text and its

transmission (e.g., canon criticism, literary criticism, and the structuralist approaches in all their variety).

5. It is easy to see how biblical material can be extracted from its context and function as instructions which abstract the reader from the challenge of the messianic way, as it intersects with an order which is passing away, into the world of fantastic speculation and out of touch with reality. Accordingly, the temptation to wrest verses out of context in a particular book must be resisted and the wider fabric of the narrative heeded. Nor should those of us who are on the "left" of contemporary theology ignore those parts of the canon which do not fit so easily with our particular views of the world. Most middle-class Christians, like the writer of this article, actually practice the compromises which characterize the outlook of books like the Pastoral Epistles with their social conformity and theory of male supremacy. We may not tolerate these solutions, but we cannot fail to recognize that such compromises are the normal stuff of our existence. At the very least the unpalatable parts of the canon can place a mirror before our rhetoric and remind us of the frequency of the distance which exists as compared with our practice. A realistic self-criticism must accompany the critique of contemporary ideology. In this situation this must be a corporate activity which recognizes the fallibility of our judgements while affirming the necessity of keeping to the task of proclaiming justice and peace, however costly that may be.

The use of the Bible must not be separated from the narrative of Jesus' proclamation and inauguration of the reign of God. It is that context which is necessary to prevent decisions about the present and the future becoming wildly unrealistic or deeply compromised. Discipleship involves sharing the way of the cross of the Son of Man as he goes up to Jerusalem. What is offered the disciple is the sharing of the cup of suffering of the Son of Man rather than the promise of sitting at his right hand and his left when he reigns on earth. There can be no escape from the painful reality of the present witness with its need to endure the tribulations which precede the vindication. That is the mark of the realism of the struggle, the recognition that over-optimism and rapid solutions are not what is promised, and that patient endurance is needed in the face of injustice. That is the challenge which faces those who wish to live out the messianic narrative in their own lives.[14] Jesus promises his disciples persecution and the need to be ready to bear witness before the courts of the powerful. They can expect to maintain

---

14. See further the suggestive comments in Hauerwas, *Peaceable Kingdom*.

a critical distance from the institutions of the old order. The decisive question is not so much (to use the words of Klaus Wengst) "How can I survive this situation with the least possible harm?"[15] Rather, the one question which is important is: in this situation, how can one bear witness to the way of the Messiah? Life along the usual lines may no longer be an option for the disciple who takes seriously the need to take up the cross of the Messiah rather than the sword of violence. The consequence is social separation and a refusal to join in the normal pattern of society. So, by contradicting and resisting, the disciples dispute that the world belongs to those who claim to rule over it. Something like this seems to me to be what the New Testament witness is demanding of those of us who are seeking to bear witness to and work for the reign of God. It is going to have a decentered quality[16] consistent with identification with the one who died "outside the city," reflecting the distorted world in which we live and the incompleteness of God's project of establishing a reign of justice and peace. When it offers satisfaction and wholeness, questions need to be asked when that claim to wholeness ignores those at the fringes of our wholeness, whose fractured existence is a reminder of the pain of the suffering Son of Man and the struggles still endured and to be shared before the kingdom comes.

Bibliography

Boff, Clodovis. *Theology and Praxis.* Translated by Robert R. Barr. 1987. Reprint, Eugene, OR: Wipf & Stock, 2009.
Clévenot, Michel. *Materialist Approaches to the Bible.* Maryknoll, NY: Orbis, 1985.
Elliott, Charles. "Is There a Liberation Theology for the UK?" Heslington Lecture, University of York, January 1985.
Forrester, Duncan B. *Theology and Politics.* Signposts in Theology. Oxford: Blackwell, 1988.
Hanks, Thomas D. *God so Loved the Third World: The Biblical Vocabulary of Oppression.* Translated by James C. Dekker. Maryknoll, NY: Orbis, 1983.
Hauerwas, Stanley. *The Peaceable Kingdom: A Primer in Christian Ethics.* Notre Dame, IN: University of Notre Dame Press, 1983.
Lash, Nicholas. *Easter in Ordinary: Reflections on Human Experience and the Knowledge of God.* Richard Lectures 1986. Charlottesville: University Press of Virginia, 1988.
———. *Theology on the Way to Emmaus.* London: SCM, 1986.
Mesters, Carlos. *Defenseless Flower: A New Reading of the Bible.* Translated by Francis McDonagh. Maryknoll, NY: Orbis, 1989.

---

15. Wengst, *Pax Romana*, 118–22.

16. See further Turner, "De-Centring Theology," 142, quoted in Lash, *Theology*, 225: "a theological discourse which can qualify as truly cognitive is that which knows itself to be the decentred language of a decentred world."

Ogletree, Thomas W. *The Use of the Bible in Christian Ethics*. Philadelphia: Fortress, 1983.

Pixley, Jorge V. *God's Kingdom: A Guide for Biblical Study*. Translated by Donald D. Walsh. Maryknoll, NY: Orbis, 1981.

Regan, David. *Church for Liberation: A Pastoral Portrait of the Church in Brazil*. Dublin: Dominican, 1987.

Santa Ana, Julio de. *Good News to the Poor: The Challenge of the Poor in the History of the Church*. Translated by Helen Whittle. Maryknoll, NY: Orbis, 1979.

Segundo, Juan Luis. *Liberation of Theology*. Translated by John Drury. Maryknoll, NY: Orbis, 1976.

Swartley, Willard M. *Slavery, Sabbath, War, and Women: Case Issues in Biblical Interpretation*. Conrad Grebel Lectures 1982. Scottdale, PA: Herald, 1983.

Turner, Denys. "De-Centring Theology." *Modern Theology* 2.2 (1986) 125–43.

Wengst, Klaus. *Pax Romana: And the Peace of Jesus Christ*. Translated by John Bowden. Philadelphia: Fortress, 1987.

14.2

Reading the Apocalypse

Apocalypse: Is It Really so Unfamiliar?

IT PUZZLES ME THAT Christians fight shy of the Apocalypse.[1] It is not just the case that we live in the shadow of the millennium, but our culture is saturated with images which in many ways parallel those from Revelation. I switch on my television and see a sophisticated, and often surreal, world of contemporary advertising which millions of us drink in. Such images affect us in ways which we cannot quite comprehend so that we are moved to buy the advertised products. Also, my children watch films and play computer games riddled with the fantastic and bizarre. This is part of their everyday world. Yes, they can tell the difference between different kinds of reality, but the fantastic is woven into the fabric of contemporary culture which bombards them with images offering a possible link with that which confronts us on every page of Revelation. That is not to say that things are going to be easy. As it has developed, Christianity has fought shy of the weird and exotic for entirely understandable reasons. Its major spokespersons tend to present themselves as reasonable men and women who would have no truck with the zany and bizarre—all of which seem to be epitomized by the Apocalypse.

Having written two commentaries on the book of Revelation[2] I suppose there should be a feeling of satisfaction that I have managed to try and make sense of this bewildering and, to some, off-putting, text. But

1. "To fight shy of" means to attempt to avoid something.
2. Rowland, *Revelation*; and Rowland, "Revelation."

herein lies the difficulty. I am not sure that we should be in the business of making sense of the text. Of course, one can read Revelation with a sense that there is a beginning and an ending in the vision of the New Jerusalem, even if it is rather difficult to see how the intervening bits hang together. I have found myself under conflicting pressures; on the one hand to explain (that after all is what a commentary is for), and on the other with a strong sense of unease that explanation misses the point of a text like this. What does one do with a dream or vision, whether one's own or another's? Half a century of Freud and Jung has reduced the world of dreams to something which is altogether more manageable—understandable enough, given the way in which the nightmarish can be so disconcerting. The world of cool reason is altogether preferable.

There are signs in the world of psychotherapy, however, that there is a greater willingness to consider a more ancient wisdom concerning dreams and revelations. One recent development in group work is directly relevant to our question, and both extends and challenges the dominant methodology of dealing with dreams in the psychoanalytic tradition.[3] There has emerged a form of group work which explores the role of dreams and what they may tell us about the collective experience. This use of dreams harks back to a pre-modern approach in which dreams are not subject to interpretation as the result of some kind of overarching interpretative key. Rather, the components of the dream themselves become the mode of discourse for the group without being reduced to a particular meaning derived from an analytic tradition. There is much that could be said about this embryonic and suggestive development in group psychotherapy, which in certain key respects departs from the psychoanalytic tradition. Though still in its infancy, it promises to add a rather different dimension to discussion about the role of dreams and what they tell us about society as well as the individual.

Submitting Ourselves to the Revelation of Jesus Christ

Revelation makes great demands of those who read or hear it in pursuit of the blessing it offers. Always there is the temptation to move too quickly to "translate" its imagery into a more comprehensible and accessible discourse. In effect that is what most ways of interpreting Revelation have done down the centuries. For example, the book has been treated as a prophecy about the end of the world. Another way relates the visions to their first-century context, involving questions about the meaning for the original author and readers and their contemporary historical realities. A

3. Lawrence, *Social Dreaming*.

rather different way of reading the text is to regard the images as an account of the struggles facing the journey of the soul to God. There has always been another approach, one which has in different ways been used by mystics and prophets, which seems to me to be more consistent with the nature of the book itself. It is a form of contemporary application in which the book is used as an interpretative lens for viewing contemporary history. Apocalypse thus becomes an unveiling of the inner meaning of events and persons. With this approach a text like Revelation reads as a gateway to a greater understanding of reality, both divine and human, spiritual and political, which includes—but transcends—that offered by the human senses. It thereby becomes a way of illuminating the nature of politics and religion in every age. The apocalyptic imagery is no longer a code for translation into another discourse in which an alternative account can be offered of the various ciphers contained in the apocalyptic texts. Like the modern political cartoon, Revelation's imagery may strike home in ways that escape the ability of prosaic discourse. Steve Bell's pungent and insightful cartoons in the *Guardian* regularly pierce to the heart of a contemporary matter in ways even the most learned of editorials cannot match.

It seems to me that to treat Revelation as if it were a code and want to "decode" it fails to take seriously the apocalyptic medium. The function of language in a code is to conceal, to communicate something which has to be kept secret. John wrote an apocalypse—a prophecy—not a story. To interpret a visionary text requires of us particular interpretative skills—imagination and emotion, for example. Like a metaphor it startles, questions, even disorientates, before pointing to a fresh view of reality by its extraordinary imagery and impertinent verbal juxtapositions. However difficult it may be for us, we must learn to exercise those faculties which are needed to engage with such a medium. We are above all else being asked to view things differently, a point well made by William Blake:

> What, it will be questioned, when the sun rises, do you not see a round disk of fire somewhat like a guinea? O no, [responds William Blake,] I see an innumerable company of the heavenly host crying, "Holy Holy Holy is the Lord God Almighty." I question not my corporeal or vegetative eye any more than I would question a window concerning a sight. I look through it and not with it.[4]

That quotation from Blake prompts me to resort to his hermeneutical wisdom. He was asked by a learned doctor to offer elucidation of his own symbolism. Blake responded tartly in the following words:

---

4. Keynes, *Blake*, K617.

> You say that I want somebody to elucidate my ideas. But you ought to know that what is grand is necessarily obscure to weak men. That which can be made explicit to the idiot is not worth my care. The wisest of the ancients consider'd what is not too explicit as the fittest for instruction, because it rouzes the faculties to act.... Why is the Bible more Entertaining & Instructive than any other book? Is it not because they [sic] are addressed as to the Imagination, which is Spiritual Sensation and but mediately to the understanding or reason?[5]

It is not the easily explained or the straightforward which is of most use to us but that which, to quote Blake's words, "rouzes the faculties to act." That is, what is most profound stretches our imaginations and gets us to open up new perspectives on things rather than merely being told what the answers are. We are asked by Blake to be co-authors in finding meaning in his texts. When theology is a matter of the systematic and the tidy, Revelation fits uneasily into that mold. Despite initial impressions, Revelation offers insight on very practical matters like what one eats and relations with the local culture. It demands non-conformity to the expectations of the world if those demands are not compatible with the way of the Lamb.

What follows in these reflections on three passages from Revelation is not an explanation of what the text is about so much as a report of the way in which this text has "rouzed my faculties to act."

Revelation 5: "Heaven Perplexed"[6]

The slain Lamb merits the worship of the heavenly host. It is not the mighty of the world who attract fame and attention, but those who are victims of the system of the beast and Babylon, just as the Lamb was, who are promised the blessings of the age to come (7:16). Revelation 5 compels us to consider a different understanding of the meaning of success and the exercise of power. This is so difficult to hold on to when all the pressures are to conform to a culture of self-aggrandizement epitomized by Babylon. Self-offering and weakness, recognized and accepted, is itself powerful and acceptable to God, but this is not about passivity (as is suggested by the more defiant stance of the Lamb in Rev 14).

The vision of the slaughtered Lamb's place with God reminds us that the gospel offers an alternative story (though there are hints of it in the Hebrew

---

5. Keynes, *Blake*, "Letter to Trusler," K793-94.

6. The title of a suggestive essay on this chapter of Revelation by Theissen in his collected sermons, *Signs of Life*.

Bible too, where the side of the victims is taken). This stands in contrast with human society's version of the story of the fate of the victim (they were troublemakers, subversives: "it is fitting for one man to die for the people" in John 11:50 represents the sentiments of the leaders of state security forces down the centuries [my translation]). The gospel gives the perspective of the victim, of the Abels of this world, who otherwise remain silent. It is the story of the innocent victim. The Christian gospel, therefore, becomes fundamental for interpreting all human history and the distortions and delusions we tell about ourselves, the violence we use to maintain the status quo, and our ways of behaving, disguising from ourselves the oppression of the victim and the way we maintain a lie in order to keep things as they are.

Revelation is a text about the unmasking of human culture. At its start it reveals the vindication of the Lamb who was slain. The story of Jesus' death is a revelation of the false consciousness of the efficacy of the scapegoat mechanism and the violence which it institutionalizes. The gospel unmasks the fact that violence lies at the base of all human culture, and it does so by proclaiming the innocence of the victim. It offers an alternative pattern for human mimesis. The consequence of this—and this is so crucial for our understanding of Revelation—is the cross. Jesus identifies with the victims in his society and as a result sets in train a process of victimization on himself. There is a violent reaction as the political elite plot to rid themselves of a troublemaker. As the unfolding visions of John demonstrate, this leads to violence *as the gospel shows up human culture for what it is*. To bear witness to this alternative way is to risk the violence of the old system. The story of Christ's life and death subverts the "lie" of culture based on violence, as do the lives of those living according to this pattern. That provokes a violent crisis as the lie is revealed as accelerating the process of cultural disintegration, the immediate consequence of the vindication of the Lamb in the visions which follow in Revelation 6. With the gospel there can be no resolution other than acceptance of its alternative way. A society based on violence is inherently unstable. The revelation of the gospel reveals God's wrath in that the human culture based on violence is shown for what it really is.

> We can see why the Passion is found between the preaching of the kingdom and the Apocalypse. . . . It is a phenomenon that has no importance in the eyes of the world—incapable, at least in principle, of setting up or reinstating a cultural order, but very effective, in spite of those who know better, in carrying out subversion. In the long run, it is quite capable of undermining and

overturning the whole cultural history and supplying the secret motive force of all subsequent history.⁷

Revelation 13:1–18: A Vision of Two Beasts

I recall a meeting with a small Christian group in the northeast of Brazil in 1990. It was round about the time of state elections, and we were listening to the way in which the members found Scripture helped them to interpret their situation. An elderly man began to talk about the flattery and blandishments of the candidates, using, without a trace of embarrassment, material from Revelation about the beast and its heads to describe the way in which politicians deluded ordinary people with their promises and veiled threats. I have often thought about that occasion when I have read passages from William Blake and from the English Civil War radical Gerrard Winstanley. In one of his illustrations Blake depicts the beast with seven heads as various parts of the state establishment of his day: ecclesiastical, royal, legal, and military power, just as his predecessor Gerrard Winstanley had done.

The insight of my Brazilian acquaintance and these earlier users of the book of Revelation represents a long-standing recognition that passages from Daniel and Revelation offer a potent insight into the nature of state power and the need for vigilance on the part of the people of God in the face of the persuasiveness of such plausible might.

Revelation 12 finishes with the dragon standing on the seashore, angrily seeking to make war on the woman's offspring. From the sea emerges a beast invested with the authority of the dragon. In turn, this authority is exercised on its behalf by a beast from the land. The immediacy of the threat to the earth and its inhabitants, which is the consequence of Satan's ejection from heaven, is set out in this vision: there is the demand to worship the first beast. John sees the world's inhabitants falling into line and worshipping the beast. Those who refuse have to live (and die) with the consequences. In the face of this power the whole world follows after in amazement (13:4) and worships the dragon. People engage in activity which should be directed only towards God.

The references to the image of the beast and the more specific description of the wound have led commentators over the centuries to suppose that there are particular historical allusions here. The worship of the image of the beast (13:14) has been linked with the promotion of the Roman imperial cult, which was particularly widespread in the area of the

---

7. Girard, *Things Hidden*, 209.

churches whose angels are addressed by John. It had become part of the fabric of life, and John's vision, in effect, demands of readers that they unravel that fabric and weave a new fabric of living in which the persistent, even casual, participation in state religion and the social conventions that surround it form no part.

This act of worship is not a private matter, for those who worship will be marked with a mark on their right hand and on their foreheads, in contrast with the sign of those who stand with the Lamb, who are marked with the name of the Lamb and of God (14:1). It is something which is imposed on the worshippers of the beast (13:16). There are public, social, and economic consequences for those who resist, therefore: exclusion from regular social intercourse. Without the name of the beast or the number of its name it becomes impossible to buy or sell. Those "bought" with the blood of the Lamb must not do anything other than resist. The present disruption of their pattern of life is a temporary hardship compared with the wider disruption of buying and selling which will take place when Babylon, the power which enables that to carry on, is destroyed, provoking the merchants to lament, as is evident in Revelation 18, especially 18:11.

Reference to the number of its name prompts another word of exhortation in Revelation 13:18 as in 13:10. But now wisdom is required to calculate the number of a beast, just as it will be to understand the mystery of Babylon and the beast in 17:9. The mysterious number 666 in 13:18 attracts much attention. Jews were fond of working out the numerical value of letters (we need to remember that Jews and Greeks used letters for numbers too, so a = 1, b = 2, etc.). The numerical value of Nero Caesar in Hebrew is 666. Within the context of Revelation itself, however, the number seven (used of angels, churches, seals, trumpets, and bowls) implies completeness. The number 666 is three times over falling one short of the number of perfection, seven. This falling short is evident also in the interruption after the sixth seal and the sixth trumpet in 6:12–17 and 9:13–21. The beast seems to be near perfection (it is after all in 13:3 a caricature of the Lamb who was slain), but what it lacks actually renders it diabolical and utterly opposed to God in supposing that it has ultimate power and wisdom (13:4). The number is a threefold falling short of perfection, that which is almost messianic but not quite so. It has most of the hallmarks of truth and so can easily deceive. For this reason, it must, at all costs, be resisted.

In Revelation 13 we have a graphic portrait of the nature and operation of state ideology which creates support and by its activities cloaks its real goals and identity from those taken in by them. The beast is the incarnation of the powers of the devil and attracts universal admiration for acts which appear to be beneficial and for its military power. The pressure is to conform. Those who refuse to do so face social ostracism (as is evident from Revelation 13:16). As the beast has some of the characteristics of the Lamb (Revelation 13:3 and 14), we can understand how watchful one has to be to avoid being taken in by what seems superficially plausible and colluding with that which is opposed to the divine justice. We should not underestimate the effectiveness of a prevailing set of ideas to form our minds in such a way that when something different and challenging comes along we consider it wrong-headed or misguided. That is exactly the effect of what is called ideology. It makes you think that the ideas which are widely held are "obvious," "commonsense," and "normal" when in fact they often cover up the powerful vested interests of a small group which has and wants to retain power. In John's vision the task of the second beast from the land is to persuade ordinary people that what they see in the first beast is normal and admirable, so that any deviation or counterculture is regarded as strange, anti-social and, therefore, to be repudiated. John's vision helps to unmask these processes and is a pointed reminder of the falsity of the attitude that what "everybody does" must be right and is to be copied (13:3, 8). This unmasking is a necessary task. Despite the widespread assumption that it was evil men like Hitler, Stalin, and Pol Pot—and their circles of supporters—who were responsible for crimes against humanity, they would not have been able to carry out the iniquities of genocide and mass murder without the tacit support of ordinary (many Christian) people keeping their noses clean, maintaining a low profile, and, above all, avoiding at all costs being seen to be political.

Revelation 20: The Millennium[8]

In the light of Revelation 20 it is disturbing that the imminence of the end of a millennium should provoke a debate about appropriate ways of celebrating it with buildings, parties, and the like without any mention of the text from which the concept comes. This will cause little surprise, given the abrasive, this-worldly tone of the book. When we consider such proposals in the light of Revelation 20, far from the world enjoying a celebration to mark the millennium, it stands under the judgement of God for the neglect of the divine justice and the things which made for its true peace. The cosmos is a culture of death. Revelation 20 promises that those who rule will be those who lost their lives at the hands of social orders which brought about their death and dares to envision a period when the messianic reign will take place on earth, a fulfilment, then, of the prayer

---

8. On this theme see Gilbertson, *Millennium*; and McKelvey, *Millennium*.

of Jesus: "thy kingdom come, thy will be done *on earth* as it is in heaven." John sees the dragon bound, so as to prevent the nations from being deceived into living lives which, in their complacency and the pursuit of "business as usual," ignore the divine righteousness.

In Revelation 20 we are offered a vision of those who resisted the beast and those who suffered for such resistance sitting with the one who had himself been the faithful witness (1:5). They are the ones who held out against the compromises required of them in the old scheme of things (14:9, 11; 16:2). Though this passage envisions a different realm in the future, the reign of Christ is both present (1:6) and in the future (5:10) and can be entered into here and now in communities of resistance to the regime of the beast and Babylon.

We can describe the bare bones of what is in the passage, but the far more difficult question is what sense we might make of it. With its symbols and metaphors, the imagery functions to question us and to offer an alternative horizon. It demands that we allow ourselves to be interrogated by the images and disturbed by a different way of looking at things. It will be like the myopic person who puts on glasses and sees things come into focus, or the walker who suddenly finds the mist disappear from the mountaintops to reveal a very different vista from any that could have been imagined lying hidden in the fog which had hitherto passed for normality. If we allow ourselves to be challenged by what we read, digesting and pondering what is there rather than rushing to explain everything and to organize the images into a neat eschatological system, we will perhaps begin to discern that the vision of the millennium may be a disturbance to our complacency, enabling us to see that we have been wretched, pitiable, poor, and blind—like the Laodicean Christians (Rev 3:17).

Those who will reign are those whose lives follow in the footsteps of the Messiah by refusing to accept the injustice, values, and oppressive behavior of the principalities and powers. Instead, they hold out for something different, representing humanity to God and God to humanity as priests. The millennium is an age that will be marked by that alternative pattern of life which was followed by a minority in the old age of the beast and Babylon, and which provoked the ridicule of those who seem to be successful in the old scheme of things.

It is that oppressive situation in the old scheme of things that the book of Wisdom illuminates well. It criticizes the mindset of those who say, "let might be right," and "come, let us enjoy the good things when we can." These attitudes are shown to be utterly wrong. Those who continue the testimony of Jesus offer a living reproach to current values and ways of thinking (Wis 2:15). But they will be judges and rulers over the people (Wis 3:8), even if according to the values of the present they may be scorned and dishonored (Wis 4:17–19). Their style of life is seen in the millennium to be honorable and true to humanity, as they have manifested the endurance necessary to resist the might and allure of Babylon by "keeping the commandments of God and holding fast to the faith of Jesus" (Rev 14:12 my translation).

Whether they recognize it or not at the time of their resistance, those who reign have shown themselves fit to do so because they are the ones who have identified themselves with the way of the Lamb and are peculiarly qualified to rule because of their espousal of another form of governance:

> The cup that I drink you will drink; and with the baptism with which I am baptized, you will be baptized; but to sit at my right hand or at my left hand is not mine to grant; but it is for those for whom it has been prepared. . . . You know that among the Gentiles those whom they recognize as their rulers lord it over them, and their great ones are tyrants over them. But it is not so among you; but whoever wishes to become great among you must be your servant, and whoever wishes to be first among you must be slave of all (Mark 10:39–44 my translation).

In the millennium the organization of the world based on deceit and self-aggrandizement, which has led to death, destruction, oppression, and other acts described in the previous chapters, will be absent (20:2). Satan will be bound, and so the deceit, which led to the pursuit of the false gods of consumption and greed promoted by the beast of Empire and of Babylon, will no longer lead the nations astray. The messianic reign is dependent on the restraint of Satan, the earthly parallel to the liberation of heaven set out in 12:7–17. The deceiving of people and the distortion of minds and lives no longer takes place (cf. 12:9; 13:14), enabling a proper exercise of justice.

The Problem of the Apocalypse

There remains a pressing problem with Revelation. Many ordinary readers of Revelation react not with awe or discomfort, but with amazement and disgust that they should have to pay attention to the words of this book. Visions are, after all, not a sign of divine authority for modernity but of severe psychic disturbance. Would we pay attention to this text if it were not part of the canon of Scripture, especially in the light of the part that Revelation has played as a catalyst in events of human suffering?

There is no easy response to such unease. Visionaries are certainly eccentric. They may at times be damaged (but what does damage involve? And what is the criterion of wholeness by which we judge the damage?), and what they see can encourage things which are humanly damaging. They are not immediately to be rejected out of hand, however. If an elderly person with senile dementia or a person with schizophrenia is the problem, I struggle to find ways of accommodating the person who is before me to my habits of behaving and speaking. The usual ways of dealing with a person no longer work, and I am at a loss. The temptation to react by rejection, consigning to a home or an asylum, is sometimes strong. But the challenge is to learn new habits of mind and behavior in the face of the other.

No reader of Revelation can fail to be uneasy about the possibility of this text being used for interpretations that are dangerous, damaging, and oppressive. There is no way of preventing such interpretations on the grounds of our theological or historical sophistication. One cannot prevent a text like Revelation, allusive as it is, from being used in particular ways merely by asserting "this text cannot mean this."

Three points can be made:

- Revelation never countenances the use of violence by the people of God, however just their cause. They are called instead to witness and patient endurance.

- The violence and upheaval Revelation speaks of is something we need to hear about regularly. We can be lulled into a sense that this is a world without violence and injustice. That merely exhibits the limit of our horizon. The pockets of deprivation are there in this country. They are widespread elsewhere in the world and are increasing.

- At the heart of Revelation is the Lamb. His story is the ultimate criterion of all life, all interpretation of Scripture, whether Revelation or any other text: does it conform to the way of the Lamb?

Revelation has been given respectability either by subordination to the rest of the canon or benign neglect. We fear that if we attend to it the cataclysm it contains will sweep away our neat theological and ecclesiastical—as well as our political—constructions. The vision confronts us with the otherness of God. In a world where the track record of reason and pragmatism has not been entirely commendable, particularly in this last bitter and violent century of the second millennium, we might think again, and at least listen and ponder whether the Spirit may be speaking to the churches through these awesome visions.

Bibliography

Gilbertson, Michael. *The Meaning of the Millennium: Revelation 20 and Millennial Expectation*. Grove Biblical Series 5. Cambridge: Grove, 1999.

Girard, René. *Things Hidden since the Foundation of the World*. London: Athlone, 1987.

Keynes, Geoffrey, ed. *The Complete Writings of William Blake: With Variant Readings*. Oxford: Oxford University Press, 1974.

Lawrence, W. Gordon. *Social Dreaming @ Work*. London: Karnac, 1998.

McKelvey, R. J. *Millennium and the Book of Revelation*. Cambridge: Lutterworth, 1999.

Rowland, Christopher. *Revelation*. Epworth Commentary Series. London: Epworth, 1993.

———. *Revelation*. In *The New Interpreter's Bible*, edited by Leander E. Keck, 12: 503–743. 13 vols. Nashville: Abingdon, 1998.

Theissen, Gerd. *Signs of Life: Sermons and Meditations*. Translated by John Bowden. London: SCM, 1998.

14.3

"The Revaluation of All Values"

Reflections on the *Spiritual Exercises*

I teach Biblical Studies at Oxford and am an Anglican priest. I have for the last two years commuted between Oxford and Cambridge while my children were able to find appropriate points in their education to make the move to Oxford. In the context of the dislocation and readjustment resulting from a change in job, the importance of the *Spiritual Exercises* has been such that it is very tempting to begin this essay by an exhaustive description of how I came to do them, and to offer a detailed inventory of my spiritual state when I embarked upon them. It is not because I am particularly defensive that I intend to resist this. Indeed, far from it: I am the kind of person who is not usually backward in sharing his inadequacies and anxieties. But that whole process of self-revelation would be to fall into one of the traps that I have identified as a besetting sin during the time that I have been doing the *Exercises*. That process is a subtle form of narcissism, the identification of which I regard as one of the most important gifts from God which came through the *Exercises*. So I shall have to disappoint the reader who wants a detailed spiritual diary. Suffice it to say that professionally, spiritually, and emotionally I was at a low ebb. Conversations with friends had persuaded me that, whatever the other causes of the problems I might be having with my life, there was a significant "spiritual" dimension which had to be tackled. So it was that I came to embark on the *Exercises* eighteen months ago. I did so not as part of a formal retreat but in the course of living my everyday life. Circumstances made any other course of action at the time rather difficult, but I am resolved to repeat the process in the more concentrated environment of a retreat in the near future. The "everyday" element had the obvious advantage that many of the issues which were to occupy me were matters which were very much "alive" as I spent my time with the *Exercises*. My guide through the *Exercises* was a priest whose gentle direction placed so much of the responsibility on me before God. I am in retrospect profoundly grateful for his supportive, yet non-intrusive, part in the process. It was my wife, Catherine's, decision to embark on the *Exercises* six months or so before me which was a major reason for my decision to explore the same process. It had clearly been a formative experience for her, and I thought it might help me at the difficult juncture in which I had found myself.

A major hurdle in embarking upon the *Exercises* was at the very start. I found myself enormously resistant to the First Principle and Foundation. It is difficult to put my finger exactly on the problem now. I can best illustrate it by sharing some of my initial resentment (though as I recall it, I find my reaction rather naive now!). I have for many years been involved in one way or another with Third-World issues both personally and professionally. I have tentatively explored what an option for the poor might mean in the context of my work as a theologian in Oxbridge and had been part of a variety of groups and networks engaged with justice and peace issues. Liberation theology had become a central motivating influence in my life. So when there was no mention of service of humanity and solidarity with the outcast as the cornerstone of divine service and the emphasis seemed instead to be narrowly religious I initially rebelled. But, while briefly stumbling over this obstacle, I struggled to come to terms with that which stood in my way. As a result I am beginning to learn that my overriding attachment to what seems to me to be the central feature of the gospel of Jesus Christ needs to be placed before God, to seek to avoid an insidious temptation for the good intention or cause to become a mask for self-centeredness, with the consequence that the concerns of God may be subordinated to the satisfaction of self-interest.

I have to confess that in the first instance I approached the *Exercises* more as a psychological technique than as a "spiritual" discipline. I did not doubt that their ability as an aid to contemplation and self-examination had been proved by centuries of use. It was that kind of psychological "servicing" that I had in mind as I embarked upon them. What I had not bargained for was that the God who had been an object of my study and a part of the fabric of the *Exercises* that I was engaged in should also be discovered to be the gracious instigator and sustainer of the whole process. Or rather, that in praying for grace I should find myself being searched out rather than doing the searching. That is a pretty depressing confession to have to make, particularly from an ordained minister. Perhaps it is symptomatic of the outlook of our age, though I suspect that it is something far more widespread in human experience and that our age is no worse than any other. I think that it is the same disease that Deutero-Isaiah and the other prophets were talking about when they condemned idolatry and offered a vision of a God who was beyond the bounds of our definitions and meager expectations.

That idolatry can best be summarized in my case as a preoccupation with self, however dressed up it might be in more acceptable guises, which I found remorselessly exposed as I moved through the *Exercises*. It was an experience of being searched out and known, as the Psalmist puts it. Or, mindful of the imagery of the opening chapters of the Apocalypse, it was as if the deepest parts of me were being minutely examined by the many eyes of the Lamb that was slain. I found that the parts of me which I regarded as most akin to the spirit of Christ had subtly been co-opted into a regime of fear and defensiveness which led me away from God and others. I began to see how anxiety and a sense of "having to live up to my reputation" were continually impoverishing my life and conspired to undermine both a sense of self and vocation. So it was that those things which have been such an important part of my identity and potentially spiritual turned out often to be the snare which could trap me in a personal slough of despond and a self-centeredness which threatened to cut me off from God. I could resonate with Paul's experience in Romans 7 and glimpsed the importance of the Apocalypse describing the Lamb and the Beast in remarkably similar terms, for the angels of light and of darkness are difficult to distinguish. That which was good and had become such a part of the fabric of my being had been subtly recruited to undermine and diminish. While I cannot pretend that I have overcome the patterns of existence of a lifetime, I can see much more clearly the ways in which preoccupation with myself and my safety had for a time been impoverishing my service of God as well as my sense of myself. Learning what it meant to place the service of Almighty God at the center of my life has offered me a glimpse of liberation.

I suspect most people who embark on the Ignatian *Exercises* find themselves entranced by the imaginative study of Scripture in which the reader is asked to identify with various aspects of the story and in imagination understand the whole array of factors which the scriptural story evokes. My professional occupation is the exegesis of Holy Scripture and so I have a variety of reasons for interest in biblical interpretation. I have for many years been interested in the creative application of Scripture to the situations of the poor in the Basic Christian Communities of Latin America, so there was a degree of familiarity with the immediate engagement with the Scripture that I was being asked to adopt. Nevertheless, I did find that I was being made to think again about some of my attitudes to biblical interpretation as a professional exegete.

I do not believe that exegesis is an arcane activity but that it is in principle open to anyone. *Critical* exegesis (which is what most professional exegetes are engaged in) demands a degree of self-awareness of the variety of factors which determine one's quest for understanding. The *Exercises* reminded me how much of exegesis is usually confined to the reconstruction of the original meaning and context and how often the understanding of criticism is confined to the avoidance of religious prejudice. Of course, the biblical books are part of the extant literature of the ancient world and so have a place within the construction of the history of that world. I would not want to devalue the importance of the historical enterprise over the years. The historical approach to Scripture has given us a sense of the "otherness" of Scripture and some fascinating insights into how our ancestors in the faith struggled with issues relating to faith and life. Their ideas are not always the same as ours, nor may Scripture be used in any straightforward way to "answer" our contemporary questions. A historical approach will obviously generate historical interest but will also offer a resource for those who want to assess the degree of continuity which exists between their own lives and the struggles, fears, and hopes of the people whose lives are reflected in the pages of the Bible.

A historical reading of Scripture is by no means the only component of a challenging and critical exegesis, despite our ready assumption that in the last two hundred years or so we are the first to read Scripture "properly." It is easy to forget that biblical criticism did not start with the Enlightenment. Jewish and Christian interpreters have explored a variety of methods. Such interpretation has included literal and allegorical exegesis, and the recognition that texts can offer a level of meanings too easily ignored by a rather monochrome preoccupation with past history. Allowing for the "spiritual" and personal nature of the way Scripture is used in the *Exercises* I frequently found that my perspective on the text was being subjected to a searching critique, and I was offered fresh insight into the text which a narrow historical focus excluded. Above all else the *Exercises* brought home to me the awareness that the biblical texts are religious texts and are a resource for exploration of what a life in obedience to God may involve. And by religious I do not mean that narrow sense of the word which is so common today. What the *Exercises* compelled me to face up to was the need to see how spirituality informed and subverted assumptions in every component of existence, not least in my professional activity as a biblical scholar. Obedience to God, prayer, and service do not usually count as critical components but are (wrongly in my view) seen as necessarily leading to bias and lack of objectivity. There is a fear that to assert the importance of their religious dimension in some sense diminishes any critical perspective. My experience of doing the *Exercises* suggests to me that the reverse is the case. The use of Scripture in the context of worship and as part of the ongoing life of communities of faith is an important resource for exegesis which aims to be critical. What is more, the dominant concern of criticism with the analytical needs to be balanced by the opportunity offered by worship for contemplation and imagination. In this respect the Ignatian use of Scripture is particularly helpful. The emphasis on obedience to God can prevent that sense of superiority and hardness of heart which quenches the fructifying experience of reading with insight and understanding. Careful exploration before God of interests (economic, political, philosophical, as well as religious) that we bring to the text is a necessary part of developing a critical awareness: after all, "where our heart is there will our treasure be also." Where exegesis of any kind (whether carried out in an academic environment or not) is viewed merely as a theoretical enterprise cut off from our wider context in a world dominated by poverty and suffering or the service of Almighty God, important ingredients will be lacking.

I feel uneasy with the word "spirituality" with its dualistic and restrictive connotations. One of the things which Christianity demands of us is a renunciation of the resort to splits in existence. Dualism has been a part of religious experience throughout the history of the church. It takes different forms: separation between God and the world; religion and politics; soul and body; and in more everyday terms between different parts of existence. We learn to cope with the difficulties of existence by "splitting" our outlook and perception of things. Often we may see no contradiction between one part of life and another. But Christian discipleship demands something different. We are not permitted to resort to dividing our existence in such a way that we are relieved of the contradictions of life by pretending that we can compartmentalize existence. For me one challenge has always been to learn to keep together theology and the reality of our world with its suffering and injustice. It would be easy to take refuge in a theology which is exemplary in academic terms and perhaps even to offer enlightenment to those who are interested to learn more of an academic subject. It is because I am suspicious of the separation between religion and life that I am also uneasy about an approach to theology which presses for its autonomy over against the life of worship and the commitments of discipleship. I am reminded of the words of Gustavo Gutiérrez, who has always stressed the roots of liberation theology in the contemplation of God:

> Contemplation and commitment within history are fundamental dimensions of Christian practice. . . . The mystery reveals itself through prayer and solidarity with the poor. . . . Contemplation and commitment combine to form what may be called the phase of silence before God. . . . Silence is the condition for any living encounter with God in prayer and commitment. . . . Theology is talk that is constantly enriched by silence.[1]

The exploration of the things of God is not to be done outside that critical environment provided by divine worship. Everything, whether it be the preferential option for the poor, the most sublime spirituality, or sophisticated theological argument, is submitted to the judgement of God. That demands a life which is sensitive to the probing of divine grace as well as enriched by it. Too often theology done by Protestants is conceived independently of the religious demands which are such a central feature of the *Exercises*. While I do not see that environment as an infallible prophylactic against false theology or religion, I have discovered that it must be an essential ingredient of it.

At roughly the same time that I was doing the *Exercises* I was working on the Gospel of Matthew and its contribution to the study of early Jewish mysticism and was struck by the theme throughout of Jesus' solidarity with the humble and humiliated. I started work exploring the attitude of the Gospels to the poor and marginalized. But it was instead the picture of a Christ as a humble king that emerged and came to illuminate my reflections on the particular privilege of the humble to understand things which the wise and understanding were blind to.

For example, in Chapter 18 the disciples ask Jesus who is the greatest in the kingdom of heaven. He answers by taking a child and instructing the disciples to become like children. So, just as fulfilling the needs of the hungry and the thirsty in Matthew 25:31–46 means acting in that way to the heavenly Son of Man, receiving a child means receiving Jesus (18:5). I still find this to be a surprising perspective. This is not because of any sentimentality towards childhood or because I think that children are particularly innocent. Rather it is all part of the challenge of Jesus to conventional values about status, and the nature of adulthood which the Gospel so probingly explores. To place a child in the midst of the disciples is to challenge the assumption that the child has nothing of worth and can only be heeded when it has imbibed an adult's wisdom. But the adult world, at least that of the dominant elements of society, is not the embodiment of wisdom and may in fact be a perversion of it. Here is a perspective which

---

1. Gutiérrez, *Truth Shall Make You Free*, 3.

has challenged so many of our assumptions. Identification with the child is a mark of greatness, and it is the children and those who identify with their lot who have solidarity with the humble.

That is a theme which runs throughout the Gospel of Matthew. At the heart of Matthew's picture of Christ is the deliberate identification of "God with us" with the powerless and the weak rather than the strong. At the very start of the Gospel, Immanuel is a child who is faced with the brutal repression of the rulers in Jerusalem. As the child of God *par excellence* there is concern and identification with the lot of the downtrodden. Their lot is one that the humble Messiah chose to share: "Foxes have holes and the birds of the air have their nests but the son of man has nowhere to lay his head" (Matt 8:20 my translation). As a child he is the victim of persecution and deliberately offers himself as a humble king whose followers must espouse similar humility. As one in a position of eminence in my professional life, it has been a salutary experience to explore the meaning of following a humble king in circumstances where status, honor, charisma, and brilliance count for a great deal. To be like a child, to learn what "solidarity of the humiliated" means in practice (to quote the German biblical scholar Klaus Wengst[2]) is a necessary, but difficult, vocation in the world in which I live and work. But to explore that without persisting in defending myself and my vulnerable ego involves a delicate spiritual balance which I am sure will be a constant theme of discipleship.

So the *Exercises* did not allow me to compartmentalize the bits of my life. Rather, I found myself being gently pressed at a speed with which I could cope and without too much personal upheaval. For me it is a hard lesson to learn that there is no escape from taking seriously the nature of Jesus' solidarity with the poor and finding that this cannot merely be a matter of rhetoric but must also be a cornerstone of everyday living. It is that quest for integrity which the *Exercises* have enabled me to take up with renewed endeavor. Over the months since I did the *Exercises*, I have been aware of a framework for existence that the experience has bequeathed. It is at one and the same time an inspiration and a discomfort, the latter because I am continually being reminded about the "revaluation of all values" which it confronted me with. Those words of Nietzsche with which he concludes *The Antichrist* (how ironic that one of its greatest despisers should have perceived so clearly so much that is at the heart of our religion!) have come to epitomize the challenge of the gospel. In one outburst about the Church Fathers Nietzsche wrote, "Nature was neglectful when she made them—she forgot to endow them with even a modest number

---

2. This is a reference to Wengst, *Humility: Solidarity of the Humiliated*.

of respectable, decent, cleanly instincts . . . between ourselves, they are not even men. . . ."[3] That's the heart of the matter, isn't it? In a "macho" culture the way of Christ cuts across all those "respectable" virtues. Those who would be disciples have to learn what it means to take up a cross and follow him. I consider that I began to do that in earnest when I imbibed and digested the wisdom of the *Spiritual Exercises* of Ignatius of Loyola.

Bibliography

Gutiérrez, Gustavo. *The Truth Shall Make You Free: Confrontations*. Translated by Matthew O'Connell. Maryknoll, NY: Orbis, 1990.

Nietzsche, Friedrich. *Twilight of the Idols; and, The Anti-Christ*. Translated, with an introduction and commentary by R. J. Hollingdale. Penguin Classics. Harmondsworth: Penguin, 1971.

Wengst Klaus. *Humility: Solidarity of the Humiliated; The Transformation of an Attitude and Its Social Relevance in Graeco-Roman Old Testament-Jewish and Early Christian Tradition*. Translated by John Bowden. Philadelphia: Fortress Press, 1988.

---

3. Nietzsche, *Twilight of the Idols; and, the Anti-Christ*, 59.

Printed in Great Britain
by Amazon